MAKING *Love* THE WAY WE USED TO... OR BETTER

Other books by Laurie Ashner

When Parents Love Too Much
Six Keys to Creating the Life You Desire
When Is Enough, Enough?
Resonance: The New Chemistry of Love
Could It Be . . . Perimenopause?
The Estrogen Alternative

MAKING *L*OVE THE WAY WE USED TO... OR BETTER

Secrets to Satisfying Midlife Sexuality

ALAN M. ALTMAN, M.D.,
LAURIE ASHNER

CB

CONTEMPORARY BOOKS

Library of Congress Cataloging-in-Publication Data

Altman, Alan M.
   Making love the way we used to . . . or better : secrets to satisfying midlife sexuality /
Alan M. Altman and Laurie Ashner.
      p.   cm.
   Includes bibliographical references.
   ISBN 0-8092-2496-8
   1. Sex instruction.   2. Middle aged persons—Sexual behavior.   3. Sexual
disorders—Treatment.   I. Ashner, Laurie.   II. Title.
HQ31.A4938   2001
613.9′6—dc21
                                                                      00-30306
                                                                         CIP

Credits
p. 69: *Six Keys to Creating the Life You Desire*, Mitch Meyerson and Laurie Ashner, New
Harbinger Publications, Oakland, California. www.newharbinger.com. (800) 748-6273.
p. 199: *When Parents Love Too Much*, Mitch Meyerson and Laurie Ashner. Reprinted by
permission of Hazelden.
p. 213: From *Adultery* by Louise DeSalvo. Copyright © 1999 by Louise DeSalvo. Reprinted by
permission of Beacon Press, Boston.

Cover design by Monica Baziuk
Cover photograph copyright © Carol Ford/Stone
Interior design by Susan H. Hartman

Published by Contemporary Books
A division of NTC/Contemporary Publishing Group, Inc.
4255 West Touhy Avenue, Lincolnwood (Chicago), Illinois 60712-1975 U.S.A.
Copyright © 2001 by Alan Altman and Laurie Ashner
Printed in the United States of America
International Standard Book Number: 0-8092-2496-8
01 02 03 04   05 06 LB 15 14 13 12 11 10 9 8 7 6 5 4 3 2 1

For Judi . . . and twenty-seven years
For my patients and what they've taught me

Alan M. Altman

For Mitch
With extra love—

Laurie Ashner

Contents

Acknowledgments

WHEN YOU SET OUT to write your first book, you have little idea of what you're about to encounter. From the extensive experience I've had with my patients, I knew the information was there, but getting it on paper in an organized fashion that would reflect the manner in which I normally teach and share information would prove to be another story. I've always found it easier to communicate verbally, mixing humor and empathy with education . . . the theater or art of medicine. So, I had to find a co-author with the ability to write the way I speak . . . no easy task. When I was finally guided to Laurie Ashner, I felt that her psychology background and vast writing experience would serve as the perfect mix in capturing the voice and the information, while blending in an understanding of the personal issues involved in the secrets of sexuality in midlife. I was right. The ten-month gestation period wasn't always easy, but once the baby arrived, I was incredibly proud and very sure of the choice I had made. She is the consummate writer.

Judi, my wife of twenty-seven years and counting, has been there through it all—the good times and the tough times. She's taught me about how relationships can evolve and change and still remain stable and loving. Her tolerance and sense of humor, especially while this work was in progress and I was away lecturing two to three days a week, allowed me to flourish at an incredibly exciting time in my life. Finally, her sense of exploration and novelty helped instill the reason for this work.

Our sons, Matt and Josh, have brought more joy than I ever could have imagined. I only hope their children make them as proud as I am. To produce children and learn who you really are through the mirror of their lives is a humbling and awesome experience. The closeness of their relationship will translate into many years to come of love and laughter as a family, no matter where we will be. They have encouraged me in my efforts to produce this work and share my pride in its completion.

Speaking of family, a physician is only as good as his office staff. The three women with whom I have worked for the past sixteen to twenty years have eased the transition from clinician to lecturer/author by maintaining my practice and helping my patients adjust to the changes with the same caring, skill, and sense of humor that has always characterized their unique abilities. Margie, Mary, and Melissa will always be family.

I have only begun to learn the importance of agents and editors in this process. Jean Naggar believed in this book from the very beginning, and her encouragement was vital. Judith McCarthy and the wonderful team from Contemporary Books guided with a steady hand, steering the ship in the right direction in spite of my inexperience.

Margaret Seawell was my guiding light in the early days of concept and planning. Her long experience in dealing with authors in the throes of panic was immensely helpful each time I called upon her expertise. The reader should also thank her for what she made me *leave out* of the manuscript that was either inappropriate or just bad taste. Her comments on the finished product lifted me to levels of pride and confidence I had never anticipated.

Thanks, also, to Susan Devine for transcribing our tapes and taking such interest in their content, as well as to Mitch Meyerson for his input and tolerance of all the time Laurie had to focus on our work.

Finally, there are my patients, women, young and older, who shared their stories, the successes and failures in their relationships, and taught me the level to which these secrets invaded their bedrooms and impacted upon their lives. Special thanks to those patients who read the completed manuscript, N.K., D.H., S.F., and, especially, W.G. I greatly appreciate the time and effort they spent in critiquing the readability of the book, the positive feedback that followed, and their contributions to its content.

Alan M. Altman

There are so many people I could not have done without during this project. Thanks to: Marcie and Howard Tilkin, the best sister and brother-in-law anyone could have, always number one on my list, forever; Martha Rubenstein, Carrie Worley, Mary Wells, Lucinda Klevay, and Ellie Needelman, wonderful friends who always let me back in their lives after I disappear under a deadline for months; Dr. Jerald Schwab, my sounding board, my favorite philosopher, a fabulous dinner partner who can always make me smile, and a truly great guy; Dr. Steven Goldstein, who convinced me I could be a medical writer and then made sure I became one and stayed one; Judith McCarthy, a terrific and, thankfully, experienced editor who steered us to the right course and the right voice and who was enthusiastic from the start; her fabulous team of assistants, publicists, everyone who made this all a very special experience; Judi Altman, for letting me invade her life with thousands of calls, faxes, and E-mails to her husband, always with a smile and encouragement—I can't say enough about how graciously you let me borrow your husband's time for more than a year, so I won't even try; Alice Stamm and Sue Spataro, women of the Web, who have helped me with my last three books in ways that are immeasurable and who help all the women who E-mail them daily for the help they give; the remarkable upbeat staff of Dr. Altman's office, Margie, Mary, and, especially, Melissa, who always got my calls through; Sue Devine, for quick, professional transcribing every step of the way, an unexpected godsend; Jean Naggar, of the Jean V. Naggar Literary Agency, for introducing me to Dr. Altman; the patients of Dr. Altman who shared their experiences with me; Dr. Tom Cash and Paula Harper, professional experts who added so much to this book; the staff and students at CCDS, whom I had to leave to pursue this project and whom I miss every day. Most of all, thanks to Dr. Alan Altman. Alan, that brainstorming session at a picnic table in Burlington was a writer's dream, and I'll never forget it. You made this project fun; you kept it fresh and exciting for eight long months. You were always there with encouragement, laughter, and ideas when the going got tough. Then you put in all of the commas. Here's to lifelong friendship and many more books to come. You are the best!

Laurie Ashner

Introduction

*Why Don't We Make Love
the Way We Used To?*

YOU LOVE HIM. You really do. You have *history*. You know everything about him. He knows everything about you. You love the things he does, how successful he is. He's great with the kids. It's true that you've had some darker moments together. Sometimes in the middle of a fight, you may wonder if you'd be better off alone. But the reality is, you're *good* together. When you're out with other people, they say they envy the two of you.

That's why what's been happening between you lately is so scary to think about and seems impossible to share. How come he doesn't turn you on anymore? How come he doesn't seem to want to tear your clothes off the way he used to? How come you're starting to look at other men? What's happening to you? What's happening to him?

You love her. You really do. Your friends say you have it all. She was magnificent when you met her. She was not only sexy but bright and independent. She was so vibrant that people turned as soon as she walked into a room. You'd share everything with her and talk for hours. You couldn't wait to be with her. Just thinking about her would turn you on.

How come you have so little to say these days? There's so much sameness every time you make love that it seems harder and harder to get turned on. She doesn't seem interested in the same things anymore. She once seemed so independent, and now you feel that she depends on you too much. You feel like roommates. You wonder if you can spend the rest of your life with a woman who feels more like a sister than a lover.

You haven't said a word. You don't want to hurt her feelings. You don't want to make things worse. You don't want to feel embarrassed. But sometimes the silence is louder than words.

Suddenly you both have secrets too difficult to share. You may not want to face them. You might believe that if you ignore the problem it will go away. But these secrets grow too big to go away. Soon the secret is ever present and definitely in the way of your sex life.

That's exactly what happened to the four people whose stories follow.

For Carol, forty-six, it was a spring she wasn't likely to forget. Her sixteen-year-old son, possessor of a new driver's license, flunked geometry at the quarter. Two math tutors in a row quit after he stood them up or just plain refused to cooperate with them. Worse, her thirteen-year-old daughter, always a pleasure, was suddenly sullen and secretive, and Carol was getting calls from *her* teachers, too.

"Let's just say that sex wasn't my priority," Carol admits. "You think sex will wait until the emergencies are over and your husband will under-stand," she says. "But my husband said, 'If Jeffrey flunks, he flunks—it'll be a good lesson for him to go to summer school. And leave Sharon alone. She's a good kid. Why are you overreacting?'

"He'd reach for me at night, but I was just too tired. Sometimes we got started and I was so unenthusiastic, he just gave up. I said, 'I need more affection.' He said, 'If you'd just relax, I'd show you some affection.' Then I'd feel guilty. I'd really try the next time. I just never felt very aroused.

"Then both of my children finally went off to camp for eight weeks—Jeff as a swim instructor, Sharon as a junior counselor. I watched the bus drive off and thought, 'This will do us all some good; we need to be away from each other for a while.'

"We made love twice that first week. It didn't rock the world, but at least I wasn't consumed with thoughts about whether Sharon was doing her homework and whether Jeff was going to wreck my car. The summer flew. Then one day I realized five weeks had gone by and we hadn't made love again. I didn't want to mention it to my husband, because the truth was, I was never in the mood. Something about the way my husband was treating me was different, too. He was polite, even kind, but sometimes I would turn and catch him staring at me in a strange way. It was like he was looking through me, to something else. And that's when I started to get really scared."

It was a Saturday night, not long after their fifteenth wedding anniversary, when Denise and her husband, Brian, were watching a movie on television. He started to massage her shoulders. When she didn't move away, it was their signal for sex. They moved to the bedroom. "It started out to be wonderful," Brian admits. "Then, we were in the middle of sex, and I don't know how to say this, but I 'lost it.' We fumbled around like teenagers for a few minutes, and it became clear that nothing was going to happen. It was downright embarrassing. I thought, Just don't say anything. Don't make it worse. I mumbled something about being tired and we went to sleep, back to back. A week later, the same thing happened again.

"Two months later I was no longer massaging her shoulders in front of the TV. In fact, I was pretending to be asleep when she came to bed. She asked me if I was having an affair. I was thinking, Why did I turn off to her? I used to just look at her and want to make love. I'm too scared to think about why this is going on. Now we've just stopped talking about it."

Felicia, thirty-seven, isn't talking about sex with her partner either. But she feels she's the one to blame. "I never thought I'd marry again after my divorce. I met Dale in the elevator of all places. Twenty-six floors down, I knew I was interested in a man for the first time in years. We had our first date that night, and we were in love two months later. The problem is, Dale has a child with his first wife, whom he never gets to see because they live two thousand miles away. He talks about wanting to have a baby with me. He doesn't know that I've been having trouble with my menstrual cycle for months. My doctor told me that I'm not ovulating regularly anymore because I'm in perimenopause. I thought, Perimenopause! How could this happen so soon? I'm only thirty-seven!

"I worry that if I tell Dale he's going to think I'm too old, even though he's forty-five. What if he says he wants a younger woman whom he can have children with? Do I just marry him and figure that once we're married and he finds out the truth it will be too late?"

Sharon's trouble is her best friend's lover, Sean. She explains, "Janice went through a torturous divorce two years ago, so I'm really glad she met Sean. He's attractive, funny, a totally charming guy. She's my best friend, and I want her to be happy, but the truth is, I get intensely jealous every time I see them together. Since we live next door to each other, that's a lot. When Janice tells me about their trysts in the bedroom, I want to die. There's something about seeing two people so much in love that they can't keep their hands off each other that makes you think, Why can't I feel like that about someone?

"I love my husband. Still, I haven't looked at a man the way Janice looks at Sean since I was twenty. Will there never be another time that I feel so turned on by a man that I can't wait to be with him? The truth is, I have so much trouble getting excited with my husband. Sometimes sex even hurts. Even with messy lubricants, several minutes into sex it begins to feel like sandpaper rubbing against me. I find myself wondering when it will finally be over. But how can I tell him? He'd just get hurt and angry."

The truth is, he *is* hurt and angry. "She makes a big deal about our silly neighbor and this hot affair she's having. Then she never wants to make love. Why can't she pay a little more attention to what's going on with us rather than what's going on with them?"

All of these couples have a secret. It's huge and ever present. Still, they never speak about it. It's something their partners sense. But neither wants to face it. They feel that if they ignore the problem it might go away. But these secrets grow too big to go away, and when they aren't acknowledged, it's like having an elephant in the bedroom.

Talking about it is difficult because they believe that the trouble is caused by something psychological or emotional—a marital problem, a partner secretly having an affair, boredom, a lack of attraction—something they feel powerless to do much about. Until recently, scientific research would have backed them up. The old thinking was that 90 percent of sexual problems were emotional, 10 percent physical. The astonishing truth demonstrated in the most recent research is that *it's probably the other way around.* Like depression, which was once thought to be purely psychological and is now known to respond to the rebalancing of chemical substances in the brain, sexual problems are responding to the right medical treatment and information.

A decade ago, experts predicted that sexual dysfunction would become a serious public-health issue by the year 2000. With an aging population come chronic problems that can affect sexuality. The millions of prescriptions written for Viagra since its release in 1998 bear this out. Surveys find that at least one in three sexually active women are dissatisfied with some aspect of their sex life. However, researchers are finding that we can do more about the challenges of midlife sex than we've ever been able to before. We can expect more at this age than we realize. New medications, procedures, and information are reducing the need for many of the secrets in the bedroom.

Make no mistake, however: one doesn't merely take a pill or smooth on a salve and completely remove the problem from the bedroom. Sometimes that secret you've been keeping has been there for years, causing anger and insecurity that are difficult to overcome.

As a doctor who has practiced gynecology (and formerly obstetrics) for more than twenty-five years, I can tell you that it's a rare couple who doesn't have at least one secret in the bedroom. As a husband and father who recently celebrated twenty-seven years of marriage, I can intimately understand the challenges of a long-term relationship as well as the satisfactions. What I've learned is this: when medical treatment is combined with the best therapy for the emotional aftereffects of facing sexual problems, the results can be incredible.

Carol, whose summer vacation alone with her husband didn't result in the sex she had desired, learned that marriage and responsibility for two teens played a definite role in her lack of libido. But that was only *half* the picture. The other half was hormonal. After discussing this with me, I prescribed a drug called EstratestHS, a combination of the hormones estrogen and testosterone. Sex is no longer on the back burner. When her mind tells her she wants to be intimate with her husband, her body cooperates. And he appreciates it!

Felicia, who worried that perimenopause would render her unable to have a child, lost that anxiety after I provided her with some concrete information about the change in her reproductive cycle. She learned that perimenopause is not menopause and that she might have childbearing years ahead. I also suggested using natural progesterone to ease some of the symptoms of this rocky hormonal transition. She now feels that she's the one who has control overall.

Sharon now uses Estring, a new vaginal ring that releases estrogen into the vagina but doesn't send it through the bloodstream. Although she isn't always in the mood, she has found that her problems with lubrication and comfort when she makes love with her husband have disappeared. Without this worry they can be much more focused on something they both want—to ban boredom from the bedroom.

Denise has realized that she isn't to blame for her husband's difficulty maintaining an erection. He's learned how to talk to her about it in plain terms that leave no room for guilt on the part of either of them. I met with them as a couple and explained to her that 50 percent of men his age experience some degree of erectile dysfunction. She became acutely aware of the problems that arise when men notice they are having a problem with erections and then begin to worry if it will happen every time they have sex. Performance anxiety, not anything Denise had done, was harming Brian's sexual functioning. Learning this and communicating their feelings helped dispel some of the fear that had been keeping them apart. Now they are trying self-help remedies and some alternative therapies. If those don't work, they have made a commitment to see a urologist for further therapy.

How do you move a mountain of secrecy? How can you enjoy the greater level of sexual and emotional satisfaction these couples gained after years of disappointment?

This book contains a unique mix of medical information and communication techniques that can allow you to achieve more of what you desire sexually. First, for each problem or secret you'll learn what's new and promising on the medical front that may help you. Case histories from my patients who have succeeded in using these therapies will help you understand exactly what to expect. You'll learn about the following:

- Estrogen, testosterone, and progesterone: Can hormones really help your sex drive?
- Estratest, Estring, Prometrium, and other unique medications, both synthetic and botanical: What's useful and what's a waste of your money?
- What changes occur in our sex lives as we age that we need to accept?
- What about Viagra? Will it help women, too?
- What to do if sexual problems occur after hysterectomy: How you can prevent these problems, even before you get to the operating room.
- How to age-proof your sex life through simple changes in your health habits—plus some new and imaginative exercises.
- How you can maintain your equilibrium during the hormonal transition of perimenopause or menopause so that the changes in your body are much less disruptive to your sex life.
- The best hormonal and alternative remedies for mood swings, anxiety, fatigue, and other symptoms that challenge your sex life.
- The truth about the new "tighten me up" surgery: Is it safe? Is it for you?

Because sexual secrets almost always have an emotional impact on both partners, the second section of each chapter will show you how to cope with and communicate your feelings. You'll learn ways of talking about these secrets that my patients have used successfully to get back the tenderness and excitement, including:

- how not to fall into the trap of using your partner as a mirror of your own sexual adequacy
- what his affair and her affair are really all about and how you can survive and even thrive afterward if you choose to

- how to deal with the emotional aftershocks when your partner uses Viagra
- the new body image therapy and what it can do for your sex life
- what to say to a partner who tells you it's your fault he's having a sexual problem
- how to find a medical professional who will answer your most intimate questions in an open and easy dialogue
- how to talk to your partner about sex, perimenopause, and menopause without giving him a message that you are a mass of raging hormones and on the brink
- what to do when the problem responds to medication, but your emotions are still raw
- how to help your male partner avoid performance anxiety

Chapter 1 will introduce you to a five-step program. The program will guide you from acknowledging the secrets in your own bedroom — secrets you might not even be aware of — to a breakthrough that banishes them from the bedroom.

The chapters that follow will give you specific information about the problems many couples face sexually, secret by secret, and how to deal with them for the best chance at success. The information is sometimes quite graphic. The secrets you'll hear may be things you've never even dared think about. Some answers are simple, while some are more challenging. Some require medication. Some require communication. Many require both. But no matter how delicate you may think your secret is, there are answers out there.

In every relationship there are many forks in the road. You can take the path that keeps you silent about what you really feel. Or you can take the path where you learn to talk about what you feel and deal with the aftermath. If there has been a secret in your bedroom that you've been keeping, letting it out doesn't need to be scary or mysterious or the fuel for even bigger problems. Telling our innermost secrets often makes us feel closer to the people we love. It can be a catalyst for more intimacy, more excitement, more love. This book is about how to make that happen for *you*.

Making *Love* the Way We Used to... or Better

"Listen. Do You Want to Know a Secret?"

Discovering the Secrets in the Bedroom—
and a Five-Step Plan for
Ridding Yourself of Them Forever

MIKE AND CATHERINE didn't think they had a secret. In fact, they'd talked honestly about their sex life many times. "Remember how great sex used to be when we met? How your parents almost caught us in their bed when they came home from their trip a day early? Remember in the car at the parking lot at the beach, when someone came up to the window with a flashlight and we thought it was the police and we had half our clothes off? I was ready to kill your friend who thought he was being so funny."

Yet they'd both wonder, Where did we begin to lose that? It was no secret that the love was still there, having grown even deeper, but the excitement wasn't. They tried new things occasionally, but they both began to feel that the loss of interest was inevitable. They even saw a therapist once, when their daughter was having problems in high school. The therapist asked if there were problems at home that might be related. They admitted that, although there were no problems, their sex life had become pretty ho-hum. The therapist said, "Well, the bloom is off the rose. After so many years of marriage, you can't expect to feel all the magic you felt when you met. There are other ways you can connect that can also be fulfilling."

I've heard that argument many times before. While I can't say that you'll ever feel the ultimate heart-stopping passion you felt the first month you fell in love with your partner, I do know this: there are many of us who settle for predictability when we could have more excitement; friendship when we could have intimacy; medical problems that kill our sex life when we can correct them; and the status quo when we could have a relationship that is constantly evolving and renewing itself.

When you hear that less-exciting sex with your partner is inevitable as you age, do you have the same secret thought so many of my patients have had? "I don't want to accept that. I can't accept that. I haven't changed inside. I still want to feel swept away, to have real passion in my life. People keep saying that I'm being unrealistic. Why does it have to be this way?"

It doesn't. While I can't guarantee that you can get the fire back that brought you together, if you follow the five-step plan I suggest in this book, I *can* promise you "sparkles." If you're willing to discover your secrets in the bedroom and work together to banish them, you'll make more of those sparkles every time you make love.

Acknowledging the secrets is the biggest step you can take in reviving midlife sexuality. I've seen it work for my patients, and I'm confident that it can work for you. There are steps you can take to cast out and overcome even the darkest secrets. But first you have to know what those secrets are.

Acknowledging the Secret

Psychotherapist Paula J. Harper, L.C.S.W., who specializes in the treatment of sexual problems, hears secrets all the time. She says, "What's the biggest secret? *What I need.* What do I need to feel sexual, to function, to get pleasure? How can I tell my partner? Couples have to find a way to be emotionally intimate first, and that's a huge barrier. There can be tremendous fear and resistance."

What if you keep it a secret? "You'll act it out," Harper predicts, "by being resentful or unavailable, finding fault, making assumptions, blaming, or withdrawing.

"Acknowledging the secrets can be the hardest step of all. Get past this, and I believe you'll find the rest of the journey easier. Many of these secrets may have hovered around for so long that they are a protective mechanism to maintain the status quo of the relationship. In other words, we fear talking about our problems will destroy the relationship. Yet not talking is more likely to have that effect. Sometimes we sense something is wrong but can't define it. Sometimes we keep the truth out of our conscious mind because it seems too difficult to face."

The quiz that follows will help you acknowledge those secrets so you can break through these barriers. Then you'll be steered to the chapter or chapters that will help you get the information you need. Not all questions have to do with sex. Many are about your general health, because it affects your sex life. Some questions apply to you, some to your partner, and some to you both.

For each of the following statements, answer A if you agree, D if you disagree. If a question doesn't apply to you, choose *disagree*.

Questions for Her

1. I have pain in or around the vagina when we have intercourse.
2. I don't lubricate or get wet the way I used to.
3. I have pain in my vaginal area even when we're not making love.
4. The only way we can have sex is if we use a lubricant.
5. I'm frightened about resuming intercourse after not having done it for so long.
6. My partner feels that he doesn't turn me on because I don't get wet enough.
7. I'm always too tired for sex.
8. More often than not I find myself faking it in responding to my partner.

9. I wake up in the middle of the night sweating and have trouble going back to sleep.

10. Everybody is pulling me in so many different directions that sometimes I want to scream.

11. I feel I have no time for myself.

12. My husband always gets turned on to have sex when other people are around or when it's totally impractical.

13. I wish people around me would take care of their responsibilities and not put them all on me.

14. I am having hot flashes and night sweats, but I have regular periods and my doctor says it's not menopause, it's all in my head.

15. There are certain times in my menstrual cycle when my family knows to stay away from me.

16. Lately I've noticed I'm getting PMS I've never had before, and I'm in my forties.

17. I find myself forgetting things I used to remember, like telephone numbers.

18. I find that I have to make a list of everything I have to do, or I'll forget it.

19. I wish I knew more about why my menstrual cycle functions as it does.

20. The birth-control pill is bad for you, especially if you're over thirty-five.

21. My periods are closer together and much heavier, and it's not any fun bleeding every two weeks.

22. I'm worried that I won't be as desirable to my partner after I reach menopause.

23. I'm more depressed lately than I've ever been.

24. I've been on hormone replacement therapy, and, while I feel better, it hasn't done anything for my sex life.

25. I stopped taking hormones because I felt awful on them.

26. Estrogen is fine, but I hate taking the progesterone.

27. I've been hearing a lot about testosterone, and I wonder if it will help me.

28. I've been on hormones for years, and now I'm starting to have symptoms again.

29. I still notice quite a lot of vaginal dryness even though I'm taking estrogen.

30. I'm having a very difficult time trying to decide whether to take hormone replacement therapy.

31. I'm depressed about the loss of my fertility.

32. I used to really look forward to making love; now I can take it or leave it.

33. Ever since I've been on the birth-control pill my sexual get-up-and-go got up and went.

34. My antidepressant makes me feel less depressed but has really diminished my interest in sex.

35. My orgasm is very different since I had a hysterectomy.

36. My partner gets very upset when I talk about using my vibrator.

37. Our sexual relationship has changed since my mastectomy because of my partner's fear of touching that area.

38. Recently it takes a lot more manual stimulation to help my partner achieve an erection.

39. The intensity of my orgasm has decreased drastically.

40. We haven't had sex for years because of his problem, and now that he's taking Viagra he expects me to respond automatically.

41. I wish they would make a pill that changes a man an hour *after* sex.

42. I'm upset with my partner because he won't get any help for his problem with getting an erection.

Questions for Him

43. I'm worried because I recently noted that I couldn't maintain an erection for as long as I needed to.

44. Recently I've found that worry about maintaining an erection in and of itself takes away my ability to keep it.

45. I try to avoid having sex with my partner because I'm afraid I'll lose my erection again.

46. It takes a lot of manual stimulation for me to get an erection.

47. The intensity of my orgasm has decreased drastically.

48. I seem to experience erectile dysfunction only with my wife, not with my lover.
49. It takes me much longer to achieve an orgasm than it used to.
50. I don't want to take Viagra, because I think it's a dangerous drug.
51. My wife doesn't seem to get as wet as she used to, and I wonder why I'm not turning her on.
52. Ever since my wife reached menopause she's had no interest in sex.
53. My partner is always too tired to make love.
54. I'm bored with our sexual relationship.
55. I want to make love a lot less than I used to.

Questions for Both Him and Her

56. I think we have sex much less often than our friends.
57. I wish I could find a way to relight the fire of our relationship.
58. My partner wants more sex than I do.
59. I met someone recently, and I can't stop thinking about him (her).
60. At some time during my marriage I've thought about having an affair.
61. It really annoys me when my partner flirts with other people.
62. It annoys me that my partner spends so much time in sex chat rooms on the Internet.
63. I am getting more of what I need from a cyber-relationship than I am from my partner.
64. I don't know if our relationship can recover from the effects of his (her) affair.
65. The affair I'm having with my lover is the only reason I've been able to stay in my marriage and keep my family together.
66. My relationship with a coworker, though it's not sexual, is becoming more important to me than my relationship with my partner.

67. I'm embarrassed to walk in front of my partner without clothes on because of the way my body has changed.
68. Many people I see have a much better body than I do.
69. I'm distracted during sex because I'm thinking about how my body looks to my partner.
70. I wish my breasts (or penis) were larger.

Better Sex One Step at a Time: A Five-Step Approach to Reviving Midlife Sexuality

Each of the statements you agreed with above represents a secret—or at least an area you find troublesome or distressing. This book offers a five-step program for making the best of this self-discovery.

Step One: Acquire the Medical Guidance and Information You Need

First you want to know, "Is this normal? Could it have a medical cause? If it's physical, what treatments are possible? Am I really in trouble here? Do I have cancer or some other disease?"

Here's how to find those answers using this book. List the numbers of the statements in the quiz that you agree with. Use the following guide to find the chapters that will provide information that will help you.

Statement Numbers   1, 2, 3, 4, 5, 6, 51

Secret	**Rx**
"It hurts so much when we have sex that I wonder if there's something seriously wrong with me."	• What causes dry, painful sex and how to cure it. • How to reassure yourself and your partner that it isn't loss of interest causing you to be drier than you used to be when you make love. • How to talk about what you need now to become aroused. • How to safely resume your sex life when it's been dormant for a while.

Of primary interest: Chapter 2
Also helpful: Chapter 6, Chapter 11

Statement Numbers	7, 8, 9, 10, 11, 12, 13, 53

Secret	Rx
"I'm always too exhausted to make love, so I usually fake it."	• What to do when you're almost always too tired for sex. • Solving the trickiest sleep problems. • Should you ever fake an orgasm, and why. • How to get what you really need to feel awake and alive again.

Of primary interest: Chapter 3
Also helpful: Chapter 6, Chapter 4

Statement Numbers	14, 15, 16, 17, 18, 19, 20, 21

Secret	Rx
"I can't sleep, I'm forgetting everything, I feel anxious and strange, and I could take sex or leave it. What's happening to me?"	• Understanding perimenopause and why these strange symptoms are absolutely normal, needn't be scary, and don't mean you're getting old. • Your hormones, how they change as you age, and why the hormonal transition doesn't have to be a sexual transition. • What to do about problem periods and month-long PMS. • The best and quickest remedies for perimenopausal symptoms. • How to talk to your partner about perimenopause.

Of primary interest: Chapter 4
Also helpful: Chapter 5, Chapter 2, Chapter 3

Statement Numbers	22, 23, 24, 25, 26, 27, 28, 29, 30, 31, 52

Secret	Rx
"I thought these hormones were supposed to help me!"	• Understanding the truth about menopause and sex. • The newest options in hormone replacement therapy (HRT)—what can help you feel better fast. • How to go about adding testosterone to hormone replacement therapy to improve the results. • What to do if HRT helps all your symptoms—except your loss of sex drive. • What to do if HRT leaves you less in the mood for sex than ever. • What to tell your partner about menopause and how to help him express his own secret fears.

Of primary interest: Chapter 5
Also helpful: Chapter 6, Chapter 11

Statement Numbers	32, 33, 34, 35, 36, 37, 54, 55, 56, 57, 58
Secret "Libido? Where did it go?"	**Rx** • How often is normal? Is every couple in America really having sex 2.5 times a week? • Why sex feels different for some women after hysterectomy. • What's in your medicine cabinet that can be draining you of desire. • How to banish boredom in the bedroom. • Understanding the myths and realities about taking testosterone to improve sex drive so that you can make the best choice. • Understanding *manopause*—does *he* need testosterone?

Of primary interest: Chapter 6
Also helpful: Chapter 5, Chapter 11

Statement Numbers	67, 68, 69, 70
Secret "Sex is OK as long as the lights are out and I'm wearing a T-shirt!"	**Rx** • Test your body image. • How to overcome a negative body image when you're making love. • Learning how to change your body image even if you can't change your body. • Why an hour lifting weights may do more for your body image than a half hour on the StairMaster. • Can plastic surgery really improve your body image? • Advice from the top body-image therapists and relationship therapists.

Of primary interest: Chapter 7
Also helpful: Chapter 11

Statement Numbers	59, 60, 61, 62, 63, 64, 65, 66

Secret	Rx
"He seems more interested in having hot chat on the Internet than being with me, his willing wife."	• Understanding sexual affairs and the unconscious reasons they happen at midlife. • Intellectual, emotional, and Internet affairs—are they really cheating? • How to protect your relationship from the "other man" or "other woman" by understanding how they came to be so important in your partner's life. • Can an affair actually ever *keep* two married people together? • Getting past the affair and on to better intimacy.

Of primary interest: Chapter 8
Also helpful: Chapter 6, Chapter 11

Statement Numbers	38, 39, 43, 44, 45, 46, 47, 48, 49, 50

Secret	Rx
"My ever-ready man has turned into the never-ever man. Don't I turn him on anymore?"	• Understanding aging and sexual response: what's a bad night in bed and what's erectile dysfunction. • The huge shadow performance anxiety can cast over sexual function. • See a doctor or see another woman? The secret question he wonders about most, and how to answer it honestly. • Viagra: Will it work for him? Will it work for her? What the latest research shows. • Beyond Viagra: if it doesn't work, what's next? • What never to say to a man with erectile dysfunction.

Of primary interest: Chapter 9
Also helpful: Chapter 10, Chapter 6

Statement Numbers	40, 41, 42

Secret	Rx
"The little blue pill is causing more problems in our relationship than it solves."	• What they don't tell you about the emotional side of Viagra and how to deal with it. • What to do when you wonder if it's you or the Viagra turning him on. • Making Viagra work for both of you.

Of primary interest: Chapter 10
Also helpful: Chapter 9

Many people find the reassurance that comes from understanding what is going on with their body or their partner's body—both physically and psychologically—enough to set them back on track. If it isn't, they can choose whether to pursue some form of available treatment.

The decision to seek medical guidance for a sexual problem can be tricky. It's going to require that you stop blaming yourself or your partner, stop hoping for magic, and stop wishing the problem would go away on its own. Also keep in mind the latest research that continues to document that sexual problems are a lot less psychologically based than we've been taught to believe. You may well find that what you thought might be an emotional problem is, in fact, physical, hormonal, or a normal effect of aging.

Given the changes in health care caused by managed care, getting the best treatment often requires that you become informed enough to ask the right questions even before you walk into a physician's office. The problem with managed care is that physicians have less and less time to spend with patients. It's not unusual for patients to find that they get six or seven minutes with their doctor at an annual exam. This book will provide you with the medical information you need to make your next conversation with your health-care provider a dialogue, rather than a monologue where the doctor speaks and you merely listen. It will also help you choose the right kind of health-care provider.

One might ask, "Shouldn't I tell my partner that I recognize a problem first?" In truth, if you could "just do it," you probably would have done it. The support of an empathic professional can make a real difference to your confidence in approaching your partner with words that may be as difficult for him to hear as they are for you to say. More important, you can't communicate effectively without knowing what the problem is.

Step Two: Bring the Secret Out into the Open

The chapters that follow will give you the words you need and the confidence to say them. You'll learn what has worked for other men and women and what has been a disaster so you can avoid it. You'll be able to say comfortably, "This is what I sense is going on between us. What do you feel is going on? Here's what I think we can try. What are you willing to try?" You'll know what to do if your partner blames *you* for the sexual problem. You'll also learn how not to fall into the trap of allowing your partner to be a mirror of your own sexual adequacy. In other words, if your partner isn't aroused, it doesn't mean that you are undesirable.

"What if my partner won't listen or won't talk to me about it?" There are answers for that, too. You are not alone. As you will learn in the chapters that follow, plenty of people have been where you are. They have persevered and worked their way through some very difficult problems. You can, too. Once you talk about the secret, it's on the way out.

What are you both going to feel when the secret is out in the open? Probably relief. You no longer have an uneasy silence but a problem you can both try to solve. This can give you a sense of control and optimism. It can also be scary to expose the problem. You may open Pandora's box and expose a nerve that really needs work to repair. But it will be more gratifying, more satisfying, more exciting and rewarding than having an elephant in the bedroom that neither of you is acknowledging.

Step Three: Consider Therapeutic Options

Now is the time to treat the symptoms and conditions that can be treated medically. If you are going to receive medical treatment for a sexual problem, let your partner in on your plan. Do what you can to include your partner.

If your relationship with your partner has been very difficult, you might wonder, Why not just get treatment and leave it at that? If it works, and I'm better, why tell my partner? It will probably make things worse!

Many couples have taken this route with dismal results. For example, he takes it upon himself to get a prescription for Viagra. She's appalled. She says, "He's never home, I feel like a widow most of the time, and now he's suddenly here demanding sex three times a day because of this pill. I've spent three years repressing my sexual feelings so I wouldn't hurt *his* feelings. Now all of a sudden I'm supposed to turn around on a dime and function. It's going to take more than a pill."

Or *she* learns everything there is to know about her sexual response and why it isn't happening but never shares this with her husband. Her new interest in sex and the new positions she wants to try in the bed-room give *him* a solid case of performance anxiety as she takes the initiative for the first time.

A woman who finally gets in touch with her sexual needs and determines, Hey, I want more out of sex—I deserve more than I've settled for—can be threatening to her partner. He thinks, Where are all of these expectations coming from? I wonder if *she's* having an affair.

If you've been keeping a secret in the bedroom, chances are good that your partner is aware of it, too. Going for treatment together can strengthen your relationship and actually enhance the treatment.

Step Four: Deal with the Emotional Aftereffects of Successful Treatment

There can be as much emotional fallout from the cure as there was from the problem! Just as there are people who get depressed after they get a promotion, there are people who find that positive changes in their sexual lives can bring tension and pressure.

Change is change. It's stressful. It's an upheaval. You may have some surprising new feelings once you don't have this problem to distract you anymore. You may have spent years trying to protect yourself or restore a sense of order by shutting down your emotions and sexual feelings. The chapters ahead will help you put a voice to these feelings so that you and your partner can work *with* them instead of against them.

Step Five: Engage Each Other in a Search for New Ways to Reconnect and Make Sex Fun Again

Do you realize that human beings are the only species that has sex for recreation? Once your secret is out in the open, it's a matter not only of being able to function but also of getting back a little bit of the fire. That's probably one of the more challenging things to do, even for people who have not had a sexual problem. However, you *can* do it.

You and your partner have the capacity to recapture the spirit of fun and adventure you once had. There are many techniques and new things you can try. Sometimes you will need to alter your ideas about sex or take on different expectations to bring back some of the excitement. You will learn how to achieve this new mind-set in the pages that follow.

Secrets can slowly and painfully erode a relationship, especially if those secrets are related to sex, the most intimate sector of a couple's life together. This book will help guide you in exposing and eradicating the secret with knowledge. You deserve a sexual relationship that is fulfilling and exciting. No matter how long something has been missing, you really do have a good chance to achieve what you desire. The chapters that follow will show you how.

THE SECRET

"It Hurts So Much When We Have Sex That I Wonder If There's Something Seriously Wrong with Me."

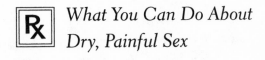 *What You Can Do About Dry, Painful Sex*

"WHAT HAPPENS TO ME," Lynda, forty-two, admits, "is that he'll do something incredibly sweet. Or he'll come behind me, kiss my neck, and run his hands down my body. I go to bed that night with every intention of making love. I'm thinking, This is going to be one of our best times. His hands feel good, and I'm aroused. Then he touches me, intimately, and gets this look on his face. I'm absolutely dry. This isn't the first time. We go on in spite of this. It really hurts at the time and even the next day, but how do I even explain this? What's stopping me from getting wet? Why isn't my body getting turned on?"

Melanie, fifty-three, married recently for the second time after being widowed four years ago, says, "I tell Rob that it hurts when we make love. But he doesn't really understand. He'll say, 'Come on, let me try this,' or 'Relax, while I do this.' He doesn't realize how much it hurts when he keeps touching me. I think, You can do that forever and nothing's going to happen, because this has nothing to do with you. It's just how I am now."

Both of these women were troubled by pain during sex. Once you fully understand why this happens, however, it is a problem that can be easy to solve. In this chapter you'll learn:

- what causes dryness, and what you can do about it with or without medication
- what else can cause painful sex, and how can you make it more pleasurable
- how you can talk to your partner when sex is painful without making him feel either of you are at fault
- how your partner can help you both make sex a pleasure again, instead of a frustrating, uncomfortable experience

Does Less Lubrication Mean You've Lost Interest in Him?

Lack of lubrication may not mean you aren't turned on by your partner. While stress, boredom, and not feeling sufficiently aroused are often blueprints for dry, painful sex, there are physical reasons why a woman may not lubricate. The most common physical cause of vaginal dryness in midlife is dwindling levels of estrogen.

To understand why this happens, let's take a look at what lubrication is and what causes it. As a woman becomes sexually aroused, blood moves into her vaginal tissues. This stimulates the glands of the vagina to secrete a moist, sticky substance. The increased blood to the vessels in and around the vagina causes release of lubricating fluid through the tissue of the vaginal walls to the inside of the vagina, just like increased blood flow to the skin can cause sweating.

Estrogen, the principal hormone that gives women their "female-ness," is important in this process because it promotes blood flow to the vagina and keeps the tissues healthy and elastic. Estrogen levels *begin* to decline when women are in their late thirties. After a woman has her last menstrual period (known as her *menopause*), her body stops producing most of its estrogen, causing even less blood flow to the tissues of the vagina and bladder. This is one of the chief reasons lubrication becomes difficult. Some women also report feeling less sensitive to stimulation because the tissues of the labia and clitoris are less engorged and responsive.

Why isn't your body producing its own estrogen anymore? When a woman is in her reproductive years, estrogen is made by the maturing egg cells inside her ovaries. As these egg cells are stimulated to grow by the brain, they produce estradiol. Estradiol is the main estrogen the body makes prior to menopause. In fact, the estradiol-making capability of these egg cells is what runs the cycle. When the estrogen levels are low at the time of the menstrual period, the brain alerts the ovaries to begin making estrogen for the new cycle. The stimulated eggs are the primary source of estrogen in a woman's body.

As you approach menopause, these eggs, which are growing older, are not as responsive to the brain's signals. While you are born with two million eggs, at puberty only 400,000 remain. By the late thirties, only twenty thousand or so remain. Even though usually only one egg ovulates per cycle, you lose hundreds more in the process. That's why the number of eggs depletes rather rapidly. By the time you reach your forties, the eggs that are left are the ones that haven't reacted to stimulation throughout your lifetime. Patients laugh when I tell them, "You know, these eggs that are left are pretty lazy eggs. They haven't responded, and they don't want to respond no matter what the rest of your body is telling them to do." The result is that you have much less estrogen in your body than you are used to, and this causes the symptoms that affect your sex life as well as many other different physical functions.

When you reach menopause, there are no more egg cells to make estrogen. Most of the estrogen made in the female body after menopause begins in the adrenal glands, which sit on top of the kidneys. They continue to make a malelike hormone that the body can ultimately turn into estrone—a different and slightly weaker kind of estrogen. This takes place in adipose tissue, or fat cells, and is why women who are very overweight can get into trouble with estrogen. They have a higher risk of cancer of the uterus because they have more fat cells that make more estrogen postmenopausally. The fat cells act like an estrogen-making factory.

Trouble lubricating during lovemaking is often the first tip-off to a woman that she is approaching menopause. It's often one of the main symptoms that brings a woman to my office. "I was really worried that something was wrong with me," said Gloria, forty-seven. "During sex my mind was saying one thing and my body was doing the opposite. I had no idea that I was approaching menopause because I'd been irregular for so long that missing a few periods didn't exactly ring a bell. I was relieved to know that it wasn't something serious but that many women experience this."

Suppose you're quite sure you're years away from menopause. What other physical causes can leave you dry during sex? Oral contraceptives can cause vaginal dryness and decreased lubrication. The birth-control pill and how it affects a woman's body is discussed in depth in Chapter 4. For now, realize that if you are taking the pill, it may be diminishing cervical and vaginal secretions. One option is to change the pill you are using and see if that improves matters, as it often does. Fifty percent of the time, when my patients change pills for this reason, they notice some improvement. But if this happens with many different pills, you may need to use another form of birth control or a vaginal lubricant.

Another cause of vaginal dryness and decreased lubrication can be breast-feeding, or lactation, which more women are doing in their late thirties and into their forties. When women breast-feed, their prolactin level goes up, because it's the hormone responsible for breast-feeding. Prolactin can act as an antiestrogen and thereby have an antiestrogen effect on the vagina—leading to dryness and painful intercourse. It's something that is seen so commonly that gynecologists call it "breast-feeding vagina." However, the last thing you want to do is treat the vagina with estrogen while you are breast-feeding. So I recommend that women use a lubricant such as Astroglide (see the following section) if needed.

Last, it also pays to look into your medicine cabinet if your dryness persists and consider what other kinds of medications you're taking. Antidepressants can cause vaginal dryness, as can antihistamines and even some medicines for high blood pressure. If you are taking these medications, it's important to let your health-care provider know about them. Perhaps he or she can suggest some alternative medications that won't cause this problem.

The Best Topical Treatments for Easier Sex

When lack of lubrication is the only thing causing you pain during sex, there are plenty of topical, nonhormonal treatments available over the counter that can help replace the lubrication your body isn't making. Here are the pros and cons of the most popular ones.

Astroglide

Astroglide is currently the favorite among my patients. Invented by a NASA subcontractor hunting for a sealant for an O-ring, it definitely helps things *take off*, women who use it agree.

Astroglide is a clear, thin, nonstaining, odorless, and tasteless liquid. It's very slippery and feels so close to the "real thing" that it's hard to tell the difference. It doesn't need to be placed in the vagina necessarily, either. You may find that your partner enjoys having it massaged on him during foreplay. It's not at all like medicine, and many couples routinely use it as part of their sex play no matter how wet the woman gets. One women revealed, "We were going through the Astroglide so fast, I thought it was evaporating. Finally I figured out that my husband liked it so much he was using it to masturbate. After the first shock of realizing he was doing *that*—and so much of *that*—we had a great conversation about sex. There was a new openness between us. I hid the Astroglide, though. I told him to get a bottle of his own!"

Astroglide is pH neutral and won't irritate the vagina. It's inexpensive and available at most drugstores. The only disadvantage occurs when you use too much of it. Like too much of the real thing, there can be so little friction that neither of you will feel much of anything.

K-Y Jelly

A clear gel, K-Y's popularity grew when couples discovered that Vaseline and other petroleum jellies ate their way through condoms. K-Y, which is water based, was the best, most widely available substitute. Recently

K-Y lubricant, which is thinner than the jelly, became available. It won't stain, doesn't have an odor, is virtually tasteless, and won't irritate the vagina. Whether placed in the opening of the vagina or on the penis, it will make penetration easier. It's a little more gooey than Astroglide, however, and some women say it feels less like the real thing.

Replens

There are couples who complain that the necessity of hunting around the medicine cabinet for the lubricant—or having to stop and put on the lubricant—breaks the mood. There are also women who are reluctant to let their partners know that *their* lubrication isn't natural (we'll discuss the wisdom of keeping this secret at the end of the chapter). Replens was created with these complaints in mind.

Replens, which is nonhormonal, contains polycarbophil, which has the advantage of lowering vaginal pH (increasing the acid level). This can help guard against infection, while increasing the quantity of vaginal secretions. It is sold over the counter in a package containing a month's supply. You apply it several times a week because one application lasts forty-eight to seventy-two hours. It feels more like a lotion than a lubricating jelly and works by clinging to the mucous membranes or lining of the vagina, simulating natural lubrication.

The advantage is that it's already there when the desire is to have quick and/or spontaneous sex. The obvious disadvantage is that if you haven't been anticipating sex, you may not have been using it. It isn't going to work as well as a fast lubricant.

Where it *does* work wonderfully is for women who feel dry not only during sex but throughout the day. When they exercise or even just walk around they feel a dryness that is uncomfortable and irritating. Replens is one product that promises to keep the vagina moist all day long, not only as a prelude to intercourse. Gyne Moistrin is another product similar to Replens.

Oils and Lubricants from the "Sex Stores"

Exotic in name, flavorful, often expensive, the name of the game here is *adventure*. Oils and lubricants you find on the shelves of the "sex stores" will definitely ease penetration. Whether they will also stain your sheets and perfume your bedroom with noxious scents of faux choco-late or other flavors is a matter of what you buy. But if the idea of tak-ing some "Pure Pineapple Passion" or "Strawberry Fields Forever" to bed with you seems more exciting than a tube of K-Y, why not? You'll know enough to throw it into the trash the next day if you're itching like crazy because this stuff has provided a happy home for a yeast infection. There are components in these lubricants that occasionally can cause an aller-gic reaction or irritation. If you are sensitive to scented or deodorant soaps, you may also be bothered by these lubricants.

When Sex Keeps Hurting and Lubricants Don't Help

Angela, fifty-three, says, "I told my older sister about Astroglide, want-ing to help, and she said, 'Angie, I've used that stuff. Trust me, in a cou-ple of years it's not going to help you at all. Now, no matter how much I use, after two minutes it feels like he's rubbing sandpaper against me. We've just stopped having sex. You'll see.'"

Angela's sister's experience is more common than one might think. For the first three years or so after menopause, women who have been having problems with intercourse due to dryness generally find they get all the help they need from the over-the-counter lubricants. But the vagina is an estrogen-sensitive organ. When it continues to be deprived of estrogen, changes occur.

Throughout the reproductive years, estrogen plays a crucial role in keeping your vagina healthy without any awareness on your part. It stim-ulates the creation of the vagina's tougher outer layer of cells, known as the *epithelium,* that line the inside of the vagina. It's this lining that pro-tects the delicate tissues underneath.

When a woman reaches menopause and her body stops producing estrogen, the change in hormone levels makes the vagina not only drier but also thinner and more easily injured. She may even experience lit-tle tears in the lining after intercourse. There is simply less tissue there to cushion against the friction that occurs during intercourse.

Another problem that comes from a thinner lining is less defense against infection. The acid level of the vagina can change because these cells are involved with maintaining the acid level of the vagina. Women who are postmenopausal can tend to have higher pH levels (less acid) in the vagina, which can mean a change in the bacteria that normally live in the vagina and that play an important role in keeping it healthy.

The thinner lining also causes a loss of elasticity. The vagina foreshortens, which means there is less depth to it. The opening becomes narrower. All of these changes are known collectively as *atrophy*. Over-the-counter lubricants do little to help. These changes definitely affect your sexual arousal, because if you begin to anticipate pain every time you have intercourse, you're going to try to avoid it. Also, this anticipation can cause "performance anxiety," which by itself can further decrease lubrication.

Many women are startled by these changes. They are eating right. They are exercising. They look and feel good. Many are no longer having hot flashes, the other major symptom of menopause. But if they haven't wanted to take the next step—replacing the estrogen their body no longer produces on its own—they are eventually going to notice the effects in the genital area, even if the rest of the passage through "the change" was an easy one.

Fighting Back with ERT

Estrogen replacement therapy (ERT) remains the best therapy for coping with and even reversing these changes. A woman can be all tightened up, foreshortened, and narrowed, yet reverse those changes within a few months of ERT. She may not get *all* the elasticity back, but she can certainly get enough to allow more than adequate sexual function.

Estrogen replacement is exactly what it says—replacing the estrogen a woman's body has ceased making. Be aware, however, that most women don't take estrogen alone—they take progesterone, and perhaps even testosterone, in a regimen known as *hormone replacement therapy* (HRT). In future chapters, particularly Chapters 4 and 5, you'll learn quite a bit more about HRT: why it's necessary to take progesterone with estrogen if you have your uterus; the advantages to other organs in your body, such as your bones, heart, and brain; the risks and benefits. For our purposes here, however, since we're talking about vaginal dryness, we're going to discuss estrogen alone and how it can help forestall changes to the genital area that cause painful sex.

If you considered taking estrogen before and decided to pass, be aware that modern advances in medications and new regimens are making it a safer and better option than ever. Still, the number one fear many women have about using estrogen replacement is the fear of increasing the risk of cancer of the breast. A large number of studies have been done to see if estrogen really increases this risk. Most of these studies can be divided into three groups. There is a group of studies that shows up to a 30 percent increase in the relative risk of cancer of the breast on hormone replacement therapy. The largest group of studies, however, shows no increase in relative risk at all. Another group of studies even shows a small decrease in relative risk. The most important information to take from this and to use in guiding your decision is that it's good news for women that there is *no* consensus. Remember, all the studies that demonstrated an increased risk in cancer of the lung from smoking were consistent, and increases in relative risk were on the order of 800 to 1200 percent. There was tremendous consensus that smoking was causing cancer of the lung. There is no such consensus about hormone replacement therapy and breast cancer. If one chooses to believe the worst-case scenario—that there is a 30 percent increase in relative risk—that means one to two more cases per year among ten thousand women, which is not considered to be a statistically important increase. That needs to be weighed against the protective effects you can get from estrogen.

Let's look at this breast cancer situation in another way. As a student of evolutionary biology, I find it difficult to accept that we have evolved into the complex organism we are only to have estrogen—our major reproductive hormone—cause cancer of the breast. Evolution passes on characteristics that help perpetuate a species, not kill it. What I *am* able to accept is that we have changed the biology; we have changed *how* we expose the breasts to these hormones. Let me explain what I mean.

A very long time ago, young women began having their periods in their mid-teens. They would ovulate a few times, become pregnant, and, if they lived through childbirth, they would then lactate (breast-feed) for seven or more years. So these women would not ovulate for eight or more years because of pregnancy and lactation. Then they would stop breast-feeding, ovulate a few times, become pregnant again, and repeat the scenario. After following this pattern a few times, they would die in their forties—from a cold or from being eaten by a saber-toothed tiger. These women may have ovulated only seventy or eighty times in their lifetimes.

What do we find now, in the "modern" age? As a result of better nutrition, young women are having their first period at age nine, ten, or eleven. Then, because of schooling and entry into the workplace, they very often put off first childbearing until their late twenties or early thirties (or beyond). Thus, they expose themselves (and their breasts) to twenty-plus years of incessant ovulation without interruption by pregnancy or lactation, unless they happen to be on the birth-control pill. "So what's wrong with ovulation?" you ask; "It's natural to ovulate." It's *not* natural to ovulate like that. Each month, after estrogen starts the process of ovulation, progesterone stimulates the breasts to enlarge and prepares them for pregnancy. That's why they call it *pro-gest-erone*—for gestation. The way progesterone makes this happen is by causing *proliferation* of breast cells—cell division that produces more cells so the breasts enlarge. That's why they get sore before a woman's period. When no pregnancy occurs, this cell proliferation *regresses* (withdraws), the breasts go back down to normal size, and the soreness disappears. With incessant ovulation, this scenario repeats itself over and over again twelve to thirteen times a year, up to 350 to 450 times a lifetime. Proliferation, regression; proliferation, regression. Stay with me now, because here's where it gets complicated.

The only difference between proliferating cells and malignant cells is that proliferating cells know when to *stop* dividing, stop producing more cells, while malignant cells don't; they just keep going. If the breasts are constantly exposed to proliferation every cycle, the chances are greatly increased that one of those proliferating cells will have a mutation occur and turn into a malignant cell that won't stop dividing. This slowly becomes a cancer that is finally discovered ten to twenty years later.

So it's not the hormones themselves but the way we are exposing the breasts to the hormones that causes the problem. That's why I say we've changed the biology. Incidentally, the same process of incessant ovulation is responsible for the increase in ovarian cancer, endometriosis, ovarian cysts, and infertility in modern times. Even the breast cancer we see in women twenty to thirty years of age may be because of this very early exposure to ovulation. Progress is good for society, but such a drastic change in our biology has its price.

There have now been numerous studies done that show women who develop cancer of the breast while on hormone replacement therapy tend to have more benign disease and fewer recurrences. Also, studies are now beginning to show that women who have had cancer of the breast and *then* choose to go on hormone replacement therapy may in fact live longer and have fewer recurrences. This is all early research, and it is still a concern to prescribe hormone replacement therapy to women who have a history of breast cancer, but it is enough data to allow us to start questioning the dictum that once you've had cancer of the breast you can't take estrogen.

There really are new choices for ERT, products that past generations of women never even dreamed would become available. They include orals, patches, creams, gels, and even rings.

The Orals

We talk about estrogen as if it's one single hormone, but there are really three kinds: estrone, estradiol, and estriol. If you had your blood tested before menopause and estrogen was detected in your blood, it would be estradiol—specifically 17-beta estradiol. After menopause it would basically be estrone. Estriol is an estrogen made only during pregnancy by the placenta. When you replace estrogen, you don't normally replace all three kinds of estrogen but one. Which one depends on what you're taking and how you're taking it.

The estrogens that come in pill form include Premarin, Estratab, Estrace, Cenestin, Menest, Ortho-Est, and Ogen. Most of them are plant based except Premarin, which is conjugated equine estrogen, which means it comes from pregnant mare's urine. The advertisements for all of these estrogens are becoming almost humorous because each one is trying to out-"natural" the other ones. Premarin claims that it is the only truly *natural* estrogen because natural means "existing in nature." Pregnant mare's urine is about as natural as natural gets. The horses aren't particularly pleased about that, but Premarin's manufacturers make much out of pointing out that their product is natural even though it goes through ninety purification steps prior to pill formation.

Estrace, on the other hand, is plant based, which means something is taken from a plant, brought into the lab, and altered so that it becomes the kind of estrogen that your body used to make. Estrace is 17-beta estradiol once it comes out of the lab, the same estrogen a woman's body makes before menopause. Hence Estrace's manufacturer argues that *its* product is the only truly natural estrogen.

The makers of Ortho-Est and Ogen also claim that their estrogens, which are mostly plant based, are the natural estrogens because they are comprised of estrone, which is the major estrogen released in a woman's body *after* menopause. Estratab is a product similar, but not identical, to Premarin, but it does not come from any animal matter. It, too, is plant based, and hence the people who make Estratab feel that it is natural as well—and that they don't have to bother horses getting it. Cenestin, one of the newest oral estrogens, is almost identical to Premarin but is plant based instead of animal based. The Cenestin pill itself also has a more modern coating and structure (remember, Premarin is over forty years old), so blood levels of the hormone remain more stable and fluctuate less, making the effect more even.

There are, of course, makers of herbal remedies that are quick to say that none of these are natural! The real point is that any of these estrogens will successfully treat painful intercourse if it's caused by dryness or atrophy, whether somebody thinks they are natural or not.

What's good about having so many different choices is that there is something for everyone. You can work with your doctor to individualize your estrogen therapy to find one that is most comfortable and effective for you.

The advantage of taking estrogen orally is that swallowing a pill is quick and easy. It's absorbed systemically, which means you'll get the advantages to all parts of your body where estrogen plays a healthful role in addition to the vagina, such as your bones, heart, brain, and skin.

One disadvantage of oral estrogen is that some women don't absorb the medication very well from the gastrointestinal tract. For example, I had one patient, Jeri, fifty, who was on a relatively *high* dosage of estrogen replacement given to her by her internist. After four months, she was still complaining about hot flashes and vaginal dryness. After testing her estrogen levels, taking even *more* estrogen wasn't the answer. For patients like Jeri, the problem isn't the estrogen but how it's delivered to their systems. I prescribed the estrogen patch—which I'll discuss next—and it made her problems disappear rapidly.

You may find that the advantages of oral estrogens far outweigh the disadvantages. The question is, which one do you use and how do you take it? If you've decided that oral estrogens are something you'd like to try, here are some suggestions you can discuss with your doctor:

1. All oral estrogen comes in different dosages. Premarin and Cenestin, for example, come in 0.3, 0.625, 0.9, and 1.25 mg. Estratab comes in 0.3, 0.625, and 1.25 mg. My bias is to take the lowest level that has the desired effect. Start low, and you can gradually build up to a higher dose if you need to. This also means that if you try a low dose and nothing happens, don't immediately conclude that estrogen doesn't work for you. The use of hormones almost always takes some fine-tuning.

2. There isn't one brand that is more effective than another. However, one might cause you side effects while others do not. While all oral estrogens are somewhat similar, there are some mild differences in how women react to these different kinds of estrogen. I find that woman are a little bit less sensitive to Estratab, for example. They don't tend to get as much breast tenderness or bloating. Premarin and Cenestin, both conjugated estrogens, are so similar that I tend to prescribe Cenestin, which is plant based, over Premarin, which is animal based, because I know exactly what's in it. No matter how hard they try, they can't make the pregnant mares urinate *just* estrogen. There are other compounds in Premarin that aren't listed on the label. A woman may go to

two different doctors and be prescribed two different estrogens, not because one is more effective but because each doctor tends to have one or two favorite estrogens. An important fact to remember is that all oral estrogens are first metabolized to estrone by the liver regardless of source.

3. *When* to take it can be as important as what you're taking. Most hormone medications are absorbed better if you take them after a meal, when the digestive juices are surging.

4. Estrogen therapy isn't just for women in menopause. I have patients who are perimenopausal and are supplementing their erratic estrogen levels to relieve symptoms. Don't let your doctor tell you that you're still having menstrual periods so you can't take estrogen. There is much more about the ins and outs of HRT to come, but suffice it to say you can benefit from additional estrogen long before your menopause, and it's really a question of how much your symptoms bother you and how motivated you are to rid yourself of them.

The Patch

The patch is applied directly to the skin of the lower abdomen or buttocks and is either left on for a week or replaced twice a week, depending on the brand. Current brands of estrogen patches include Estraderm, Climara, Alora, Fempatch, Vivelle, and Esclim.

The delivery of medication through the skin by using a patch will really become much more common in the future. For right now, one of the major benefits of using an estrogen patch is the steadiness of the estrogen dose that gets to the bloodstream. When you take a pill, the blood level of the medication slowly rises and then comes down. When you take the next pill, that level goes up again. So there is a hill-and-valley effect when there are changing levels of medication in your system. When you use a patch to add estrogen to the body, the estrogen is absorbed through the skin *directly* into the bloodstream without first going to the liver. There's constant release of estrogen from the patch into the bloodstream. This means there are more even levels of estrogen in the system. Also, the patch delivers 17-beta estradiol, which is the estrogen the body makes normally before menopause, although in my opinion that is not necessarily preferable for HRT users, as I'll discuss later.

Another advantage is that by going in through the skin, the estrogen does not have to go into the gastrointestinal tract and the liver. When you take a medication orally, it goes into the stomach, where it is broken up by the stomach acid and then goes into the small intestine. From there it's absorbed into blood vessels that go directly to the liver. This is very important and makes a lot of sense if you're Mother Nature, because it protects the individual from poisons that may be taken in by mouth. The liver detoxifies everything first, which means it gets rid of anything that could be bad or poisonous before it enters the systemic bloodstream. Poisons work only when there's too much of them to be handled by the liver. So oral estrogens first go through the liver, where they are metabolized to estrone, while patches deliver estradiol directly into the bloodstream without it being metabolized to estrone.

A problem with estrogen going through the liver first and then into the bloodstream is that estrogen can cause a tumor in the liver called a *hepatoma*. This is extremely rare, but the risk does exist. A selling point of the patch is that the medication bypasses the liver, and you don't run the risk of getting this tumor. Also, there is some data suggesting that oral estrogen can increase your risk of gallbladder disease and/or gallstones. By bypassing the liver, you tend to diminish that risk as well.

An important disadvantage of the patch is that it can be irritating to your skin. You can get a rash that needs to be treated with cream. Some women find that it's annoying to have little red blotches here and there from their patch. However, there are a lot of patches to choose from. Some may irritate your skin and others may not. Also, dirt or lint can collect around the edge of the patch. A new elastic patch may help prevent that.

A second disadvantage of the patch is that you wear it on your skin where it can be seen. Patches are about the size of a silver dollar. Vivelle, however, has just come out with the Vivelle Dot, which is ultrasmall. Still, if you wear a patch, while you are making love your partner may reach around, feel it, and say "Hey, what's that?" If that man is your husband of thirty years, that's one thing. But, Brenda, forty-three, had this to say: "I had my menopause at thirty-seven, and I didn't love having this red flag (or clear plastic thing) announcing it to the new man in my life or every woman in the locker room at the health club. I used to take it off, but that got expensive. Today I'm forty-three and engaged, and I could be wearing the patch on my forehead and he wouldn't care."

More important, there is a potential disadvantage to the patch that affects more than just the skin or the liver. Many women who choose to go on ERT or HRT are not only concerned with the vaginal changes that make sex uncomfortable but also want the rest of the benefits they can receive from taking estrogen as well, including protection against osteoporosis, heart attack, and stroke. Estrogen protects you against stroke and heart attack in two major ways. First, it works directly on arteries that feed the heart, allowing them to widen to let more blood flow through them. Second, it changes the level of cholesterol in your body, increasing the good cholesterol (HDL) and decreasing the bad one (LDL). This protective effect occurs in the liver, where cholesterol is made. If you bypass the liver by using the patch, you will not get this effect early on, and it may take a number of years before you *do* see the benefit. For this reason, many physicians do not use the patch as a first line of therapy for women beginning hormone replacement, especially if they already have cardiac problems.

Estrogen Creams and Gels

Estrogen creams have been around for some time. They include Premarin, Estrace, Ogen, and Ortho Dienestrol cream. Either you use an applicator to put the cream inside the vagina or you massage the cream on the opening between the labia or outside the labia to help get estrogen directly to these tissues.

Creams are a popular choice among women who don't want to take hormone replacement therapy but who want to deal with the vaginal dryness. But you must remember that when you use estrogen vaginally it is still absorbed into the bloodstream. It may not happen at first, though. When you have vaginal atrophy and you massage estrogen into those tissues, you're going to get very little absorption into the bloodstream, because the atrophy is so bad that absorption doesn't take place. As you improve the vagina by using the estrogen, absorption will occur. The healthier the vagina, the more the absorption. If you are worried about absorbing vaginal estrogen into your bloodstream, you should use very little of it only one or two days a week.

One more thing to consider is that creams are, frankly, not as user-friendly as pills. Their use requires placing a glob of medication into the vagina, which can (and often will) leak out. You do this about twice a week at night, so if you aren't good with schedules, it's easy to forget to do. You have to use an applicator to place the cream into the vagina. You usually get one applicator with the medication. Some women complain about having to reuse the applicator: "I don't want to stick this dirty thing in my vagina." They feel they should boil that applicator. Nothing is less necessary. You can just wash it out. As clean as a woman keeps herself, the average, healthy vagina is still full of bacteria (as is the mouth). These bacteria are useful bacteria and essentially not harmful.

You don't want to use your estrogen cream before sex, especially if your sex play includes oral sex. It won't poison your partner, but it definitely tastes unpleasant. In any case, be assured that millions of women use estrogen cream, love the fact that it's being absorbed in the area where they need it, and don't worry about the risks of estrogen replacement therapy as *much* as women taking orals.

Estrogel, which is an estrogen in *gel* form, is available in Europe and will soon be available in the United States under a different name. The gel is rubbed on the skin, usually of the upper arms. It's quite possible that Estrogel may revolutionize HRT in the United States. With gel, you avoid the stickiness of the patches and the frequent rashes where the patch was. Basically, you get all the advantages of a patch without any of the annoyances. For the first time, women will be able to think of their HRT as a "cosmetic" gel that is rubbed into the skin as opposed to a "medicine" that has to be ingested.

Nontraditional Estrogens

Triestrogen is an estrogen that is available orally and as a cream. It's made up by compounding pharmacies (pharmacies that make prescriptions by hand). You still need a doctor's prescription to get it. Triestrogen consists of estradiol in small amounts, estrone in small amounts, and larger amounts of estriol. Recall that estriol is made in a woman's body only during pregnancy by the placenta. Many women feel that it's very safe since it's associated with pregnancy. There is also a feeling among consumers that estriol is the one estrogen that *protects* against breast cancer, but there is little data to support this, and I caution my patients who have chosen to use it for that reason.

Certain herbal products such as black cohosh, dong quai, and ginseng contain components called phytoestrogens, which are not estrogens but estrogen*like* compounds. These products are discussed fully in Chapter 5. One of the benefits of herbal estrogen is that it is not very strong, but that's also a drawback. It often will have only the most minimal effects on these vaginal changes and not provide adequate cardiovascular or bone protection.

Beyond the Topicals: Estring

You might feel that smoothing on salves and creams is an unnatural, messy, time-consuming task. Or perhaps you are still having a problem with dryness and/or a lack of elasticity even while you're on HRT or ERT. You'll find Estring a welcome alternative.

Estring is a soft, flexible, halo-shaped plastic ring placed in the vagina that has estrogen (estradiol) inside it. Very small amounts of estrogen leak from the ring on a daily basis. Estring was such a breakthrough for so many women because there is very little absorption of estrogen into the bloodstream from the vagina due to the small amounts released daily. This meant that it was a godsend for women who have problems that prevent them from using estrogen if it gets into their bloodstream, such as women who have had breast cancer or are at high risk for it. There is only minimal absorption from the vagina in the first couple of days of usage.

Caroline, fifty-seven, a patient of mine who is a breast cancer survivor, is very enthusiastic about Estring. "It took me long enough to get over my breast cancer and start moving on in my life. Then it started to become next to impossible to have intercourse. My vagina was simply getting smaller and smaller, and there was nothing I could do about it. My oncologist said that I shouldn't take hormone replacement therapy or use estrogen creams. Lubricants didn't help. After speaking with other breast cancer survivors, I found this was a very common problem. I felt that I'd struggled to feel sexual again after my breast cancer and all that followed, but now my sex life had no chance without estrogen. That's when I first heard about Estring. Or course, when I started with it, I had every question in the world. Was it going to fall out? Would he feel it during sex? What are the side effects? How long would it take before it worked?"

Although Estring begins to release estrogen the moment it's in place, you may find that it takes about two to three weeks or even longer for you to tell that it is having a positive effect on your vagina, and your urinary tract as well. The lack of estrogen can also cause the bladder to lose its elasticity. Then the bladder can't stretch and hold as much urine as it used to, so you have to urinate more frequently. Using the ring will help the bladder regain elasticity as well.

One ring is effective for three months and then should be replaced. Some of my patients find that if they use it for one three-month interval, their problems with dryness disappear to the point where they don't feel the need to replace the ring. Six months later they use it again for another three months. In other words, you can use Estring as you learn you have a need for it.

In terms of side effects, some women experience an increase in vaginal fluids, but this, of course, is one of the side effects you want. Some women see a yellowish mucus buildup on the ring when it's removed, but this is not dangerous. Any itching, bad odor, or other problems should be reported to your doctor or health-care provider.

Will either you or your partner feel Estring during sex? Most women and their partners don't. If, however, you do, you can remove it. It's easy to reinsert. One more thing my patients often ask about: there has not yet been a report of a man pulling out of the vagina after sex and finding the ring wrapped around his penis!

When Hormones Don't Relieve Vaginal Dryness

While most women who take ERT or HRT find a great deal of relief of vaginal dryness and atrophy, some get only minimal change. Unfortunately, being on hormone replacement therapy doesn't mean the vagina is definitely going to respond to the level you want it to. What you can do is either increase the estrogen a bit or use Estring along with HRT.

Something else to consider is the kind of estrogen product you are on. There is a form of estrogen replacement therapy known as SERMs (selective estrogen receptor modulators) that are loosely called selective or "designer estrogens" even though they are not really estrogens. While SERMs *look* like estrogen and *act* like estrogen in some places, they act like an antiestrogen in others. Raloxifene, sold as Evista, is one of these SERMs that may be prescribed as ERT. Raloxifene acts as an antiestrogen in the uterus but also in the vagina and bladder. Therefore, it will not work to combat vaginal dryness and may, indeed, make it worse.

The perfect selective estrogen will have a beneficial effect on heart, bone, brain, vagina, bladder, skin, and more, while having an antiestrogen effect on the uterus and the breast. Science has not yet developed the perfect SERM. But, so far, Evista *may* have the ability to protect against breast cancer while offering reasonable protection against cardiovascular disease, uterine cancer, osteoporosis, and resulting fractures. A concern about Evista is that it can cause or increase hot flashes. Since hot flashes result from a change in the temperature control area of the brain, some researchers worry that Evista may have some *anti*estrogen effects in the brain. Only more studies will resolve these concerns.

What Can I Do If I Don't Want to Take Estrogen?

When sex is painful after menopause, when it requires lubricants, medication, etc., many women think, Let's just forget about this now. I'll come back to it later, when I'm way past menopause. You might assume that the urogenital changes eventually stop, as the hot flashes usually do, but it doesn't work that way. Hot flashes are caused by the withdrawal of estrogen that occurs with menopause. Eventually the body adjusts, so the hot flashes can disappear. Vaginal dryness and bladder problems do *not* come from withdrawal of estrogen but from chronic low levels of it. Without some kind of intervention on your part, the changes will continue, and any symptoms you have will persist and even worsen.

What option do you have then, if you can't or choose not to take estrogen? Doctors often say "Use it or lose it" when it comes to sex. Lack of use promotes vaginal atrophy, while frequent intercourse helps maintain elasticity. Some women find this message irritating. "Reminds me of the pressure to have sex when I didn't feel like it many times in my life" was the way one woman put it.

However, "Use it or lose it" is a very important concept postmenopausally, not only for the health of the vagina but for your overall health. Human beings need to "use it or lose it" in terms of many organs of our body. The heart weakens if you don't exercise. The bladder is another example. Urologists have been telling men and women for years that the answer to having to get up several times a night to urinate isn't drinking less water but drinking more. The bladder will maintain elasticity only by keeping the water going through regularly and letting it stretch the bladder. Even the brain will atrophy if you don't stimulate it by reading, learning new things, following intellectual pursuits, and thinking.

The sex organs are the same. Yet there can be many reasons why you may find that "Use it or lose it" is a problem. The most frequent one is the lack of a ready, willing, and able partner:

"He isn't interested. Ever since his prostate surgery, that's been that."

"It's difficult, it hurts, and he isn't understanding about this. He thinks I should just give him oral sex. I don't want to go through it anymore."

"I never was that into sex to begin with. It isn't that important to me."

"I think sex is great. But I haven't had a partner since my divorce, and I don't see one on the horizon."

"I'd have sex, but since he developed diabetes, he has a problem performing."

I had one patient, forty-eight, who came in for her annual exam, and it was obvious that she had begun to lose elasticity. I asked her if she was sexually active, and she said, "Not since my divorce five years ago." I asked her if she had any thoughts of resuming sexual activity at some point in the future. When she said, "I hope so," I explained that she would need to begin to do something about the atrophic changes she was experiencing *now*. I pointed out to her that sexual intercourse isn't the only way to increase blood flow to the vagina and keep it healthy. For patients who don't have a willing or able partner, I suggest they take the advice from the song made famous by Carly Simon: "Nobody Does It Better." Although she wasn't singing about masturbation, doctors and sex therapists definitely recommend it as a remedy because it works to keep the vaginal walls healthy, elastic, and responsive.

There is a particular kind of masturbation that best keeps the vaginal walls healthy, elastic, and responsive. Massaging the outside of the vagina, stimulating the clitoris, is the type of masturbation most women are familiar with. It should increase some blood flow to the area, as well as be enjoyable. It also keeps the nerve supply to the clitoris "trained." In other words, if you use a nerve pathway, signals get used to moving along it and functioning. When you don't use a pathway, it gets lazy. By achieving an orgasm through masturbation, you're basically keeping the circuits open.

But this isn't enough. With the subtle changes that inevitably take place after menopause, some kind of penetration of the vagina becomes necessary to keep it physically fit for intercourse. In other words, it takes more than this outer massaging to maintain the length and width of the vagina as well as maintain its elasticity. If you don't have a partner or if you have a partner of the same sex, the easiest method is to use digital penetration, which basically means to use your fingers. This can stimulate the vagina and stretch it as well. The use of vaginal dilators or vaginal inserts can be very important in helping maintain the length, width, and elasticity of the vagina. They can be used with or without clitoral massage, preferably with. If you are unable to achieve orgasm, the stimulation can still help increase blood flow. Masturbation can also be done with a vibrator that includes a portion that is inserted into the vagina. Of course, you need to be careful with anything you place inside the vagina by inserting it slowly, gently, and often using a lubricant.

How to Safely Resume Sex After a Hiatus

Colleen, fifty-eight, was divorced for ten years when she met Mike, sixty-four, on a flight to visit her son. "We both had children who had moved to California, and neither of them was setting the world on fire. It was reassuring to hear that Mike had so many of the same frustrations I was having. Mike admitted he was on that flight to try to talk some sense into his own son, who was constantly broke and calling home for money. Well, obviously we talked up a storm. And when we got back home it was natural to meet, and soon one thing led to another. I never thought I'd ever fall in love again. I hadn't had any kind of sexual relations in over ten years. I'd been on hormone replacement therapy, but even with the hormone replacement therapy I wasn't sure I could have sex. I wanted to talk to my doctor about it, but I lost my nerve."

Colleen was like many women in similar circumstances. She wanted to know the best approach to resuming sex after being away from it. With men becoming more active or able to resume sexual relations because of new therapies such as Viagra, some women who haven't had any intercourse in years find that it's almost like being a virgin again, with no pill to instantly make intercourse possible.

Whether it's been six months or six years, what's important here is not to force yourself to go through the experience without any prior preparation. Friction from intercourse could cause tears and bleeding in the vaginal walls due to the loss of elasticity. See your gynecologist and ask if there is evidence of vaginal atrophy. As mentioned before, estrogen cream will often bring dramatic improvement within weeks. Clinical studies on Estring, the vaginal ring mentioned previously, showed that it provided relief or improvement of vaginal and urinary symptoms in most women within three months. You can also help prepare the vagina by first gently placing your or your partner's finger through the vaginal opening. Once that has become easier, you can move to a series of dilators, which will eventually prepare the vagina for penetration. Dilators can be obtained discreetly through reputable companies like Good Vibrations, a mail-order company that also has retail stores in San Francisco and Berkeley. It doesn't sell its customer lists to anyone and has built its positive reputation on tactfulness and protecting customers' privacy. Contact information is in the appendix.

Communicate with your partner, even if it's simply to say, "It's been a long time. Let's work together and see what we can do."

What Else Can I Do About Dryness?

Here are some suggestions that every woman should be following to keep the vagina healthy:

- Drink enough water to keep yourself hydrated. This is good for the bladder as well as the vagina.
- Wear underpants with cotton crotches. This helps air circulate and is especially important if you are prone to yeast infections.
- Avoid deodorant soaps, douches, and hygiene sprays, which can be drying. Avoid frequent bubble baths if you have vaginal problems.
- If you develop a symptom, such as itching, don't try to rid yourself of it with soap and a washcloth. There are natural oils on the skin and lining the vagina that need to stay there to keep tissues healthy. If you have chronic problems with itching and infections, shower instead of taking a bath. Toilet paper is a serious offender. The formalin in the paper can be irritating. Using a spray bottle with water and a soft washcloth to pat yourself dry, although inconvenient, is sometimes a necessity.

What Else You Need to Rule Out When Sex Is Painful

While the most common reason sex is painful for women is that the vagina isn't lubricated enough, there are other conditions that women need to be aware of. If you have these symptoms, it's important to consult with your health-care provider.

Frequent Infections

You may have spent your entire life up to now never experiencing any kind of vaginal infection. All of a sudden, you find you're having one after another. Why? When estrogen levels go down, the vagina is less resistant to all kinds of infections. The thickness of the lining of the vagina, called the *vaginal mucosa*, is very important as a protector against infection and disease. With the lack of estrogen, part of the loss of elasticity happens because the mucosa gets much thinner, and that allows bacteria or infectious agents to enter into the vaginal wall more easily. The big three common vaginal infections that women get are yeast infections, bacterial vaginosis, and trichomoniasis. Each of them can occasionally cause pain during intercourse. Each has a specific therapy and is often treated with over-the-counter remedies. But if you experience any persistent infections, definitely see your gynecologist.

Vaginismus

Vaginismus is a condition where there is spasm of the muscles at the opening of the vagina upon touch or penetration. Repeated painful sex can cause vaginismus. It can also have a psychological cause, usually a traumatic sexual experience. The memory of that experience causes everything to tighten up. Unfortunately, vaginismus can become a vicious cycle. You feel pain, you get spasms, and that makes it more painful, causing more spasms.

A combination of physical therapy aimed at learning to relax enough to be able to tolerate penetration and psychological therapy that treats the underlying issues has helped many women overcome this condition.

Vulvodynia

Vulvodynia is a serious and very troubling problem. It is essentially pain in the vulvar area, mostly at the bottom of the opening of the vagina, the perineum, and sometimes along the labia, on the sides. It's such severe pain that if I touch the area with a Q-Tip, a patient with the condition will often jump away. Most patients who have vulvodynia also have vaginismus as a reaction to the pain.

Vulvodynia is a complicated problem that has to do with nerve supply and the way nerves receive the sensation of touch or sensation of pain. It's as if the nerves are overstimulated and give a pain response instead of a normal "Oh, that feels good" response. There are theories that it's caused by chronic infections or that it's an autoimmune phenomenon of some sort, which means that the body is attacking its own tissues in the vaginal area.

There are many different kinds of treatment for vulvodynia. The existence of many different types of therapy for a problem in medicine usually means none of them really work well. That's unfortunately the case with the treatment for vulvodynia. Neurologic drugs like amitriptyline and neurontin are being used with some success. Occasionally, surgery to remove the involved tissue will work.

Because treating vulvodynia is so tricky, if you're diagnosed with this problem it's important to see a specialist in touch with all the potential therapies. Your gynecologist can usually direct you to one in your area.

Herpes

The most important infection to rule out when sex is really painful is herpes. It is the most common cause of really painful intercourse from an infection.

Herpes is a viral disease that is very prevalent in society. It is usually transmitted sexually from one person to another. It is possible to have intercourse with someone who has herpes and not get it, but if you do get it, usually symptoms will appear within a couple of weeks of exposure.

The first symptom is a little reddened area that begins to become hypersensitive to touch. Then blisters develop on that red base. Soon after, the blisters will lose their "roofs" and ulcers remain. These little ulcers then gradually heal.

The first episode of herpes can be so painful that some women are unable to urinate. The first infection will last longer, sometimes two weeks or longer, and usually be far more extensive and wider spread around the area of the vagina and anus.

The problem with herpes is that it can be recurrent. Some women will never get it again after the initial infection. Some will get it once a year. Others will get it once a month, and it can be debilitating.

Getting a diagnosis of herpes can be psychologically devastating in itself. I tell my patients that the best thing that ever happened to herpes was AIDS. AIDS, which is a deadly disease, put herpes in its place. It made herpes seem to be nothing more than an annoyance. It has a very strong effect on sexuality, however, because of the potential for transmission. I've seen women who report they have lost their sexual drive because they're frightened that they're going to give herpes to someone. However, there is much hope for herpes sufferers.

Although there is as yet no cure for herpes, medications such as Zovirax, Famvir, and Valtrex can reduce the duration of the outbreak. Continuing the medication for an extended period of time can prevent recurrences. Zovirax can, on average, reduce a ten-day outbreak to five days. Famvir and Valtrex work a little faster. Three days is the reported average.

It's important to begin taking these medications the moment you feel a symptom of a recurrence. Generally, women who have herpes learn what it feels like when they are about to get an outbreak. Sometimes the first signal is a tingling or a pain that goes down their leg. If you take the medication right away, you may even be able to keep the infection from coming out.

More and better treatment options are arriving. Researchers predict that in the next two years a new herpes vaccine will be available. There is much more that can be said about herpes, but it is beyond the scope of this book. If you find that herpes is affecting your sexuality, discuss this with your doctor.

How to Talk to Your Partner About the Pain and Dryness You Experience During Sex

Vaginal dryness is definitely a challenge most women will face but one that has many remedies. While you're experimenting with different options, how can you approach your partner so that he'll see this as you do—a part of the process of aging that has its challenges and solutions—rather than rejection of him or evidence that you're "no longer sexual"?

Usually, if you notice vaginal dryness, he's going to notice it, too. Most discerning men will notice you're not lubricating as you used to. He may feel he's not stimulating you enough.

In the midst of sex, simple statements will probably work best: "Can we slow down? I need more time." Or "This is hurting me. Can we do something different?" Or "I'm turned on, but somehow my body isn't following my mind." Or even, "Tonight doesn't seem to be my night."

Later, in discussing the problem with their partner, some women find that a frank approach is best:

> "I told my husband, 'I'm noticing that I'm really dry, and it's not anything you're doing or not doing. I'm going to talk to my doctor about it the next time I see her.' He was relieved."

Once you've discussed your problem with your gynecologist or health-care provider and have gotten information or decided on a treatment, you can choose a comfortable time to share the details with your partner. Be sensitive to your partner's level of comfort. Some men are interested in all of the facts. Some, however, are like Jean's husband. She says: "For a man who can use all kinds of four-letter words in the middle of sex, it's amazing that he turns red and looks completely grossed out when you say 'vaginal dryness' at four o'clock in the afternoon. He's really uncomfortable with the word *vagina* altogether. Say *menopause* and he finds a reason to leave the room. He tells me, 'Honey, I don't need to know every detail about it. If you're going to the doctor, and it's helping you, that's all I really want to know.' In the end, all he understands is that I wear this patch and that it is helping my symptoms. It's fine, actually. I save the details for my sister."

Sandra, fifty-four, is divorced and has found a way to discuss her needs comfortably with the men she becomes sexually involved with: "I've dated several men over the past few years, and what I've found works best is to put things positively. Obviously, I don't say, 'Look, we've got to use some Astroglide or it'll feel like you're ripping me apart.' The first sexual relationship I had after this started happening, I admit I just used the Astroglide in the bathroom and hoped he'd think it was him turning me on. Now I just say, 'Let's use this; it makes it more fun.'"

Chances are, if *you're* really OK with the changes that are occurring in your body and any special needs you have, he will be, too. Talking to your partner rather than trying to hide the trouble has a bonus you might not suspect. As he ages, as he experiences changes—*and he will*—he will be that much more comfortable sharing his feelings with you. You can have the kind of sensitive and honest communication that makes intimacy so rewarding.

THE SECRET

"I'm Always Too Exhausted to Make Love, So I Usually Fake It."

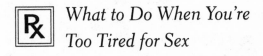

What to Do When You're Too Tired for Sex

YOU HAVE A PRESCHOOLER to pick up at noon and a preteen to drive to soccer practice at 3:00 P.M. Your list of things to do has only one thing crossed off, and it's already 11:00 A.M. When your husband asks you what you do all day, you feel the hairs rise on your neck. Then he comes home, after sharing a pitcher of margaritas with friends from work, with his mind on sex. You're just too tired. So you fight about his drinking with his friends.

The next day you have an intimate conversation with your sister, the only person who still understands you. You say, "It wasn't the margaritas. It wasn't even that he stayed out so late. I like having the house to myself, and I have my nights out, too. What scares me is that I'm always too tired for sex. I'm too tired on vacations, for God's sake. I hardly sleep at night. I wake up sweating to death and have to toss the blankets off, which makes him think I'm crazy because he says the room is cold. Even after a full night's sleep, I wake up tired. I really worry about what's happening."

Sleep problems *do* become more common as we age. A life of rising expectations can leave us depressed, anxious, and too tired for much of anything, including sex. But there's a much more common cause of this problem, and there are new answers to the too-tired-for-sex dilemma. You don't have to live with it.

In this chapter you'll learn:

- how a lack of estrogen can cause a reduction in REM sleep—and subsequently make you feel tired all day
- how night sweats cause sleeplessness—and why you might not even know you're experiencing them
- the best treatments for your fatigue if you choose not to try estrogen, including the latest studies on botanicals, including Remifemin (black cohosh), Promensil, and soy
- why strength-training exercise (lifting weights, not walking) may be the best thing you can do to decrease feelings of fatigue
- how best to manage the exhausting "taffy-pull" of midlife by creating boundaries with the people you care about, without guilt

The Secret Sleep Robber

When you're tired because you aren't sleeping well, you may automatically think it's stress, anxiety, and depression. But if you're a woman over the age of thirty-five, you need to also think about estrogen.

The most common complaint of both perimenopausal and postmenopausal women, whose bodies no longer produce normal amounts of estrogen, is lack of sleep. In fact, researchers maintain that almost every woman will have some kind of sleep disturbance once she is past menopause due to the lack of estrogen. Often the biggest trouble isn't falling asleep but waking up in the middle of the night, unable to fall back asleep. Janet, fifty-one, who had her menopause two years ago, describes it this way: "I wake up at 3:00 in the morning, absolutely alert, like I could make a pot of coffee and call someone on the phone. Then at 7:00 A.M., when I should be getting up, I'm falling off my feet. No, I haven't wanted to make love. I have friends who tell me that they love to have sex before going to bed because it's so relaxing it helps them sleep better, but for me it's too stimulating right before sleep."

Sue Spataro, a registered nurse who has run a website known as HotFlash! for three years (www.pinksunrise.com), specializes in helping women get information about menopause. "Women E-mail me personally with their health questions all of the time. Sometimes I look at the times those messages were written. You'd be surprised how often the time is 2:15 A.M. or 3:30 A.M."

You may be thinking, But I haven't reached menopause yet, and I'm having this problem. In the transitional years before menopause, known as *perimenopause*, which begins for some women as early as their thirties (more about this in the next chapter), you can still experience estrogen deficiency because the levels of estrogen in your body often fluctuate widely.

How exactly do declining estrogen levels become the culprit in sleep disturbances? For one, insufficient levels of estrogen can rob you of REM sleep. Second, loss of estrogen can cause night sweats that you might not even be aware you're having but that are waking you up. The other thing that can wake women up is urinary frequency, also caused by low estrogen. Let's look at each of these problems separately.

What's REM Got to Do with It?

There are actually two kinds of sleep, rapid eye movement (REM) and non-REM (NREM). During REM, also known as *dream sleep*, the higher brain centers are more active. Your eyes dart about underneath your closed lids. Your pulse rate, blood pressure, and breathing pattern change as you dream. NREM sleep is a less-active kind of sleep where your metabolism slows along with the brain-wave rate. This allows the body to repair itself. We usually have about five ninety-minute cycles of sleep a night from REM to NREM and back again, with the REM phase getting longer with each cycle.

Researchers have found that low estrogen levels lead to a loss of REM sleep. You might wonder, If I'm more active during REM sleep, what's wrong with being deprived of it? Wouldn't that be a good thing?

Think of REM sleep as playtime for your brain. During REM sleep the brain is free from the type of control and structured function it exerts while awake. You can dream wildly. If you are robbed of REM sleep on a chronic basis, no matter how much rest you get, you're still going to feel drowsy during the day. People who don't get enough REM sleep become anxious and irritable. They also have difficulty concentrating, remembering, and/or learning new tasks. Not exactly a blueprint for great sex!

Night Sweats

A night sweat is a hot flash that occurs while you're sleeping. You may not realize it's happened until it's over. That's when you wake up, perspiring, sometimes with your heart pounding.

A classic hot flash is a flush and a sweat that starts low in your body and works itself up, becoming an overwhelming feeling of warmth. Chills can occur afterward because of the sweat. This can last anywhere from forty-five seconds to ten minutes.

"I have one every morning at 4:00 A.M.," one woman admits. "You can set the clock by me." But many women are never aware of when a hot flash will hit. There are women who never have hot flashes during the day.

Some women have only one component of the classic hot flash. For example, they only feel warm, with no flushing or sweating. Some just sweat but don't feel overly warm or flush. Some just flush without any other symptoms.

Don't assume that if night sweats are the cause of your problem you'll easily recognize this. Sometimes night sweats can be so mild you wake up feeling the room is too hot, kick the blankets off, and go back to sleep. Or you end up in a thermostat war with your husband, who says he feels like he's sleeping in a meat locker while you feel you're living in a sweatbox. Lauren, forty-four, a mother of three, says, "I always thought I was sweating because the room was too hot, even though my husband said he was a Popsicle. Even after I heard of perimenopause, I had no idea these were night sweats."

You're not alone, however, if you have experiences like Sharon, fifty-three, who couldn't possibly mistake her night sweats for anything else: "I wake up with my T-shirt soaked and my hair drenched, and even the sheets are wet. I have to get up and change clothes and get a different blanket—otherwise I freeze. It's embarrassing, even with a man I've lived with for twenty years. I try not to wake him, but he's a light sleeper. He jokes that he's ready to start going to sleep wrapped in a towel."

The trouble is that waking up with night sweats can also rob you of your cycles of REM sleep. Night sweats can also cause feelings of anxiety, which may make it harder to go back to sleep.

What actually happens to the body during a hot flash? This analogy can help you understand it better: Think about sitting in a hot tub. You immerse your body in water that is probably about 105 degrees and stay in there for fifteen to twenty minutes. When you get out, a number of things occur. First, your body temperature is so high that the thermostat in your brain says, "We're too hot," and dials down to a lower temperature. The body hears that instruction and responds by cooling itself.

There are two main ways that the body cools itself. The first is vasodilation. This means the blood vessels near the skin expand or open wider. When they dilate, more blood goes to the skin, and therefore the heat can leave the body more easily. The reddish flush you see is the blood vessels dilated near the skin. The second way the body cools itself is to sweat, because evaporation of water on your skin causes cooling as well.

Because of the vasodilation in the skin, when you get out of a hot tub and stand up, sometimes you feel dizzy. So much of the blood goes to the skin that there's a lack of blood to the brain, and sometimes people feel faint. Some feel nauseated because of the lack of blood to the gastrointestinal tract. Basically, the blood goes where it's most needed.

That's what a hot flash is like, minus the hot tub. When you're going about your business (or sleeping) with a body temperature that is perfectly normal, something in your brain suddenly, and without reason, turns down the body's thermostat. The body responds like it normally is supposed to respond, by cooling and by carrying out those two main reactions of vasodilating and sweating. It makes no difference how cold the room is, either, as Caroline, fifty-seven, will tell you, remembering a particularly bad hot flash: "It was about twenty below in Manhattan, and I was on a bus that wasn't even heated. It came over me all at once, and I had to throw off my coat and get off the bus immediately into the cold air."

What we don't know, however, is specifically what turns the body's thermostat down and sets this whole process in motion. Contrary to popular opinion, hot flashes and night sweats are not caused by low estrogen levels. Eight-year-old girls have low estrogen levels, yet they don't have hot flashes. Most eighty-eight-year-old women have low estrogen levels and don't have hot flashes. It's not the low level of estrogen but the *withdrawal* of estrogen that's causing the symptoms. In other words, a woman must have estrogen in her system and then lose it to experience these changes.

There are three types of estrogen withdrawal that women encounter. First, there's the erratic period of perimenopause—the transitional years before you reach menopause. You have normal levels of estrogen circulating through your bloodstream one day and they're down the next. These changes are sporadic or episodic, not permanent. Estrogen withdrawal can also occur at two specific times in the normal menstrual cycle. When you're about to ovulate, your estrogen levels go way up and then shoot way down. The second time it happens in the cycle is right before a period, when the estrogen levels go down again. We are now aware that women who get headaches at these times in the cycle are getting them because of estrogen withdrawal, almost like a hot-flash experience. These problems can now be treated safely by raising the estrogen level at those times in the cycle.

Even women who are taking birth-control pills, which prevent ovulation, can experience estrogen-withdrawal headaches and night sweats. This happens on the week off the birth-control pill, when they aren't taking the medication.

The third type of estrogen withdrawal is the absolute withdrawal you get when you have your menopause and your ovaries no longer produce estrogen. It can take years before the symptoms of this withdrawal cease and you no longer have hot flashes, but most women will see a gradual decline in the frequency and the intensity of these hot flashes within a few years as their bodies adjust to the lack of estrogen.

Getting Rid of Night Sweats and Getting Back REM Sleep

There are four strategies that may help you begin to get a better night's sleep when night sweats are the culprit: behavior modification, medication to prevent night sweats, hormonal treatment, and herbal therapy. Let's look at each of these in depth.

Behavior Modification

If night sweats are waking you up, many women have found the following strategies, which involve making a few lifestyle changes that might be helpful in coping with hot flashes:

- **Avoid the hot-flash triggers.** These include smoking (which can also bring on earlier menopause), hot and spicy foods, sugar, caffeine, alcohol, red meat, chocolate, hot tubs, and saunas. Chances are, if you begin to keep a calendar of your symptoms, you will discover your own hot-flash triggers.
- **Think ahead.** Use a fan while you're sleeping, put moist towelettes in your freezer to use when you're overheated, use a top sheet that breathes, and keep a glass of water at your bedside and a fresh, cool pillowcase nearby. The Sharper Image store offers a device that you wear around your neck that cools your entire body. One of my patients swears by it and has found it useful while she's gardening on a hot day as well.
- **Take multivitamins.** Deficiencies in nutrients such as B_6, B_{12}, riboflavin, folic acid, and pantothenic acid have been shown to impair sleep. Vitamin E can often help with hot flashes, and if it helps with hot flashes, it can help with sleep. Try 400 units twice a day. Vitamin B_6 at 500 mg twice a day can be helpful to some women. Understand that more is not better. You've got to be careful not to take too much of any of these because too much can give you symptoms beyond the ones you're trying to control. Remember, even though vitamins are generally good for you, adverse reactions can still occur.

- **Take your calcium.** Some sleep clinics are using calcium and magnesium as a substitute for tranquilizers. In addition, calcium has been shown to reduce PMS symptoms. Try taking 1,500 mg a day.

Medication

Several nonhormonal prescription drugs on the market have been proven successful in treating hot flashes. Bellergal is one medication that is effective in reducing hot flashes and also appears to reduce nervousness, irritability, and palpitations. It does contain phenobarbital, however, which means it can be habit-forming as well as sedating.

Clonidine is another medication that is effective in treating hot flashes. Unfortunately, the side effects of dizziness, dry mouth, and insomnia do not make it a best bet for women already suffering from fatigue.

The antidepressant Paxil has recently been shown to be useful in treating hot flashes and may be a good alternative for women who don't want to take hormones.

Hormonal Treatment

What can quickly make night sweats a distant memory and restore REM sleep? Estrogen replacement therapy. As an insomnia treatment, nothing works as well if your night awakenings are really due to hot flashes caused by estrogen withdrawal.

In the last chapter we discussed the variety of ways a woman can replace estrogen and the wide variety of pills, patches, and creams that provide estrogen to the body. For night sweats, the pills and the patches will be most effective. Those women who have estrogen withdrawal symptoms on the birth-control pill can also wear a low-dose patch during the week off, take one of the newer pills, Mircette, which provides estrogen all month long except for two days, or take a traditional low-dose birth-control pill like Loestrin 1/20 *without* any pill-free interval. The use of natural progesterone, available as Prometrium, which has to be taken at bedtime, can also be an interesting therapy because of its sedating effects. This is above and beyond the effect that estrogen alone can have. More on natural progesterone in Chapter 5. Discuss these options with your health-care provider.

Herbal Remedies

What if you were able to get hours of rest and deep relaxation through something you could buy over the counter? What if this sleep remedy didn't cause a morning hangover, a growing tolerance, or an addiction? This is the promise of herbal therapies, and no wonder so many women are trying them.

I have some problems with herbal therapy, which I will go into in depth in Chapter 5, where I discuss problems women have using herbal medications to ward off symptoms of menopause or perimenopause. Basically what troubles me is the fact that these remedies are not regulated by the FDA, so the companies that make them do not have to follow standards for dosage, sanitation, or even to assure the consumer that what they say is in the bottle really *is* in the bottle. Sleep can be a more serious problem than many people realize. Chronic insomnia can be a symptom of many underlying problems. It can put you out of balance both physically and emotionally. But, frankly, doctors hear about sleep problems so frequently that some of them have stopped listening very well. One woman told me, "I told my doctor that I was waking up at 1:00 A.M. every morning and that I couldn't go back to sleep and that this was something very different for me. All I got was 'Don't go to bed until you're really tired.' Hell, I'd already tried *that*. I mean, come now, of course I knew not to toss and turn in bed endlessly, or have dinner in bed, or drink coffee at night. I only told my doctor because when nothing worked I was really, really worried. But it was like 'Tough luck, happens, hope it goes away, and here, I'll throw you a bone.'"

You may feel very much alone, as if no one really takes your problem seriously. The health-food stores are open late, with people eager to help and listen. But if you start introducing things into your system that you really don't know anything about, and if no one can prove they *do* what the manufacturers claim they'll do, frankly, you can mess yourself up even worse.

Still, I am no stranger to the health-food store. You will find many physicians, nurses, and other health-care providers roving those aisles. My advice is that when you're looking for something to "cure" a problem rather than a vitamin or mineral to enhance your general health, do it *carefully*. Do it slowly. Find the most reputable source for these medications you can and *be aware*.

That said, here are some of the most commonly used products being offered on the sleep front, as well as herbs that are helpful for increasing your energy. I have listed those approved by Commission E in Germany, the only country with such a regulating commission.

Valerian

WHAT IS IT? Valerian consists of the dried underground stems and roots of the *Valeriana officinalis* plant. It has been used for centuries as a sedative and is often called "nature's Valium." Proponents say it reduces nervous tension, promotes sleep, and controls menstrual cramps. It can be taken as one or two commercial capsules at night, or one teaspoon of the tincture can be mixed in a quarter cup of water. It can also be taken several times a day at lower doses for a calming effect.

WILL IT WORK? When 128 people were given either 400 mg of valerian extract or a placebo in a clinical trial, the herb was shown to improve the *quality* of sleep. The people taking valerian, however, woke up just as frequently during the night as the group taking the placebo.

Germany's Commission E approves it for treating sleep disturbances due to excitability or restlessness. The FDA includes valerian on its "Generally Recognized as Safe" list, which refers to its safety rather than its effectiveness.

WHAT TO WATCH OUT FOR. Valerian acts as a stimulant for 10 percent of the people who try it. Although valerian has not been shown to be addictive, any time people regularly use sedatives to go to sleep, they run the risk of becoming psychologically dependent on them. I tell my patients who are interested in valerian to use it only occasionally, not longer than a week or two at a time. It can also take a while to find the optimum dose that will work for you, so don't drive a car after taking it. Side effects of too high a dose include blurred vision, headache, excitability, and nausea. If you have impaired kidney or liver function, talk to your health-care provider first.

Melatonin

WHAT IS IT? Melatonin doesn't grow in the ground. It is a hormone that is secreted by the pineal gland at the base of the brain. The pineal gland secretes the highest levels of melatonin at night. The melatonin you can buy at drug and health-food stores is a synthetic version of this hormone.

Melatonin made big news several years ago when its ability to fight jet lag and "traveler's insomnia" hit the news. There were many other reports that melatonin might slow the aging process and function as an antioxidant.

Melatonin supplements are available as capsules, liquids, and tablets, and the usual dose begins at 0.3 mg.

WILL IT WORK? One double-blind trial of six volunteers, an admittedly small sample, found it took them less time to fall asleep and to experience REM sleep after taking 0.3 to 1 mg of melatonin one to two hours before bed. Most of the other studies are what's called anecdotal—based on people saying it worked rather than any actual studies. But there are many claims that people taking melatonin have had great success readjusting to a new time zone more quickly.

Melatonin is being studied actively by sleep researchers throughout the country with some positive results. None of the other promises—that melatonin is the fountain of youth, for example—has been confirmed in clinical studies.

WHAT TO WATCH OUT FOR. There is little information about the long-term use of this drug. Although many people find it helps them fall asleep, there have been reports that some feel depressed after taking it.

Passionflower

WHAT IS IT? Also known as *apricot vine, maypop, passiflora*, and *wild passionflower*, this herb probably will not stimulate any passion, unless your true passion lies in calming yourself down. Passionflower has a strong reputation as a sedative and natural tranquilizer. The recommended dose of the solid extract is usually 150 to 300 mg per day. Herbalists claim that a half-teaspoon of the tincture can be taken up to three times per day for a calming effect.

WILL IT WORK? Germany's Commission E approves passionflower for nervous unrest. The FDA, however, banned it from over-the-counter sleep aids because there weren't enough studies to prove its sedating and tranquilizing effects in humans. However, there haven't been reports of serious side effects or interactions with other medications. It has not been shown to be addicting.

WHAT TO WATCH OUT FOR. Expect a very mild effect, not the kind you would have taking a sleeping pill. More isn't better. Too much of *anything* can be harmful.

Kava-Kava

WHAT IS IT? Kava, as it is commonly called, comes from the root of a flowering shrub that grows in the South Pacific called *Piper methysticum*. South Pacific Islanders drink kava cocktails as part of ceremonial life, much as we use wine. However, kava enthusiasts say it promotes relaxation without affecting mental alertness or causing addiction. They also claim it promotes sleep without suppressing REM sleep or creating a morning hangover. The recommended dosage is 50 to 70 mg kavalactones three times a day.

WILL IT WORK? In 1997 a double-blind, placebo-controlled study involving 101 participants over a period of twenty-five weeks set out to determine kava's effect on anxiety disorders. The participants took 70 mg kavalactones three times a day. The kava group showed a significant improvement over the placebo group in terms of reduced depression and anxiety.

In two more placebo-controlled, double-blind studies of eighty women who had reached menopause, the kava groups had significant reductions in hot flashes, as well as significant improvements in mood and sense of well-being.

Germany's Commission E approves kava for nervous anxiety, stress, and restlessness. Proponents of kava often talk about an improved quality of sleep rather than sedation. In other words, it may not help you *get* to sleep but give you more restful sleep.

Kava is one of the more promising remedies to come out of the health-food store for treatment of anxiety, but keep in mind that it isn't standardized here in the United States. We don't really know what happens to kava as it crosses the Atlantic and makes it to the shelves of American stores. A steadily increasing number of brands of kava is flooding the market, so getting kava from a reliable source is very important.

WHAT TO WATCH OUT FOR. There have been reports of allergic reactions such as yellow discoloration of the skin and nails, in people who take kava for an extended period of time. Kava can also interact with alcohol or barbiturates and increase their effects. If you have been taking benzodiazepines such as Valium, Xanax, or Klonopin regularly, don't add kava to it. If you're interested in trying kava, develop a plan with your health-care provider to wean yourself slowly from the benzodiazepine first so that you don't experience withdrawal or other adverse reactions.

Ginseng

WHAT IS IT? The ginseng root has been used in traditional Chinese herbal medicine for more than five thousand years. There are two main types: American and Asian. Ginseng has a reputation for combating fatigue and depression but has also been touted as a remedy for vaginal dryness and hot flashes.

Ginseng seems to be popping up everywhere, even in chewing gum and candies. Consumer watchdog groups in the United States were quick to report that some of these over-the-counter ginseng supplements contained little or no ginseng at all!

WILL IT WORK? If you're looking for a mild stimulant, ginseng may provide it. Proponents point to two studies involving more than five hundred people who received ginseng along with vitamins and minerals. The participants reported a boost of energy and a feeling of well-being.

WHAT TO WATCH OUT FOR. There's nothing like taking ginseng at 4:00 P.M. when you need a pick-me-up and then finding out that you're too stimulated to go to sleep later. If anxiety is one of the symptoms you struggle with, ginseng is probably not a good bet. It may also be a potent phytoestrogen. There have been reports of women having uterine bleeding after menopause from taking ginseng. In any case, women on HRT should discuss ginseng with their health-care providers. Not even the most ardent fan of ginseng is claiming it's the new HRT.

Thirteen Tips for Getting a Good Night's Sleep Without Herbs or Drugs

It's not unusual for a patient to tell me, "I've tried all of this stuff, and I still can't fall asleep!" For millions of people, bedtime is an invitation to hours of worry. However, while a man can be too tired at twenty, thirty, forty, and beyond, women are especially vulnerable to fatigue and sleep problems during midlife, when their hormone levels are changing. Small annoyances like a truck driving by or a humidifier that goes on and off turn into major obstacles to sleep. Thoughts become obsessive: "Did I pay the gas bill, or didn't I?"

Here are some practical tips you can try, regardless of what is keeping you up at night:

- **Develop an attitude of not caring.** Trying to fall asleep is a paradox. The harder you try, the more difficult sleep will become. Sleep is about letting go. Say to yourself, It really doesn't matter if I fall asleep. My body will get enough rest just lying still. And it's true.
- **Wake up at the same time each day.** The best way to fall asleep is to get up early and consistently. If you can't fall asleep, the antidote isn't getting more sleep in the morning to make up for the lack. Reset your internal clock by getting up even earlier. You will feel tired for a while, but you will see the payoff as you fall asleep more quickly at night.
- **Avoid weekend jet lag.** A common mistake people make is to sleep late on the weekends. This is like flying across time zones. You unconsciously reset your internal clock, making Sunday night a nightmare for falling asleep.
- **Avoid hidden caffeine and any alcohol.** Everyone knows not to drink coffee before bedtime, but did you know that chocolate,

colas, some aspirin products, and many common foods and beverages contain significant quantities of caffeine? Read the labels before you get an unexpected surprise. Avoid alcoholic beverages. They may help you fall asleep but disturb the quality of your sleep and wake you up at 3:00 A.M.

- **Take time to practice letting go during the day.** Just as the mind can become conditioned to stimulation, it can become conditioned to relaxation. Take time each day to breathe deeply. Do five minutes of stretching exercises. Learn to meditate. One of the best books I can recommend on this topic is *The Relaxation and Stress Reduction Workbook* (New Harbinger, 1988), which contains hundreds of tips for learning how to relax your mind and body.

- **Stop the nighttime drama.** Avoid stimulating movies, books, and so forth while lying in bed. Condition your mind to see your bed as a place where you sleep, not where you figure out your business problems. Don't take your laptop to bed to do your office work there. Move the TV out of the bedroom. Get up when you can't sleep and go to another room.

- **Exercise both the body and the brain.** Physical exercise doesn't have to be an hour of killer aerobics. Take a walk. Get fresh air. Mental fatigue is also an important helper in being able to sleep. Studies have shown that daily mental activity increases the amount of REM sleep. Challenge yourself by learning chess, doing puzzles, or learning to play a musical instrument.

- **Avoid a heavy dinner.** When you're going through a phase of having trouble sleeping, make your largest meal of the day lunch, which is what we all should ideally do anyway, even if we're not having a bad night's sleep. Don't add digestion to your body's nightly tasks. However, a high-calcium snack an hour or so before bed may help, because calcium has been shown to promote sleep by calming the nervous system.

- **Develop a sleep ritual.** There should be something you do every evening before sleeping that's regular and comforting. Maybe it's a hot bath. Maybe it's a few stretches. Make a routine for yourself that never varies and that tells your body, "This is the time to wind down."

- **Keep your room cool (sixty to sixty-five degrees).** Let the blankets provide the warmth. Get separate blankets so that if you have to kick yours off in the middle of the night you don't freeze your partner.
- **Be realistic about sleep.** Many people wake up during the night two or three times. This doesn't necessarily mean you have a sleep disorder. But if you wake up and agonize, It took me so long to fall asleep, now I'll never get to sleep again, you've got trouble. It's my opinion that anticipating not being able to fall back to sleep keeps more people up than any other single factor.
- **Put your alarm clock under your bed.** This tip comes from Sue Spataro, who runs the HotFlash! website (www.pinksunrise.com), a resource for women approaching perimenopause and menopause. Sue says, "When you can't see the clock, you can't get as anxious about how long you haven't been able to fall asleep as you will by looking at it every ten minutes. Don't worry, the alarm will still go off in the morning if you leave the clock out of sight!"
- **Sleep at the other end of the bed.** One man told me that he woke up and found his wife's feet almost in his face and her head at the foot of the bed. "What in the world are you doing?" he demanded. She said, "I'm sleeping facing the Western Wall; what do you think?" She was joking, but the truth is, when you've rolled around for hours trying to find a comfortable sleeping position, turning yourself completely around may turn your sleep problem around.

Muscling Your Way to Better Sleep and Less Fatigue

While there's much you can do in the evening to encourage a good night's sleep, there's even more you can do during the day to prepare for it. Strength training has often been touted as one of the best remedies for PMS symptoms, and it's gaining accolades as well from women who are peri- and postmenopausal. In fact, strength training has been shown to minimize hot flashes and help banish fatigue.

Strength training is different from aerobic exercise such as walking, running, or taking a spinning class, although those activities do build strength. It involves working your muscles against a resistant force, whether that force is weights you lift or machines that provide resistance. Huge rubber bands, available for about $10 from your fitness store, can also provide resistance, as can the weight of your own body. You can even use cans of soup or full containers of milk.

Strength training will build muscle mass. What does that have to do with fatigue? Your metabolic rate slows as you get older. If you think of metabolism as a fire in the furnace that's keeping your body going, that fire is now burning a little lower. When you were young, that metabolism was running high and hot. Most of the food you took in got burned up by the fire or energy. Very little was stored. As you get older and that fire lowers itself, very little of the food you take in will get burned, and most of it will get stored. The point of strength training is to increase your muscle mass, make the body work at a higher level, and bring that fire up higher, so that now when you take in food it will get burned instead of stored. Muscle burns seventeen to twenty-five times as many calories as fat. And the more energy expended, the more you will feel tired enough to fall asleep at night.

Most women will rapidly see results from strength training if they start out doing it two to three times a week. The optimum would be three to four times a week. With aerobic training, you can get on the Stair-Master or the treadmill or run outside *daily*, but with strength training you have to give your muscles rest after you've done it. Many trainers recommend a forty-eight– to seventy-two–hour break between strenuous workouts, to give time for the muscles to rest afterward and, more important, to grow. However, you can strength-train every day or combine strength training with aerobics *if you work your muscles in groups.*

There are six main muscle groups. They are the shoulders, the chest, the legs, the back, the biceps, and the triceps. You can exercise different groups on different days. Many women who enjoy strength training will work two muscle groups a day. They'll work their chest and their back on Monday. Then they'll work their shoulders and their legs on Tuesday and the back of the arms (the triceps) and front of the arms (the biceps) on Wednesday. Another way to do this is to do one exercise from each muscle group every day that you exercise.

Doing these exercises correctly is a must to avoid injury. Doing them hard enough is a key to making them effective. Sitting down at a Cybex machine and lifting ten pounds up and down with your legs while you listen to music isn't going to do much if it's easy and quick for you. One session with a personal trainer can teach you the correct form and get you started feeling what it's like to really work your muscles without strain but with enough intensity. It's wonderful if you can afford regular coaching, but there are tapes, books, television programs, and Internet sites that will help you get the coaching you need. While joining a gym is great for some, you don't need a health club. You can get a set of five-, ten-, and fifteen-pound weights and do just about every strength-training exercise there is to do in your own home.

Will you gain weight if you give up some of the time you've given to aerobics and exchange it for strength-training sessions? You may actually lose more weight if you work your muscles hard enough. When you build muscle mass, you increase metabolic rate, and you tend to lose weight. You certainly lose fat weight. You may notice some extra pounds on the scale at the beginning of your program, because muscle weighs more than fat. But if you stay with it, you'll generally find that your system, working at the higher metabolic rate, will cause you to lose weight or at the very least, lose inches off your waist, making your clothes feel looser.

Many women were conditioned throughout their twenties and thirties to see aerobic exercise as the only way to go if weight loss was the goal. Running, jogging, and step classes were the vogue. Aerobic exercise is still important for your heart, but it's my opinion that extreme running, in particular, is not good for women as they age. The pounding on the pavement is hard on a woman's internal organs. It exerts a profound pull of gravity on the uterus and the bladder every time your foot hits the pavement, especially in women who have had multiple vaginal deliveries. It can lead to eventual prolapse or protrusion of the uterus and bladder out of the vagina. Also, common injuries include problems with the lower back, knees, ankles, and feet.

Fatigue and Faking It: The Big Dilemma

You're tired. Bone tired. Enter your partner, who is eager, ready, and going to be disappointed. Dare you say no again?

"Faking it" is one way many women handle the secret that they aren't feeling sexual because they're tired, depressed, or just not in the mood. Lauren, a forty-six-year-old high school teacher, admits: "Of course I fake it. If I didn't, sex would go on forever. If I make a lot of noise, if I touch him while we're doing it, and kind of let my hand roam around down there, it hurries him up. His ego is satisfied, and I get to go back to what I need to do."

Deanna, thirty-seven, and a mother of two, admits to faking her satisfaction but for a different reason: "It has always taken me a long time to be satisfied by a man. It just seems easier to say, 'Honey, that's great, I'm going to come,' than 'Honey, here's what you need to do and you need to keep doing it until I tell you to stop doing it, and that might take the next hour.' I mean, what man is willing to give you oral sex for an hour?"

Kris, fifty-five, says, "I was with my twenty-two-year-old daughter watching that famous scene in *When Harry Met Sally* where Meg Ryan fakes an orgasm at a restaurant. My daughter turns to me and says, 'Why would any woman be so stupid as to fake an orgasm?' I didn't answer, having done it myself. I thought, It was different for the baby-boom generation. The sexual revolution made women aware that we could have orgasms, and we felt like we were expected to have them if we were really with it. At the same time, we were taught to soothe men's egos."

Obviously there is a pro side of faking it, as these women point out. You avoid a discussion, you soothe his ego, you get your time back. There are many other reasons women fake a satisfaction they don't feel. Some women are scared: "What would he think if he really knew how little desire I actually have? If I never pretended, we'd never have sex."

As tempting a solution as faking it is, the cost can be high. You perpetuate the myth that every sexual experience has to end in a toe-clenching, bed-rocking orgasm for it to be successful. This simply isn't true. As your physiology changes, it may become more and more difficult to reach that peak, even though you still feel pleasure during sex. Your secret thought may be "Can my lover really ever understand that I still enjoy sex, even if I don't have an orgasm?" He can. As one man put it, "In my marriage I've learned that there are going to be times when she needs sex and I don't want anything to do with it, and there are going to be times when I need it and she isn't interested. We've had to work on what to do at this point. Sometimes we'll just say no. But there are times, like the other day, when she was getting dressed for work. Something about the way she was pulling on her nylons looked so sexy to me that I suddenly wanted her badly. She had a million things on her mind. But she said, 'How about a quickie?' I knew it was for me and not necessarily for her. In plain terms, she knew she wasn't going to 'get off,' while I knew I would. It's like a gift. She doesn't need to come every time. Why should she need to fake it? What mattered to me was that she was willing to be with me, just because I wanted her."

Many women conclude, after years of sex, I've been faking it long enough. What's in it for me? I deserve some pleasure. The expectation of another night of ho-hum sex can begin to cause resentment. She's simply not that interested in soothing his ego anymore. If she stops faking it suddenly, he feels the wallop of performance anxiety.

Perhaps the worst part of "faking it" as a solution to the too-tired-for-sex dilemma is that you may never deal with whatever is overwhelming you and draining you of sexual feeling. Some women eventually find that their fatigue has a medical reason, such as thyroid problems, a systemic illness, even iron anemia from irregular or heavy menstrual periods. Any woman who has been "too tired" for more than three months should discuss this symptom with her doctor, who can help her screen these factors out. However, for many more women, it's not these physical factors that turned them off to sex. It's what I call the "taffy-pull" of midlife that's so overwhelming.

Are You Caught in the Taffy-Pull?

You've probably heard the advice before: "If you're too tired and busy for sex, make a date with your partner. Make an appointment for sex." But plenty of women tell me they feel like this just makes sex one more demand in an incredibly long list of things to do. Mary, forty-nine, who is dealing with her father's illness as well as financial problems, says, "At night I'm really tired, physically tired. At the end of the day I don't have any time left over for myself. I don't feel loving. I don't even feel feminine."

The "taffy-pull" of midlife can definitely leave you feeling exhausted. It may seem that everyone is pulling you in different directions. Your children need you, your job has its requirements, your marriage creates other responsibilities, and your aging parents call at 10:00 P.M. with their problems, just when you were ready to go to bed. In midlife most women are also reassessing everything—their careers, their marriages, their relationships with their parents and their children—and that can be emotionally draining. Coming to terms with difficult issues in relationships or financial concerns may result in insomnia. Too much of the taffy-pull of midlife can lead to depression—a retreat from all feelings because you can no longer cope.

What's the solution? The real Rx for being too tired for sex may not be more time alone with him but more time alone with yourself. Time alone can give you a sense of balance and renewal, which can give you more energy for everything. How do you get that time? By learning to set boundaries with the people in your life who depend on you.

To set boundaries with people you care about, you need to genuinely believe the following: You have needs. Those needs are as important as other people's needs. You can help others, but you do not have to be everyone's answer to everything. If you consistently take on other people's responsibilities and problems, you help create people who have no more idea than you do about how to meet their own needs or find their own answers. Sometimes saying no is a gift to the other person, who grows and becomes stronger by learning more self-reliance.

People who don't know how to set boundaries often feel resentful, and this can play out in the bedroom. Unconsciously you turn off to sex because you end up feeling "You never give me what I need, so I won't give you what you need."

How can you begin to set boundaries? First, assess how weak or strong yours are at the present moment. Do you feel that the needs of others are a priority? That you're often smothered by others? That you have little privacy? That you can't say no? That you take on other people's problems as your own? That you are often rescuing others from the consequences of their own actions? That your own needs always come last?

If you answer yes to these questions, consider that you may not be having relationships with the people in your life but *enmeshments*. Julie, sixty-six, discovered this after having hip surgery: "You'd think people would appreciate you for making them such a priority your whole life and help you in return when you need it, but they just resent you. After my surgery I had to *ask* my family for help. My husband complained that he was coming down with every symptom of every illness in the world himself. He was too 'sick' to help me. My children did the absolute least amount they could get away with."

Julie saw a therapist and confided her secret fear: "As much as I resent it, I think my husband loves me because I do all these things for him. If I stop doing them, he might leave me for someone else who will."

The therapist was frank in her reply: "He's not going to leave you. He's attracted to competent, insecure women. Let's work on helping you keep the competence and get rid of the insecurity. It will be better for you both." She then helped Julie set some new rules in her relationships. Julie took the following steps:

- **Discover what your needs are.** It may have been years since you've really thought about it. Do you need more acknowledgment? More appreciation? More time to yourself? Once you know what you need, you can be that much clearer in expressing it to people you care about.

- **Practice letting go of control.** Begin with small things. It's amazing the solutions other people can come up with when they are forced to think. Consider that these people—these adults—have as much capacity as you do for solving their problems or taking on their own responsibilities, although they may choose not to use it. It's incredible how many responsibilities they can take on their own shoulders when no one is doing it all for them.

- **Make a list of every responsibility you took on today.** This was the list one woman wrote about her day off: "Watered plants, paid bills, fed cats, hunted under bed for child's library books, mailed bills, called for dinner reservation, picked up dry cleaning, etc." Next to it, write whom you could have delegated that responsibility to. Vow to delegate at least one responsibility a day.

- **Announce today that beginning tomorrow you are no longer going to function as anyone else's calendar.** Keeping everyone else's schedule in your head is exhausting. Cut these people off from reminders at age twelve and over. Your teen can't remember when the tutor is coming? He or she misses the appointment and pays for the tutor. Your husband can't remember to make an appointment with the dentist? Tell the receptionist to phone him at his office; you aren't making his commitments anymore. Your daughter missed soccer practice because she forgot? Guess she doesn't get to play in this weekend's game. She'll do better next week. Buy a big calendar for the family to write their appointments on, hope they use it, and if they don't, let them face the consequences. You're not being selfish. You're teaching other people responsibility. Think about how you learned to be so competent.

- **Make it a priority to have at least a few hours a week that are totally your own and see if that helps your relationship with everyone in your family.** Tell your partner, "I think if I had more time for me, I'd be more interested in sex. Let's try this and see if it makes a difference." Just don't fall into the trap of feeling you have to exchange sex for his emptying the litter box. If your time alone is merely ransom for sex later, you haven't really set a boundary.

- **Realize that people are stronger than you think.** There's a trick to dealing with the chronic complainers and drainers in your life: Stop parceling out solutions. Have you noticed that they don't take your suggestions anyway and that you feel even more tired and drained after a session of "yeah, but"? See if this sounds familiar.

> **You:** "Have you thought of talking to your boss about all that overtime and how other people seem to get around it, leaving you stuck?"
>
> **Them:** "Yeah, but he doesn't care, as long as the job gets done."
>
> **You:** "What if you said, 'I simply can't put in any overtime tonight?'"
>
> **Them:** "Yeah, but then I'll probably get a bad review."
>
> **You:** "So? You hate the job anyway. Why not look for another one?"
>
> **Them:** "Yeah, but all the other firms want someone young who is willing to work for nothing."
>
> **You:** "Have you talked to a headhunter?"
>
> **Them:** "Yeah, but they never come up with anything good."

You're probably exhausted even reading that! I remember one patient who was clinically depressed after a series of health problems and family troubles. She was fighting it, though. She was seeing a therapist, exercising, doing everything she could to combat it. She'd start to see the mist lifting when her husband would come home and complain and whine and make her feel more depressed. She'd give him suggestions she'd gotten from therapy, but he just shrugged and complained some more. Finally she told the story to her therapist, who said, "Next time he does that, instead of trying to help him, say, 'Well, honey, you better see a doctor, because there's no sense in the two of us going down the tubes together.' His depression is his responsibility just as yours is yours. He's really not your problem to solve."

My patient learned to listen to her husband start to complain and say, "That must be terrible; I hope you can figure something out," and go on quietly to work on overcoming her own depression. She did, and the complainers and drainers in her family have either sought help after seeing how well she's feeling or found another victim to complain to.

We forget that other people are stronger than we think. Another patient of mine, Mara, forty-nine, and her husband, Ron, fifty-three, wanted to move to Arizona badly. They felt the economy and opportunities would be better for them and that the more relaxed environment would be good for their teenagers. The trouble was that Mara had two parents in their midseventies, with a growing list of health problems. "I just couldn't abandon them. I never even mentioned that I wanted to move, because I didn't want to hurt their feelings. Then one day, my mother calls me up and says, 'Guess what? Your father and I are moving to Florida.' Just like that. Here I felt they were so dependent on me I could never leave them, and they had their own plan for how they wanted to live the rest of their lives."

■ **Adopt the following as your Personal Bill of Rights** (adapted from *Six Keys to Creating the Life You Desire*, by Mitch Meyerson and Laurie Ashner, New Harbinger, 1999):

> I have the right to say no to requests I do not want to meet.
> I have the right to ask for what I want.
> I have the right to have and express my feelings.
> I have the right to be happy.
> I have the right to be listened to and understood.
> I have the right not to be responsible for others.
> I have the right to say "I don't know."
> I have the right to make mistakes.
> I have the right to leave abusive people.
> I have the right to my own personal space and time.

The real road to having more energy for sex and everything else is learning to focus a bit less on everyone else and more on you.

Talking to Him About Being Too Tired for Sex

Claire, fifty-one, complains, "My husband simply wants sex at the worst times. He says, 'Come on, let's do it,' as if that's supposed to make me spring into lust. Then he sulks all night if he doesn't 'turn me on.'"

What do you do about partners who grope for you when you're monitoring your ten-year-old child's sleepover and there are twelve children in your basement? Or who refuse to listen no matter how many times you've told them you need a little more romance than their pressing their crotch up against you while you're putting dishes in the dishwasher? A partner who does that may be just as ambivalent about wanting sex, regardless of what he or she is saying. Let's face it. Couples learn how to seduce each other. They know what works and what doesn't. For example, if he comes up and grabs her where he knows she doesn't like it, or asks for sex when he knows she's too tired or overwhelmed, chances are he knew this wasn't going to work on some level. It's often unconscious.

How can partners do a better job of communicating and avoid such games? Here are a few suggestions for breaking the silence and having a discussion about being too tired for sex.

- **Choose a time when you haven't just said no to sex to talk with your partner about your fatigue and about what you need.** If he's hurt or angry because you've just said, "Honey, not tonight," this probably isn't the time to get the understanding you need.
- **Talk about your feelings.** You can end the old "You never want sex anymore—what's wrong with you?" battle by admitting: "I'm worried about being this tired, too. I'd love more pleasure in my life. I want a solution to this, but going ahead and hoping it pleases you isn't going to solve anything. I'd like to talk about it with you sometime when you're open to listening."
- **Dare to be honest.** Cathy, forty-eight, says "My first husband couldn't have cared less if he pleased me. But Don, whom I've been going with for a year now, is different. He wants to work at it and work at it until he satisfies me. There were times I literally had to grab his hair and pull him away from me while he was giving me oral sex and say, "Stop already. Please. It's just not going to happen!" I finally had to tell him exactly where I was at: "There are times when I'm going to come. There are times when I'm going to come multiple times. There are times when I'm going to come quickly. There are times when it's going to take longer for me to come, and there are times when I'm not going to come. That's got nothing to do with anything that you're doing or not doing."

- **Say no gently.** "I don't have the energy right now. Can I give you a rain check?" will go a lot further than "I can't believe you asked me. Do you ever think of anything else but sex?"

In midlife, as at most stages of life, the people who have the best lovemaking aren't the ones with the most energy or the most time. They are the people with the best communication. Actually, fatigue is one of the easier obstacles to overcome, if you work at it. It's certainly far easier than raising a declining libido, which involves so many different factors. You need to ask yourself one question, however: is fatigue really a sign of boredom? If so, you have more than one secret in the bedroom. The chapters that follow can help.

4

THE SECRET

"I Can't Sleep, I'm Forgetting Everything, I Feel Anxious and Strange, and I Could Take Sex or Leave It. What's Happening to Me?"

 Understanding Perimenopause: The Hormonal Transition Doesn't Have to Be a Sexual Transition

"I WAS MOODY and tired no matter how much sleep I got," admits Alicia, thirty-seven. "I kept walking into rooms and forgetting why I had entered them. As for sex, well, I was so frightened that something was seriously wrong with me, I couldn't respond. Then one day I had the worst menstrual period I'd ever had. I was changing pads every hour. I thought, Oh God, what if I have cancer?"

Alicia didn't have cancer. She was just having symptoms millions of women have had, usually beginning sometime after age thirty-five.

Do any of these sound familiar? You're having a hard time recalling phone numbers or your E-mail password. You can't concentrate. You're vaguely anxious, terribly tired, and having trouble sleeping. PMS seems to last for weeks instead of days. Worse, your next menstrual period seems to come too closely on the heels of the last one and seems to be lasting forever.

It may not occur to you that the changes in your menstrual cycle are related to your other symptoms, but if you're a woman thirty-five to fifty, what you may be experiencing is perimenopause, the hormonal transition that will ultimately lead to menopause. The hormones that once gave you a sense of equilibrium, steadiness, even of femaleness are suddenly fluctuating—and sometimes wildly.

Why does perimenopause often become a secret in the bedroom? A few examples:

- Your physician drops the ball and tells you your symptoms are all in your head and hints that you should talk to a psychotherapist. You become too embarrassed to talk about your symptoms with your partner or anyone else, because if the doctor who delivered your children and was so wonderful at those times suddenly thinks you're losing it, what will everyone else think? You suffer in silence, read books about Alzheimer's disease and cancer, and hide them under the bed so no one in your family will know. When your partner reaches for you, you're too anxious to respond. You are *scared*.

- Your physician is thorough and tells you *exactly* what this is. But the word *perimenopause* throws you for a loop. It's depressing. You're only thirty-eight. Your partner, at forty-five, is getting more handsome every day. It's hard enough to think about facing forty, let alone that menopause might be on the way. Will he think you're old or less of a woman if you tell him? You keep it a secret. When he mentions that maybe the two of you should have the third child you've talked about now that *his* career goals have been achieved, you want to die.

- Your physician is understanding, knowledgeable about perimenopause, and very helpful. Your partner shrugs when you mention perimenopause and says, "I wish they could give *me* some estrogen. You think *you're* forgetting things—let me tell you what happened to *me* today." You both start taking ginkgo, and he says, "Isn't this great? My mind is so much clearer." You don't feel a thing. The symptoms become your secret. He doesn't want to hear that you have PMS all month long anymore or how in the middle of a meeting you got the unexpected-period-from-hell. For the most part, you don't want him near you. And when you look at your seventeen-year-old daughter in full, beautiful bloom and the nineteen-year-old boy who can't keep his eyes off her, you wonder how you're supposed to continue to live on this planet. Sex suddenly feels like a responsibility, a talisman to your lost youth, and it frustrates you that you're so rarely in the mood.

How do you get the perimenopause secret out—and out of your sex life for that matter? In this chapter you learn:

- why perimenopause isn't menopause and what causes the unpredictable symptoms
- the best treatments for perimenopause—and why many women do well with no treatment at all once they fully understand what's happening to their body
- why the pill is one of the best treatments for a difficult perimenopause, and how to find one that won't interfere with your libido
- why you may still be able to conceive a child if you want to and what you need to do immediately if this is your goal
- how to talk to your partner about perimenopause
- how to revive your sex life and get off the sexually draining perimenopausal roller coaster

What Is Perimenopause—and Why Is It Killing My Sex Life?

Some women are so used to having irregular bleeding patterns—missing periods, fifteen-day-long periods, heavy, clotty periods, twice-a-month-periods—that they take it as a matter of course. But if you've never had those experiences and they suddenly begin to happen to you, it can be scary.

Sometimes a particularly heavy bleed brings a patient to my office long before it's time for her annual exam. Or for two months she doesn't get a period and knows she isn't pregnant. These women are frightened, but most of the time they needn't be. While there can be other causes, if a woman is in her late thirties or forties, more often than not these symptoms are the normal beginning of perimenopause.

Some of my patients don't have such noticeable changes in their cycles. A patient might notice that her cycle is shorter—perhaps twenty-five days when it used to be twenty-eight—but it's happened so gradually that she barely notices. Even cycles that begin to range from twenty-one days to forty days don't necessarily ring a bell. A woman may think, Something is throwing my period off. It must be this new diet.

What's equally important are the symptoms they don't immediately tell me about. Perimenopause can masquerade as insomnia, moodiness, fatigue, forgetfulness, depression, and weight gain. These symptoms are real libido killers. Some women feel as if they have PMS all month long. That can sap the energy out of anyone's sex life. Yet many women don't think of these symptoms as something that modern gynecology can help diminish and even cure. Here's a sampling of the complaints women recently brought to my office that absolutely *did* have to do with perimenopause and responded to the appropriate treatment:

> *"I'm just so short with my husband these days. Everything he does irritates me. When he touches me it's irritating. I just want to say, 'Get away from me!'"*

Touch that used to be pleasing—especially sexual touch, such as the breasts or the clitoral area—can suddenly stop feeling good due to changes in the levels of sex hormones. These areas of your body can even become hypersensitive. Touch can be irritating. Breast tenderness is a culprit in not wanting to be hugged or touched. Some women find that their breasts haven't been this tender since they were pregnant. Also, mood swings are typical of perimenopause because your hormone levels fluctuate. This can certainly all add up to irritation instead of pleasure at the prospect of having sex.

> *"I wake up at four o'clock each morning and can't go back to sleep. Finally, I fall asleep at six—not good, since I have to be up at six-*

*thirty. My internist told me that waking up early and not going back
to sleep easily is a sign of depression."*

Early-morning waking is one sign of depression—but when you're
a woman aged thirty-five to fifty-five, fluctuating levels of estrogen may
be causing your new wakefulness. This is discussed in much detail in
Chapter 3, but suffice it to say here that when your hormones begin
to go out of balance, so do your sleep patterns. Waking up and being
unable to fall back to sleep is one of the most common complaints
women have in midlife. It's a sex-life killer because after a month of
this you can want to take the head off any person who comes close to
you. He says, "How did you sleep?" You say, "Why do you keep asking
me that! You know I was up all night. Don't hug me! I don't want your
sympathy! And you're snoring again. Why won't you see a doctor about
your sinus problems?"

*"I wrote a check the other day, and the guy behind the counter asked
for my phone number. I gave the first three numbers, and suddenly
I couldn't remember the rest. I started getting really anxious, and
he looked at me like I was someone who was trying to pass off a bad
check. I finally just made a number up. Two minutes after I left the
store it came to me. I was mortified and frightened."*

It may make you think, Oh, God, is this the beginning of
Alzheimer's disease? But these strange bouts of forgetfulness are quite
common for women during perimenopause. For some it's just a can't-
get-that-phone-number-off-the-tip-of-my-tongue type of thing. But you
aren't "losing it" if you're like one of my patients who stood in her living room trying to remember her brother-in-law's name for ten minutes
and was absolutely terrified. You aren't going crazy. First of all, like so
many people of our generation, you are experiencing information over-
load. Today there is so much more daily data to input, and so much more
stress, that people are having unprecedented short-term memory problems. But also, dwindling estrogen levels during perimenopause begin
to play mind games here. It's no wonder you keep losing your train of
thought.

"My two girls and my husband know that there are times when they just have to get out of my way—for four or five days. I never had PMS, but this seems worse than anything I ever read about PMS. I'm a bull in a china shop—you can't say anything to me or I start to cry, snap, slam doors, go off. I'm sorry the minute after I do it, but it's too late."

Perimenopause is often confused with bad PMS. But PMS is usually predictable during one's early reproductive years. As bad as it can be, it often comes right on schedule, a few days before you menstruate. Now you *can't* predict it. You have your regular PMS symptoms: you feel bloated, your breasts ache, you're eating bowls of potato chips—whatever your regular pattern is. You're waiting patiently for your period to come, when the storm will subside. But it doesn't come. Sex is the last thing on your mind as you watch your stomach becoming bigger and rounder, and you can't even stand to be in the same room with yourself.

"I had my hair done recently, and I don't know what she put on it, but it's falling out."

It's true that coloring your hair can damage it. But hormonal fluctuation can also cause changes in the hair as well as the skin. If you were ever pregnant, you may have noticed that about three months after delivery your hair started to fall out in clumps. That's because hormones have a profound effect on hair growth cycles. So just as there is an effect after pregnancy, when hormone levels drop, there can be an effect during the perimenopausal transition, when hormone levels are changing.

One of my patients told me, "I must be pretty vain to be worrying about my hair thinning when so many of my friends have real medical problems." Yes, it's true that no one ever died from dry skin or a bad hair day. But in terms of how sexual you feel at midlife, having a clear, soft complexion and beautiful hair can make you feel good. When your hair shines and falls exactly the way you want it to and your skin is glowing, you feel young, vibrant, and sexy. If that's vanity, shouldn't you be allowed a little vanity?

"I feel so dizzy and spacey lately. Is this a bad allergy season or something? I've never had this before."

Feeling out of sorts, out of balance, and vaguely anxious is very typical of perimenopause. Plenty of women make the rounds of allergists, internists, psychiatrists, and marriage counselors because they're having palpitations or sweating or feeling anxious. Unfortunately, sometimes the last person they confide in is the gynecologist, who might sit them down, go over their menstrual history for the last six months, and assure them, "There's nothing seriously wrong here—you're just perimenopausal. This is part of a normal transition."

I've had dozens of patients who have actually cried in my office when they heard that. They weren't crying over the fact that they were in perimenopause. They didn't care if this was menopause itself. They were just so relieved to find out that there wasn't anything seriously wrong with them. They were normal. They were going to be OK. My simply validating their symptoms meant so much to them. Other doctors had told them, "You can't possibly be anywhere near menopause; your blood tests are fine, and you're still having periods. It's all in your head, so take Prozac." They were finally learning that there was a name for what they were experiencing and they weren't going crazy.

I Think I Have This! What Causes It?

Like many women, you may have given little thought over the years to why menstrual cycles occur. It was enough to know that you got your period once a month. If it came on schedule, great. If you could cope with the forewarnings of cramps, bloating, cravings, or fatigue, and if you didn't miss cycles for unexplained months at a time—well, the physiology of it all just wasn't that interesting. But now things are changing and you want to know how to deal with those changes. It helps to understand the normal menstrual cycle and the process a woman's body goes through during the reproductive years. With that knowledge you can easily comprehend how it begins to change as you approach midlife. Understanding the hormones your body produces, what they do, and how hormone levels fluctuate during the decade before menopause makes many women immediately feel steadier and less frightened. What you thought was cancer or something just as serious turns out to be a totally normal hormonal change.

Here are the basics.

What Is a Normal Menstrual Cycle?

Your cycle is considered normal if it's twenty-eight days, plus or minus two days, although the range of normal can be anywhere from twenty-one to thirty-five days. There are four "chemical messengers" or hormones working together in perfect synch that cause the normal cycle to occur. Two of them are made by the pituitary gland in the brain, and two of them are made by the ovary. The ones made by the pituitary gland are follicle-stimulating hormone, or FSH, and luteinizing hormone, or LH. FSH stimulates some of the follicles or eggs in the ovary to grow and produce more estrogen during their growth. LH, on the other hand, causes the most successful estrogen-making follicle to finally ovulate, or send out its egg.

The two main hormones made by the ovary are estrogen and progesterone. (We'll get to testosterone later.) Estrogen has many effects, but in the cycle itself it causes the lining of the uterus to grow and thicken. Progesterone, on the other hand, is made by the ovary only after ovulation and won't be made if ovulation doesn't occur. It stops the growth of the lining of the uterus and prepares that lining for pregnancy. That's why it's called progesterone—pro-gestation.

In a normal twenty-eight-day cycle, ovulation occurs on day fourteen. Fourteen days *after* ovulation, you get your period if no pregnancy ensues. One might ask, "Then how come so many women's cycles aren't this perfect twenty-eight days but twenty-six days or thirty-one days?" What makes the cycle different is that the *pre*ovulatory time can vary. For instance, if your cycle is twenty-six days, then you ovulated on day twelve. If your sister's cycle is thirty-five days, she ovulated on day twenty-one.

What Is Perimenopause and What Causes It?

As you age, your estrogen levels get lower because the ovaries no longer make as much as they used to. While the last period that you have is called your menopause, perimenopause is the time leading up to it, when estrogen levels fluctuate and finally decrease. Estrogen levels begin to decline in your early thirties, but most patients notice it at around thirty-five to forty-five. The mean age of menopause, or the last menstrual period, is fifty-one, but the range is thirty-five to sixty-five, which means the last period can occur anywhere in that time period. Perimenopause can happen anywhere in the thirties and forties.

Only 10 percent of women will have nice regular periods and then wake up one morning and never see another one. The other 90 percent will see a gradual change where their cycles can get closer together or farther apart and experience this transition called perimenopause. Think of it as a hormonal imbalance. What's important to understand here is that *perimenopause is not early menopause.* Your body is still making the hormone estrogen. It's just that these estrogen levels are erratic and unpredictable. Unlike a woman who stops menstruating for a year and knows that this is menopause, you can be in perimenopause and have no idea that you are in it.

Scientists and doctors used to think that perimenopause began because the egg follicles in the ovary produced lower amounts of estrogen. We now know that early in this perimenopausal transition these follicles are overstimulated by rising FSH levels and actually *overproduce* estrogen. Most women, in fact, produce more estrogen in early perimenopause than they did in their twenties. Another result of overstimulation is shorter cycles, because the ovary is being hyperstimulated and ovulation occurs much earlier than day fourteen. Cycle lengths as short as twenty days can occur. Later in perimenopause, the estrogen levels finally get lower and ovulation may be delayed or not occur at all. Here the cycles get longer and periods become farther apart. That's why perimenopause can be so confusing, even to doctors; sometimes too much estrogen, sometimes too little estrogen. This makes symptoms erratic and treatment complicated unless someone is really tuned in to it.

Based on these facts, a perimenopausal woman can experience estrogen-*dominant* symptoms from overproduction of estrogen and later estrogen-*withdrawal* symptoms from declining estrogen levels. Let's look at each of these symptom complexes in depth.

Estrogen Dominance: Too Much of a Good Thing?

How do you know if your symptoms are coming from too much estrogen or too little? Estrogen dominance will often give you the symptoms of bloating or breast tenderness almost the same way as you might feel if you were pregnant. Your breasts may even feel a little larger. Remember that estrogen also has a growth effect on the lining of the uterus. Because of this thicker uterine lining from higher levels of estrogen, you can wind up with polyps or fibroids and have heavier or more frequent bleeding. This is a time in a woman's life when surgical interventions such as D&Cs and hysteroscopy become necessary. As I explained earlier, you can also have shorter cycles because the ovary is being overstimulated and works too quickly. As one woman put it, "I feel like I'm having my period every three weeks!" And, in fact, she was.

Sometimes you have cycles that don't include ovulation. Even though estrogen levels may be higher, your system can't mount an estrogen surge when it's supposed to, and ovulation can't occur. This can lead to heavy, irregular bleeding as well as surprise bleeding. A patient complained of getting her period without warning: "It was the strangest thing," she told me. "No cramps, no bloating, no nothing. I'm a teacher in the inner city, and you get a couple of times a day to head to the ladies' room, and that's it. Had I decided to use that time to make a phone call instead, I would have ruined my outfit."

Ovarian cysts are also much more common without ovulation during this estrogen-dominant time. I recall the time when Greta, a forty-two-year-old woman, was referred to me with an ovarian cyst. Her own gynecologist had recommended laparoscopic surgery to remove the cyst. After an ultrasound reassured me that this was a benign cyst, I suggested that she go on the birth-control pill to stabilize her hormone levels and get rid of the stimulation for the cyst. Within six weeks, the cyst was gone and the surgery had been avoided. This was another instance of perimenopausal estrogen dominance.

Estrogen Withdrawal: What Happens When There's Too Little of a Good Thing?

For as long as you've had your periods, you've had some experience with estrogen withdrawal; you just didn't realize it. In a normal cycle, estrogen levels get lower at two times—right after ovulation at midcycle and before the menstrual bleed. Most women don't notice this change at all. But perimenopausally, when estrogen levels become lower overall, what wasn't noticed before suddenly becomes more obvious. What are the symptoms? Marie came in to see me complaining of headaches, palpitations, and night sweats. She had been to her allergist, her internist, her dermatologist, and no one could figure out what was going on. Her internist told her she was probably having panic attacks and wanted to put her on Xanax or Valium. On taking her history, we figured out that the symptoms were occurring at midcycle and right before her period. This was classic cyclic estrogen withdrawal of perimenopause. Other problems that can be noticed include sleeplessness and fatigue. In other words, any of the symptoms a woman can have postmenopausally she can also experience perimenopausally, especially during these times in the cycle. Finally, menstrual periods begin to get farther and farther apart. Ovulation no longer occurs, and since estrogen levels are now lower, you don't feel the bloating and bleeding as you did with estrogen dominance. These symptoms can be treated with estrogen. More on that later.

The problem is estrogen dominance and estrogen withdrawal are not consistently early and late phases of perimenopause. They can fluctuate. As an example, I've had patients come in to my office and tell me they've had no periods for four months. They think, Wow, I've just had my menopause; I'm done. Then, a month later, they'll have a period, and they'll begin cycling normally. This can make therapy very confusing and difficult for both patient and doctor.

Why Didn't My Doctor Tell Me About Perimenopause?

As you can see from the preceding stories, many physicians do not recognize perimenopause or understand it well, which is why becoming an informed patient is crucial. Here's what can happen if you're lacking the information you need:

> "My doctor took my blood levels, told me they were normal, and I couldn't be in menopause because there was still estrogen in my bloodstream. Six months later another doctor told me the first one had definitely missed the boat. She told me that a woman can have FSH levels that the lab would call menopause one day and something entirely opposite the next, and therefore the tests are a waste of time. The suggestion I got about my bleeding problem was, 'Have a hysterectomy. You've already had your children. See if it helps.' That was out of the question. I wasn't about to donate my uterus to medical science. Besides, I didn't even have insurance! I wanted to say, 'Doctor, would you like to have your testicles removed while I have my hysterectomy?' Then the doctor I saw for a second opinion said there were still at least three or four levels of therapy I could go through that would probably solve my problem before I had even to think about a hysterectomy."

> "I had a small cyst on my ovary—and a lot of spotting every month. The spotting never bothered me, because it had been going on for years. But the first doctor I saw took an ultrasound and starting talking about laparoscopes, D&Cs, and hysteroscopes. I was terrified. It wasn't so much the cyst but the irregular bleeding that she thought was such a concern. The second doctor looked at the same ultrasound and said, 'Let's repeat the ultrasound in eight weeks and try you on the birth-control pill for a couple of months. What you're experiencing is pretty typical of perimenopause. That cyst may go away on its own.' It did."

> "I was told that, since I was still having my periods, I wasn't having perimenopause and that, at thirty-five, it was impossible that this

could be the problem. I had PMS twenty-five days of the month. I knew that something wasn't right."

This is not to say that you won't find excellent doctors out there who understand perimenopause and will be enormously helpful to you. These doctors will also rule out the many other medical conditions that can mimic perimenopausal symptoms. Your thyroid, your diet, stress, the medications you're taking—it all needs to be considered. But each of *these* women's symptoms were caused by perimenopause. When it was treated, they saw their symptoms disappear.

What's the Best "Treatment" for Perimenopause?

Many of the women I've seen require no formal treatment at all once they understand what's going on in their bodies. Understanding estrogen dominance or estrogen withdrawal and the symptoms these conditions cause is key. Just knowing what's happening each month can be enough. Often patients will say, "Now that I understand this, and I know what it is, I can deal with it. I mean, it's not that bad. It's just that I was really scared, and I didn't know what was going on."

Knowledge can be very powerful in giving one a sense of control and with it the strength to endure symptoms. Keep in mind that perimenopause is not something new or something that just recently began happening to women in the last couple of decades. Your mother had it too, only she had no idea what to call it, and she was probably told that it was all in her head. Sue Spataro of the HotFlash! website (www.pinksunrise.com) remembers growing up on Long Island, New York, back in the sixties. "Everyone knew everyone else. My friends all had stay-at-home moms, who were very active in their kids' lives and in our community. This meant we were always in somebody's basement or garage doing some kind of messy craft or playing games and just generally being kids. One of the moms was always around.

"Then something started to happen to these women. All of a sudden they didn't want any of us girls to come over to their houses to play after school. Instead of baking cookies on a Saturday afternoon, moms were taking naps with the drapes pulled and the house quieted. There were women who developed drinking problems when previously they had barely touched a drink. Marriages, good ones, were breaking up left and right. Some moms were being sent to South Oaks, a nearby psychiatric hospital, and all anyone would whisper was 'She had a nervous breakdown.' My friends were very upset; they had no idea why their moms became antisocial, abandoning all their activities. These women had become a shadow of their former selves. My hunch today is that these women were experiencing perimenopause, no one understood it or knew how to help them, and they literally felt they were going crazy."

Sad but probably true in many of the neighborhoods across America in those days. Today's women have the knowledge that they aren't losing their minds and perimenopause is not all in their heads, and this, alone, may be the right medicine.

Consider one patient who told me, "I was terrified that this bleeding at the wrong time of the month meant cancer. I didn't want to tell my husband about any of this, because I knew he'd just say 'It's nothing; you worry too much.' I felt out of control because my hormones were whipping me around. Now I know it's not anything like what I feared, just perimenopause. I can't always predict what's going to happen, but I know *why*. I'm relaxed enough to feel sexual, to stop worrying so much, to do what I can to get control of these symptoms and go on with my life."

Other women can't tolerate the symptoms as well. Each woman's decision about whether to treat her symptoms or how to do so depends on the level of her symptoms and how much they disrupt her life.

Treating the More Difficult Perimenopausal Transition

Some women find perimenopause to be more of a wild roller-coaster ride than a simple transition and find their lives seriously disrupted. Enissa, for instance, remembers, "I was bleeding twenty days out of every month. The fatigue hit me so hard I would lie in bed half the day. I didn't want to go anywhere or do anything. When my doctor diagnosed perimenopause, all I could think of was, Fine, but when is it going to end? He told me that even blood tests couldn't answer that question. I decided to do some reading about perimenopause, tough it out, because I hate taking medications. One day my mother was over, and she was complaining the way she has every day of her life. I can usually turn her down in my mind to a distant drone, but that day I turned and I raised my hand, and I almost slapped her. She stared at me, openmouthed, and I felt terrible. I almost hit my eighty-year-old mother, who is sick and has no one but me to talk to. All I could think was that I wasn't going to have a marriage left or a family left if I had to go through this much longer."

Enissa was experiencing a difficult perimenopause, and it was having far-reaching, frustrating ramifications. If your perimenopausal symptoms are disruptive and even painful, you have two major options in treating them, which are the two options you really have in treating any kind of medical condition: you can treat the symptoms, or you can treat the source.

Treating the symptoms usually means taking different medications or vitamins or making lifestyle changes to treat each of the annoyances separately. You treat the weight gain with exercise and diet and depression or anxiety with medications. Mood swings might be helped by certain vitamins. Bloating and breast tenderness can be treated with diuretics and dietary changes. Libido problems may respond once the other symptoms subside or with the use of vitamins, herbs, or exercise.

Then there are women who tell me flat out, "I don't have time for all of that. I *do* exercise. I *do* eat right. I can't stand another minute of this. I want things back the way they were. Is that too much to ask?" I don't blame them for feeling that way. As a physician, I always feel that it's better to treat the source than the symptoms. If you treat the source, you don't have to run after each of the symptoms.

Remember that, in perimenopause, the main problem is erratic estrogen levels. Wouldn't it be wonderful if we had a treatment that would stop the ovary from its erratic functioning, thereby eliminating these fluctuating levels and at the same time providing stable levels of estrogen and progesterone to the body? In fact, we do. It's called the birth-control pill. Low-dose birth-control pills created especially for women over thirty-five are one of the best treatments for perimenopausal symptoms.

You may think, the pill? Isn't that supposed to be bad for you? Doesn't the pill cause cancer? The pill has come a long way in forty years. Not only are researchers almost completely positive that the pill does *not* cause cancer, but there are many *noncontraceptive* benefits to the birth-control pill that are quite healthful to women. Studies indicate that only one year of oral contraceptive use reduces the risk of endometrial cancer by 50 percent, and that this protection lasts for at least fifteen years after discontinuation of the pill. After five years of use, the risk of ovarian cancer is diminished by 60 to 80 percent even if you stop taking it. In addition, you'll get these benefits while you're on the pill:

- less benign breast disease
- fewer ovarian cysts
- fewer uterine fibroids
- fewer ectoptic pregnancies
- more regular menses (including less flow, less PMS, and less iron-deficiency anemia)
- less rheumatoid arthritis
- stronger bones

Is there any risk to taking the pill once you're over thirty-five? In truth, you can safely forget the dire warnings from the 1970s about the risks of stroke and heart attack in women over the age of thirty-five. These risks are very small and are even lower with the introduction of low-dose (20 mcg) birth-control pills, except in women who smoke, who should not take them. If you're not a smoker, you can safely take the low-dose pill into your fifties and as an added bonus receive protection against the development of osteoporosis. There remains a very small risk of phlebitis or blood clots.

"But the pill is not *natural*," some patients tell me. "I'm not sure I want to put chemicals in my body that aren't natural to stop my ovary from ovulating." Let's first look at what natural really is. Natural used to be having your first baby in your midteens, and if you lived though delivery, you breast-fed for six or seven years because there were no super-markets to run out to for milk. All this time, you were not ovulating. Then after weaning, you would ovulate a few times and start the whole sce-nario over again. You died relatively early. You could count on your hands and feet the number of times women in those early days ovulated in their entire lifetime.

Today women begin ovulating at around age ten and most often put off first childbearing until the late twenties or thirties. This means there are twenty or more years of *incessant* ovulation. That's not neces-sarily good or what nature intended. This is not to say that women should have their first child at fifteen, but the constant ovulating is why we see so many more problems today with endometriosis, infertility, ovar-ian cysts, ovarian cancer, and breast cancer. Turning your ovaries "off" and giving them a rest via a low-dose pill may be the best and most nat-ural thing you can do for yourself. (See Chapter 2 for more on incessant ovulation and breast cancer concerns.)

As a treatment for perimenopause, most women find the pill to be just what the doctor ordered. Kate, forty-six, for example, was suffering from irregular periods, mood swings, fatigue, and headaches and told me that she had been enduring this for a number of years, trying to treat the symptoms one by one. She was taking Fiornal for her headaches and fluid pills for her breast soreness, and it wasn't doing much good. Her sex life was down to almost nothing. "My moods were just all over the place, and let's face it, who wants to have sex when you're exhausted and your head is pounding? My husband was sympathetic at first, but after a while I'm sure he didn't believe me and just thought I was a hypochon-driac or just turned off to sex. Even my friends didn't want to hear about it anymore." I gave her a prescription for a low-dose birth-control pill. She came back three months later and said, "Where can I build a statue to Loestrin 1/20? I can't believe how much better I feel!"

Pill Problems and Remedies

There are so many forms of the pill on the market that almost all of my perimenopausal patients who want to can find one that really helps their symptoms. However, the pill isn't perfect. There are some symptoms you can get *from* the pill, especially in the first three months. For example, it's not uncommon in the beginning to feel a little nauseated and to have some breast tenderness or irregular bleeding. The treatment for this is to just keep going on with the pill. The lining of the uterus has to get used to this new level of hormone. Therefore, the lining may shed irregularly until it gets to a nice thin level that can be supported by this low level of hormone. Usually by the third or fourth month all of these problems will be gone.

What if they aren't? Here are the most common problems and what to do about them.

Headaches

Years ago, when doctors heard a woman complain of headaches while taking the birth-control pill, the usual response was "We'll have to look at other birth-control methods. You probably should stop taking the pill." But now we know that the important question to ask these patients is "When are you getting these headaches?" Frequently they happen during the *off* week—the week during the placebo pills. During this week off the pill doesn't provide estrogen, and a woman's body hasn't been making it either, because the pill shuts down a woman's natural production of estrogen. This is another example of estrogen withdrawal. I will sometimes prescribe a very low-dose estrogen patch for use during the week off the pill, and for many of these patients, the headaches disappear.

There is another, easier way of avoiding estrogen withdrawal on the birth-control pill, which is to continue to take the birth-control pill without a week off. Is this dangerous? Not at all. When the pill was originally developed, there wasn't a regimen of three weeks on and one week off. But it was felt that women might be uncomfortable not having a bleed once a month to "prove" they weren't pregnant. The truth is women can take birth-control pills, especially the low-level pills, for three or four months at a time with no week off. At that time they should skip a week and allow a bleed to occur; otherwise they might notice spotting. There is no medical reason why this bleed is necessary every month, however. Women who have problems with withdrawal symptoms during the week off will benefit from this strategy in using the pill without endangering their health. If you choose to try it, however, coordinate it with your health-care provider.

Breast Tenderness

If breast tenderness continues after you've been on a particular pill for more than three months, try a different pill. Since estrogen is usually the culprit in sore breasts, check to see what dose of estrogen your pill contains. Many practitioners begin their patients on midrange (30–35 mcg) pills, such as Estrostep, OrthoCept, OrthoTriCyclen, Nordette, or Triphasil. Moving down to a 20 mcg pill such as Loestrin 1/20, Alesse, or Mircette may stop the breast tenderness.

Break-Through Bleeding or Spotting

With the new low-level pills available today, this is not an infrequent problem. The lower the level of estrogen in the pill, the thinner the uterine lining is going to be. Sometimes that lining is so thin that women find they have little or no bleeding on their week off the pill. That's actually a benefit, because maintaining a thin lining is what makes the pill so protective against uterine cancer, which usually develops after years of an overstimulated, thicker lining. However, the problem is that a thin lining can also lose its integrity during the wrong week of the month and begin to shed, in which case you'll experience this as spotting or break-through bleeding. If that happens to you once, do nothing and wait and see what happens next month. If it happens repeatedly, it's a signal that you need a bit more estrogen. While some doctors will advise you to take a higher-dose pill, that's often not necessary. You can stay on the same pill but take a booster of estrogen, such as seven days of 20 mcg of Estinyl, while you're taking the pill, during one week, once or twice a year. That's often enough to stop the break-through bleeding. See your gynecologist for this.

Clotty Periods and Heavy Periods That Last for More Than Five Days

Usually when you're on the pill you get periods that are much lighter than you used to have. If you get a heavy period instead when you first begin taking the pill, wait a couple of months to see if it continues. If it does, try changing pills. If you're currently on a monophasic pill, try a triphasic, and vice versa. A pill with a different kind of progestin might help. For these problems, I often recommend Nordette and Triphasil, because they have a stronger progestin. You might also want to have an ultrasound, just to make sure that there isn't a polyp or fibroid in the uterine lining or cavity causing the clotty bleed. It's possible that your doctor couldn't feel it during the pelvic exam, because they can be inside the uterus. In any case, both polyps and fibroids are common during the perimenopausal years and are easily treated.

Bad PMS

If you're being treated for PMS symptoms with the birth-control pill, be aware that three things can happen: your PMS can get better, stay the same, or get worse. Getting PMS on the pill is also possible. This is usually due to the progestin component in the pill. Therefore, if the pill is making your PMS worse, ask your doctor about switching to a pill with a different progestin.

Loss of Libido

Changing the pill from a monophasic to a triphasic or the other way around sometimes helps women who lack libido. Some women unfortunately will still have considerably less libido no matter what pill they try, simply because of the loss of normal cyclic changes on the pill. Also, more important, the pill can lower testosterone levels, which is how most birth-control pills decrease acne. Because of this, instead of stopping the pill, a newer option is to take testosterone supplements with it. Estratest HS or testosterone cream may help. DHEA has occasionally been used here. The pill and its effect on libido are discussed at greater length in Chapter 6.

Nausea

This is common in the first few months on the pill, and I usually advise my patients to stay with it because it often disappears. It is especially prone to happen if you miss a pill and then take two in one day. If nausea continues, a lower-dose pill might help.

Depression

When a woman hasn't had depression before and suddenly experiences it while on the birth-control pill, the pill should be changed either to a lower dose or from monophasic to triphasic. If this doesn't help, I'd advise going off the pill, especially if she went on it to treat or lessen her perimenopausal symptoms. The last thing she needs is *more* moodiness.

In general, the most important thing to remember when taking the birth-control pill to counter or treat perimenopausal symptoms is that if your problems were truly caused by fluctuating levels of hormones, they shouldn't be occurring now that you're on the pill. If they are, you need to look to another cause. There is no reason to stay on the pill if it doesn't help or if it makes things worse.

What About HRT When You're Still Having Periods?

My office fills up with patients who are perimenopausal and were started on HRT. It can cause more trouble than it's worth. HRT consists of taking estrogen every day and adding a progesterone to protect the lining of the uterus. The progesterone can cause bleeding either monthly or irregularly. The problem is that if you give a perimenopausal woman HRT, she will bleed from the hormones that were given, but since her ovaries are still working and still producing estrogen (even though it's in erratic amounts), she will also bleed from her *own* estrogen and occasional progesterone. The reason the birth-control pill is so successful in treating perimenopausal symptoms is that it suppresses the ovary; it stops the ovary from functioning. Most people don't realize that HRT levels of hormone are much lower than the levels in birth-control pills and don't suppress the ovary.

So, should you ever use hormones other than the birth-control pill for perimenopausal therapy? It's possible if you take the estrogen or progesterone *alone*. It has to do with which of the two kinds of perimenopausal changes are troubling you. If your problem is estrogen dominance with irregular bleeding and sporadic ovulation, sometimes doctors recommend a progesterone *alone* in the second half of the menstrual cycle to help women regulate erratic cycles.

If the trouble is coming from estrogen withdrawal (you're waking up sweating, you are fatigued, you're depressed), your doctor might recommend that you augment your estrogen level using a low-dose oral estrogen or estrogen patch.

It's a rare patient, however, who will benefit from taking HRT in perimenopause without bleeding irregularly. While your body is still making the hormones, you are better off augmenting one or the other as needed or, better, finding a birth-control pill that will work for you. The problem is that perimenopausally it's possible for a woman to alternate between estrogen dominance and estrogen withdrawal or deficiency, and it's impossible to predict when. The birth-control pill is the best strategy because it shuts the ovaries down completely, avoiding both of these phases.

Beyond Hormones, What Else Can You Do to Treat Your Perimenopausal Symptoms?

Here are some of the best soothers of the symptoms women complain about most during perimenopause.

Strength Training

There is growing evidence that strength training helps women with their PMS symptoms. Whether that's because it is exercise, which is always a mood lifter, or because it gives women increased feelings of confidence in their bodies is not really known. However, three forty-minute sessions a week of work with weights has done wonderful things both mentally and physically for many of my patients. An added bonus is that studies show that exercising a half hour before sex increases arousal and orgasm.

Take More Calcium

Not only good for your bones, which need extra help as the estrogen in your body declines, calcium is also a natural soother. There are even claims that it helps people sleep more soundly and restfully. I recommend that you take 1,500 mg a day, through diet, supplementation, or both. Make sure you split the doses; don't take it all at once, because it won't get absorbed.

Vitamins

Vitamin E, which is an antioxidant, as well as vitamin C, along with a good multivitamin, can be very helpful. But be careful to read the labels on any vitamins you buy, especially those that are specifically touted for midlife women. One patient whose perimenopausal complaint was anxiety and sleeplessness found that her vitamins contained gingko and ginseng—substances that can act as stimulants in some women.

Antidepressants

According to the psychiatric researchers, there are no studies that definitively tie depression to perimenopause or menopause. Studies or no studies, many patients come to see me with the complaint of problems with depression during perimenopause. They complain of crying for no reason or feeling moody or being quick to anger. If you choose to treat the symptom, rather than the source of the problem, antidepressant medication is certainly an option, and there are many choices. The most common are Paxil, Prozac, Zoloft, and Celexa. These medications, however, may cause a loss of libido in some women, as well as causing difficulty achieving orgasm. There are also over-the-counter remedies such as St. John's wort or Sam-E, both of which have been shown to reduce depression without as many side effects, although studies still need to be done to shed more light on how, why, and to what extent they work.

What About Herbal Remedies for Perimenopause?

In the next chapter, I fully discuss my feelings about herbal therapies. However, suffice it to say for now that one of the problems women have from attempting to use an herbal therapy advertised to help *perimenopausal* symptoms is that most of these products contain phytoestrogens (or plant estrogens). Recall that your problems during perimenopause can come from two different directions—one is declining levels of estrogen, but the other is estrogen dominance, or too much estrogen. The last thing you need when you're having symptoms from too much is more estrogen in *any* form. One patient recently told me that she tried black cohosh because her sister recommended it. Black cohosh is an herb commonly used by women who have reached menopause. They like it because of its estrogenic properties. The trouble was this patient, unlike her sister, wasn't near menopause and actually was having problems because of estrogen dominance in her system. What happened when she took the black cohosh? "It was terrible. I felt like howling at the moon. I was screaming at everyone; I couldn't sleep. There was no other explanation for it."

Had this patient been having symptoms caused by low levels of estrogen, the black cohosh might have helped. It's important that you discuss your symptoms with your doctor regardless of whether you intend to go a medical route or an herbal route in treating them.

If you are intent on taking the herbal route, the following are herbs that have been judged *effective* for perimenopausal symptoms by Germany's Commission E, which is the only regulatory agency in the world to really look at herbal therapy: balm, black cohosh, chasteberrry, ginkgo, ginseng, passionflower, St. John's wort, and valerian.

The Perimenopausal Pregnancy

I did a lot of OB work in my first two decades of practice and delivered many midlife moms. I learned one thing very quickly: there is a huge difference between a couple who is having a midlife baby when they've *just* gotten married and a couple having a baby after they've been married for twenty years. To the first couple, that baby is a "love child." If it puts a damper on their sex life, they think, Who cares? If we're not making love, so what? We've got this baby. Just look at what we've both produced! We're going to bring her up a hell of a lot better than we would have when we were both twenty-five years old. *He's* even apt to say "Do whatever you want to do. I'll stay home with the baby. You go to work if that's what you want to do." He may see this as an opportunity to do what he couldn't do years ago. He was obsessed, then, with building his career. That career may be solid gold today, but it can feel less important. Having this baby with a woman he loves and who excites him is an opportunity to do something meaningful. When their middle-aged friends no longer want to come to their house—they can't cope with the baby crying and the chaos—the couple often doesn't care. Their new bonds are quick friendships with other older parents met in the Lamaze class or at the preschool picnic who are equally excited by this late chance at having a family.

Then there is the couple married for twenty years and unexpectedly having another baby. Of course you can't stereotype couples, and some are thrilled, but I've had plenty of midlife moms and dads tell me they were frankly pretty angry about an unexpected pregnancy. "How could we *do* something so stupid? We never get any sleep. I have to go to work. We're so exhausted. This is really a nightmare."

She's angry because he's so upset. She comes in for a checkup six weeks after delivery and when I tell her she can resume sex she says, "Sex? You've got to be kidding. Please don't tell him I can have sex again. Give me a note that says I can't have it for the next six years. I'm so exhausted I can hardly keep my eyes open. He changes one diaper a month and thinks he's father of the year."

It's important to remember that perimenopause is not menopause. Even with sporadic ovulation, *you may still be able to get pregnant.*

That's another reason why the birth-control pill is so useful for the peri-menopausal patient.

Helping Yourself Through the Emotional Side of Perimenopause

Many of my patients tell me, "Compared to perimenopause, menopause is a snap." It's true that perimenopause can be a time of tremendous emotional upheaval. The whole unpredictable nature of it—one day you're crying, the next you're bleeding—can make you feel like you're on an emotional roller coaster. When you go through a rough time like this—and it's added to the other challenges of midlife, such as taking care of your parents, dealing with work problems, and taking care of your kids—there's no question that it can affect your sexuality.

Perimenopause tends to kick up emotional issues that can be as confusing as the fluctuating hormones. First, the knowledge that you are coming off your reproductive years can fill you with mixed emotions. Some women are thrilled to be done with that part of their lives, while others are upset. Even women who don't want to have more children may feel a pang when they realize that it's no longer going to be an option.

Kelly's story is a case in point. Her marriage to Jim was her second and his third, and they had accrued four children along the way. With a house full of preteens coming and going, all in joint custody with other parents, just managing the family "calendar" kept Kelly's mind consumed for years. "I was never sure how many of us would be sitting down at the table for dinner. Just keeping track of who was at whose house was a major undertaking."

The last thing anyone imagined was that Kelly might want to have a baby. Then Kelly's doctor told her that her irregular periods and headaches were probably symptoms of perimenopause. "My first thought was that Jim and I had never had a baby together. In fact I was the one who didn't want one. But now that I knew that it might never happen, I wanted a baby."

Jim looked at her astounded. He told her flatly that he wasn't about to start all over again with babies and felt overwhelmed thinking of college expenses for the children they had. Fights over sex sprang up between them. She went off the pill, complaining that her breasts ached and it was making her fat. Jim accused her of trying to get pregnant. She stopped feeling any desire to make love to him, angry that he wouldn't even discuss her feelings.

"Finally I knew I had to talk to someone. The counselor assured me that what I was going through was normal. She said most women feel some ambivalence about perimenopause. 'It's saying good-bye to a particular part of your life, a lot of things regular menstruation is symbolic of.'"

In the end, Kelly knew she didn't really want a baby. What she wanted was reassurance that Jim was committed to her. "The only reason my own father stuck around was to raise us. So much of my identity was tied up in being a mom. What was going to happen when the kids no longer needed me so much? Who was I going to be then? Having a baby seemed the answer. If I got pregnant, it would be another fifteen years before I'd have to face those questions again."

Your emotional reaction to perimenopause may or may not have to do with entering the end of your reproductive years as Kelly's did. But it will probably coincide with midlife. It's a time when we start to question everything we were once so sure of. Kelly's crisis led to a deeper understanding of herself and the value of her marriage. For many women, however, perimenopause heralds a time of questioning whether they want the relationships they have. Janice, fifty-four, says, "Our kids went off to college, and we had nothing to distract us from each other. One day I found myself looking across the bed wondering, Who is this man? What is he thinking about these days? Why does he stay? Why do I let him stay?"

Carmen, forty-seven, found that her diagnosis of perimenopause was followed by a complete loss of interest in sex. "I didn't want to take the testosterone my doctor offered; it was like I just didn't care about that part of my life anymore. Then one day, when I was talking to my sister about our family, it struck me. I'm sure that the last time my mother had sex was when she conceived my brother thirty-five years ago.

Both of my aunts also clearly felt that sex ended when you could no longer have babies. Unconsciously I had absorbed the notion that if menopause was on the way, then I was no longer a sexual person and should be done with 'all that.'"

Carmen isn't alone in tying her sexuality with her ability to reproduce. However, today, when women routinely live into their eighties, they can live thirty years past their reproductive capability, and there's no reason why those can't be highly sexual years.

For some women a diagnosis of perimenopause brings up one awful thought: does this mean I'm getting old? Sandra, forty-five, admits, "When I first heard my doctor say *perimenopause*, I thought, Oh, no, I don't want to go there yet. Can't we stop this somehow? I started saying things to my husband like, 'Do you think this dress makes me look old?' or 'Do you think I look as old as she does?' When he said, 'You know, you can't expect to look thirty for the rest of your life,' I was so angry I didn't speak to him for two days. He threw up his hands and said that no matter what he told me, he couldn't win.

"That was two years ago. I can't say that I love the notion of aging, but I'm much more at peace with it than I was during those early days. Perimenopause was a shock I just wasn't prepared for."

Prepared or not, most women will find that they have *some* emotional reaction to realizing they are in perimenopause. What can you do to help yourself get through the emotional side of perimenopause? Here are several suggestions:

- **Realize that perimenopause does not go on forever, and neither will these feelings.** Kelly, who is fifty-four today and reached menopause a year ago, says, "Menopause was a lot easier to cope with. It's final. No more *what-ifs* and *can we stills*. Perimenopause was harder. I think all the transitions in life are harder. When you finally arrive, you come out on the other side a stronger person. I have a tremendous sense of who I am now."
- **Don't forget that perimenopause is natural.** At the other side of it, after menopause, a lot of women feel a great deal of relief because they feel like they are no longer slaves to their hormonal cycling. The ups and downs of worrying about things like "Am I

going to have my period the whole vacation?" or "I can't face going out tonight; this PMS is awful" are over. Perimenopause has been called the "storm" before the "calm."

- **Get support when you need it.** Other women who have gone through what you're going through can be enormously reassuring. Support groups on the Internet abound with women who benefit from sharing their experiences and solutions. Talk with your friends. A little support can empower you to set new goals or make the changes in your life that you need to. It's always reassuring to hear you're not alone. Confidence in your gynecologist or other health-care provider can also have an impact on how you accept or deal with perimenopause. Knowing your doctor is accessible to help with problems as they arise can make this transition easier to navigate.
- **Live the questions.** Have patience with what's unresolved in your life. You don't have to have all the answers at once. Give yourself time to find the answers. As you live, they'll often come to you. If you don't get any answers, the questions may resolve themselves.

Will He Ever Understand What You're Going Through? Talking to Him About Perimenopause

"Should I tell him I'm going through perimenopause? Will he think I'm getting old?"

Chances are that if you're positive about perimenopause, he will be, too, and it will stop being a secret in the bedroom. Many women find that their partner's reaction to perimenopause is "What is it?" followed closely by "Who cares? This is no big deal. We'll handle it."

He can be enormously reassured, however, that the reason for your moodiness, sleeplessness, and lack of desire for sex when you're having your worst symptoms has a name—and it's not *his*.

Letting him in on the secret can also be helpful to your relationship. As one patient told me, "All I have to say now is 'Bad day!' and he knows to give me my space and stay out of my way. We used to fight when I'd get irritable. He took it personally. Now he knows it's something I can't always control."

Include your partner in what you are going through as much as you comfortably can. Educate him (let him read this book) so he knows that this is normal and that there isn't anything seriously wrong. Let him know that it's expected that you may be more tired than usual, or short with him at times, or not in the mood to be sexual on days that are particularly bad. Most of all, reassure him that the ups and downs of perimenopause are not forever. You may find you become closer as a couple having gone through this together.

5

"I Thought These Hormones Were Supposed to Help Me!"

 Hormone Replacement Therapy (HRT)— the New Options

WHEN LISA, fifty-three and postmenopausal, was prescribed hormone replacement therapy (commonly called HRT), she was ready to try anything. "I was having about twenty hot flashes a day. I always felt dizzy, sweaty, and tired. Nothing helped. Sex? I couldn't imagine doing anything that would make me even more hot and sweaty. We were sleeping in separate rooms at that point anyway. I was having such a tough time falling asleep that if he rolled over in bed and woke me I was furious.

"My best friend told me her sex life got better after she stopped having periods because she'd always been terrified of getting pregnant in her forties and she couldn't take the pill. She thought menopause was the end of a major monthly mess she was glad to be done with. She had few, if any, symptoms. I kept thinking, What did I do wrong to deserve this?

"So I got the hormone prescription, and my internist said, 'Take these as directed, and I'll see you next year.' I knew I'd be getting a period again from taking these pills. I was told that much. It didn't seem like the biggest deal at the time. What I wasn't prepared for was how much my breasts ached. I got nauseated and bloated, and after three months I said, forget this. As far as HRT doing anything for my sex life, I was so embarrassed about the shape my body was suddenly taking, and the acne I started getting, I had no interest in sex at all. I didn't want my husband to see my body."

The type of hormone replacement Lisa was taking consisted of 0.625 mg of Premarin, an estrogen pill that she took daily, and Provera, a progesterone supplement that she took for twelve days a month along with the estrogen. While there are many other ways hormone replacement therapy can be prescribed, this has been one of the more commonly used HRT prescriptions in the United States, and plenty of women do quite well on it. But Lisa was by no means an unusual case. There are women who have this first experience with HRT and decide, If this is HRT, then I'm not taking it. I don't need to feel worse symptoms than the ones I already had.

Some breast tenderness, water retention, nausea, and irregular bleeding are common and can be expected when a woman begins HRT. In many cases, these annoyances will stop after several months. However, when the symptoms persist as Lisa's did, they can interfere with your sexuality as well as every other aspect of your life. Nothing is a bigger downer to a woman's ability to feel sexually aroused than feeling fat, tired, and bleeding.

Researchers estimate that only about 20 percent of the thirty-seven million women in the United States who have reached their menopause take HRT. Half of the women who try HRT stop within two years. You've probably heard that women quit because of side effects, cancer fears, monthly bleeding, and weight gain. But I firmly believe that the number-one reason women who are motivated to try HRT quit after a short time is that they've received outdated medical advice, a hormone prescription that wasn't tailored to their specific needs, or little information about the latest options, or it just wasn't working for them.

When Lisa was referred to me by her internist, the first thing I told her was "You don't need to feel this lousy on HRT. No woman does."

When a woman makes a prudent choice in her life to go on HRT— and I'll explain in a moment why it's a wise choice for many women—

there's no reason to stop it because of the annoyances it can cause. *There are so many different ways to prevent those annoyances.*

I modified Lisa's prescription to find a combination of hormones that worked best for her. Three months later I modified it again. Today she's on her second year of HRT and says she has never felt better. "I feel like a desirable woman again," she recently told me, "and we're looking forward to doing a lot of traveling and other things we haven't had time for that I couldn't have even considered those first months after menopause."

In this chapter you will learn:

- how to get HRT to do what it is supposed to do—enhance your health
- how to solve the three most common problems involving HRT and sex
- how to handle the emotional issues of menopause

Can HRT Improve Your Sex Life?

While estrogen maintains the blood flow and the integrity of the sexually sensitive tissues, it's no passion pill. We have no medical evidence that taking the hormone estrogen can improve a woman's sex drive, quickness to arousal, or ability to achieve orgasm. But what we do know is that it can keep the vagina healthy and lubricated as well as improve a postmenopausal woman's health by ridding her of symptoms and protecting her from many illnesses. HRT can provide renewed energy, a sense of balance, and well-being. In these respects, HRT can improve one's sex life. What are the implications, then, for women who choose not to take HRT?

The average age at which a woman in the United States reaches menopause is fifty-one. At that point her ovaries will stop producing estrogen. One might think, So what? That's natural for a woman's body. It's natural to stop having menstrual periods and to stop being able to have babies. But because of rising life expectancy, most women will live one-third of their lives *after* their bodies have stopped producing estrogen. This has enormous implications.

For a long time it was believed that estrogen was solely a reproductive hormone, affecting only the female organs. But today we know that there's an estrogen presence in brain cells, bone cells, heart cells, and blood vessel cells, to name just a few. Estrogen *receptors* (the "cellular machinery" that allows a hormone to do its job) have been found in the skin, the liver—in fact, all over a woman's body. By taking HRT a woman can gain the following benefits:

- fewer hot flashes
- improved sleep
- better vaginal elasticity and bladder health
- a decrease in her risk of heart attack. HRT has been shown to improve a woman's ratio of "good" cholesterol (HDL) to "bad" cholesterol (LDL). Estrogen also appears to help keep the coronary arteries open and reduce the plaque inside them.
- a reduction in her risk of stroke
- a decrease in her risk of osteoporosis and osteoporotic fracture. HRT helps prevent bone resorption—the process that decreases bone density.
- a probable decrease in her risk of Alzheimer's disease. We're only beginning to understand the effects of estrogen on the brain and its ability to enhance memory.
- a lower risk of colon cancer
- a decrease in her risk of macular degeneration, the major cause of blindness in women over the age of fifty. HRT keeps a woman's eyes moist and generally promotes health of the external part of the eye as well.
- a decrease in her risk of tooth loss
- better skin tone and protective effects that ward off wrinkling. Estrogen helps preserve a woman's collagen and prevents dehydration beneath the skin.

As research continues, fueled by the fact that millions of women are approaching or have reached menopause, we're learning more about the positive effects of estrogen. What causes women who are well read, well educated, and motivated to end up not filling their prescriptions?

HRT the Smart Way

One key to avoiding the problems of HRT is getting started on the right track. A large part of my practice is devoted to helping women who have had a negative experience with HRT or couldn't find a regimen that works for them. They are sent to me by their health-care providers, or they come on their own after reading an article or book about the benefits of HRT, wondering why it hasn't worked for them. They've already gone for their yearly exams. They have complied with what their doctors told them to do. Why are they having so much trouble?

The most common reason is that a doctor gave them a prescription for hormones and said, "Take these as directed, and I'll see you next year." The patient started taking the medication, hated how it made her feel, and said, "Forget this!" To understand how easily that experience can be avoided, one has to understand a little about what HRT actually is.

When we talk about hormone replacement, most people automatically think "estrogen," because estrogen is what's missing from the organ systems that need it and is the main reason doctors prescribe HRT. But when a women takes estrogen alone, called unopposed estrogen, the lining of the uterus grows thicker. This can create a higher risk over time for developing an overgrowth called hyperplasia that can become precancerous and, later, cancer of the uterus. Before menopause, during your normal menstrual cycles, your ovaries' natural estrogen also causes the lining of the uterus to thicken, but then your ovaries also produce another hormone, progesterone, to stop the growth and prepare the lining for pregnancy. If pregnancy doesn't occur, the progesterone level automatically goes down and the whole lining is shed. You get your period.

In hormone replacement therapy, the hormones you are taking try to mimic the natural process. Estrogen is prescribed daily (see Chapter 2 for a full explanation of the various kinds of estrogen available).

Doctors prescribe progesterone along with the estrogen for women who still have a uterus. This causes the uterine wall in many cases to slough off regularly, almost totally eliminating the risk of hyperplasia or cancer. In fact, not only will progesterone prevent the increase in risk from estrogen, but postmenopausal women on hormone replacement therapy have a *lower* risk of cancer of the uterus than women on no hormones at all.

In most of the regimens of hormone replacement therapy, estrogen is taken on a daily basis. The difference between regimens is how the progesterone is added. There are a number of different regimens that really depend on the patient and whether she wants to have a period or not. The first and oldest kind of HRT is cyclic HRT, where you add the progesterone twelve days a month like a normal cycle. Usually you bleed after you take the progesterone. The second kind is continuous combined HRT, where you take both the estrogen and the progesterone daily. This is supposed to prevent the lining from thickening, thereby avoiding a monthly bleed. There are even other ways to take it, which I'll explain shortly.

In the past, the most frequent prescription for HRT was in pill form, usually Premarin (an estrogen tablet) and Provera (a synthetic progestin taken ten to twelve days a month). Too often the patient went home, started taking the medication, and her breasts ached. Or she felt depressed. Or she was nauseated. It may not have been the HRT itself but the way she was instructed to take it. Here are three common mistakes:

1. **Taking a full dosage of hormones from the start.** A woman's body reacts to these sudden hormone levels by saying "Whoa! Where did this estrogen come from?" She may feel uncomfortable symptoms immediately. My cardinal rule for successful HRT is this: *Start slowly, one hormone at a time.* I start my patients with a very *low* dose of estrogen. After a month of that, I move them up to a *regular* dose of estrogen. A woman's body will react better if she builds up levels slowly. Some of my patients find that they have to move back to the lower dose and stay there, because for them a regular dose is too strong.

2. Taking progesterone with estrogen immediately in the first month and being told this is absolutely necessary to ward off the risk of cancer of the uterus. I don't add progesterone to a woman's hormone replacement regimen immediately. After a month or two of estrogen, I first begin adding the progesterone. Now, I've had patients phone me, upset, and tell me, "I saw my internist today, and she says this is terrible. She said I have to be on progesterone if I'm taking estrogen." For the first two months of HRT, when you're going one month on a low dose and the next month on a regular dose, it's OK to go without the progesterone. It's not going to suddenly cause cancer of the uterus. I use this stepwise approach because if there's a problem, I'll know what caused it each step along the way because with each step only one component is being changed. If I know what causes it, I know how to fix it.

3. Taking a combination pill—estrogen and progesterone together—as the first type of HRT you try. The idea of combination pills like Prempro is enticing because it's easy to take just one pill. With Prempro you are taking a synthetic progestin with estrogen, and that daily dose of progestin doesn't allow the lining of the uterus to build up, so there's nothing to shed and you don't have a "period." I may get a seventy-two-year-old woman in my office who wants to try HRT, and if I tell her she's going to bleed once a month, she's going to say, "Are you crazy? I haven't bled in twenty-two years!"

But I don't like to *start* my patients on a combination pill, because if they get bloated or their breasts ache or they feel sick, it's difficult to tell what part of the pill is causing it. The prescription for HRT takes more fine-tuning than most women—and many doctors—realize. It's a lot easier to fine-tune a woman's therapy if you have two components, estrogen and progesterone, and you can change each of them if you need to or alter the level. That's important in making it a smooth transition from no hormones to HRT. There is plenty of time for combination pills later, once the body has adjusted. A newer combination pill called Femhrt will ultimately have two strengths, allowing a little bit more ability for fine-tuning, even with the use of a combination pill.

What Has HRT Done for Your Sex Life Lately?

With all the news about estrogen in the media, I have many more patients coming to me, talking about trying HRT to preserve their bones or help them avoid heart disease or Alzheimer's disease. But the major reasons women come to me wanting to try HRT are more immediate: "I'm having hot flashes. I was out to dinner the other night, and it was so embarrassing. Menopause is killing my sex life as well as everything else in my life. Do you think hormones will help?"

Robin, forty-seven, is a case in point. I talked to her about HRT when she first reached menopause a year ago, but she wasn't experiencing any symptoms she couldn't cope with and was reluctant to take medication every day. Now she was frustrated. She was always angry at herself for forgetting things. She didn't seem to have the energy she used to have. She was losing her confidence. "You know," she sighed, "my husband looks better and better as he ages. On him, prematurely gray hair looks sexy. I see women still look at him. Sometimes I think, I'm going to take him home and show him that these women don't know anything about sex. I know exactly what he loves and what really turns him on. But I end up not doing it. I'm just not with it these days. I'm so tired. I don't feel attractive. I feel like I'm losing my edge. Do you think estrogen will help? Does it really help a woman stay young?"

Estrogen has been touted at times in the media as the proverbial fountain of youth. Research has credited this hormone with giving women an increased sense of well-being, renewed vigor, energy, youthfulness, better skin and hair—and even a longer life. I have seen many patients get all of those benefits. Many of these women also have high hopes that it will make their sex lives better. Instead, for some of them, it makes it worse. Either the symptoms don't improve or new annoyances occur from taking the hormones.

The secrets in the bedroom become "My body looks so bloated on these hormones, I don't want him to see me naked." Or "I'm totally unaroused. If he told me over dinner that we could never have sex again, I'd say, 'Oh, really? Too bad. Pass the salt.'" Or "I'm still so dry when we make love, and I thought these hormones were supposed to help."

Or even "I really hoped the problem was menopause like my doctor said. But now I'm worried that something is really wrong with me."

His secrets include "She never wants to go anywhere or do anything. When she started taking hormones, I thought things might change, but it's worse, and I'm getting tired of all these doctor bills." Or "I've worked for years. We have the house she wanted. I'm finally ready for more fun and adventure in my life. She's too tired. No wonder a couple of my friends are having affairs with younger women." Or "She really doesn't look good these days. When she asks me if her dress looks tight, or her hair looks thin, I tell her she looks fine. But she's putting on a lot of weight around the middle, and to be honest, it's not exactly a turn-on." Or even "Is she going to be like my mother? Is she going to sit around every day complaining about her aches and pains? No wonder my father spent his whole life hiding in his workshop in the basement. I wish she'd snap out of it."

The good news is, baby-boomer women who have reached menopause haven't given up their place as the most innovative, far-reaching, goal-directed, sexually savvy women of all the generations to date. When they begin experiencing sexual problems due to the natural transition of menopause, they want good solid answers. HRT *can* be one of the solutions.

The more we learn about HRT, the more we find that women who are having arousal difficulties and/or problems achieving orgasm on HRT usually fall into one of four groups:

1. women who found the Provera they were directed to take with their estrogen intolerable and felt the side effects and annoyances diminished their desire to be sexual with their partners
2. women who found HRT helped every symptom—except the sexual one
3. women who were doing well on HRT but suddenly began to have symptoms again, including a loss of sexual arousal
4. women who were doing relatively well on HRT from a medical viewpoint but came face-to-face with emotional issues of menopause and their sexual selves

Let's look at each of these problems in depth.

How to Solve Your Problems with Progesterone

Bleeding, mood swings, depression, bloating, "hyperness," hair growth where you don't want it, and hair loss on the scalp are some women's complaints about HRT. These problems are often due to the progesterone component rather than the estrogen. Clearly these annoyances can diminish your sex drive. As one woman put it, "My breasts felt so heavy and swollen, I couldn't sleep on my stomach, which meant I couldn't sleep at all. I didn't want my husband to touch them."

Why not simply skip the progesterone? If you choose to go that route, remember the increased risk of cancer of the uterus from unopposed estrogen. But if absolutely no kind of progesterone works for you, there is still the option of staying on estrogen if your doctor watches you very, very closely, monitoring the lining of your uterus regularly.

I really try to avoid having a patient on an estrogen alone. When you have a problem with a synthetic progestin, there are many other ways that you can avoid suffering. Your trouble may not be progesterone but medroxyprogesterone acetate (MPA), a particular type of progesterone also known as Provera. It has been the most commonly used progesterone in the United States for hormonal replacement therapy. MPA is also found in Prempro, which is one of the single pills that has both estrogen and progesterone in it.

Provera or MPA is a strong progesterone, which can cause many annoying effects, including decreased libido. Over the last few years I've prescribed less and less MPA. Besides the annoyances, it may also actually work against the benefits of taking estrogen. The reason many women take HRT is to gain protective effects against the development of cardiovascular disease. A growing body of literature in both animal and human studies has begun to demonstrate that MPA can diminish some of the cardiovascular benefits of estrogen. MPA has also been implicated in preventing the potential widening of the coronary arteries, which are the arteries that feed the heart muscle and that are involved in heart attacks. Estrogen has been shown to be able to dilate or widen these arteries, and MPA seems to inhibit this ability.

If your major problem with HRT is the MPA or Provera, what are your options? I recommend the following choices:

- **Switch to Prometrium.** While Provera is a synthetic hormone, Prometrium is a natural progesterone that is taken orally. It's better tolerated by women. In addition, one of the most important postmenopausal hormone studies, called the PEPI study, showed that when natural progesterone is combined with estrogen, it provides better cardiovascular protection than synthetic progestins such as Provera by not diminishing the estrogen benefits. It also causes far fewer annoyances and does not decrease libido.

While Prometrium was approved by the FDA in 1998, the natural progesterone in it has been around for at least fifteen years. Women were able to get it through compounding pharmacists (pharmacists who make prescriptions by hand). But the dose wasn't standardized, and different pharmacists used different methods of preparing it. In 1998, Solvay Pharmaceuticals placed Prometrium, a standardized 100-mg dose of natural progesterone, on the market.

There are two things to keep in mind when you take Prometrium. Number one, it's very important that you're not allergic to peanuts, because the natural progesterone is in peanut oil, which helps with absorption from the intestines. A second side effect became apparent to me years ago, when my wife complained that she was getting acne from taking Provera. I had read about natural progesterone. Provera left her so frustrated she was willing to be my favorite guinea pig. I got her some natural progesterone from a compounding pharmacist.

It was the first time I had ever prescribed it. My wife's acne went away, and she felt much better on a natural progesterone. Shortly after that, when I would call home in the afternoon just to say hello, my kids would pick up the phone and say, "You can't talk to Mom; she's asleep." It was unusual, but I didn't make a strong note of the fact that she suddenly seemed to be sleeping every afternoon, thinking that our sons were wearing her out. Then one morning I was operating at Brigham & Women's Hospital, and a resident was assisting me. As usual, when doctors operate with residents, they *talk*. While discussing menopause, I explained that I was trying some natural progesterone in my practice. The senior anesthesiologist heard this and said, "Oh, we used to use that stuff to sedate people before anesthesia. In the pre-op area we'd give them a shot of natural progesterone, and it made them nice and sleepy before bringing them into the OR."

It dawned on me that this is what was happening to my wife. She was taking the natural progesterone during the day, and it was literally putting her to sleep. I warn my patients now that natural progesterone can be sedating, and that's why it needs to be taken at bedtime. This is not a problem, because taking it at night will also *help* you go to sleep. This calming effect of natural progesterone is also why very little anxiety and mood change is caused by it compared to Provera.

One additional warning: Don't confuse Prometrium with the so-called natural progesterone you can buy in the health-food store. The latter products may not offer the protection to your uterus that you need if you are taking estrogen. The biggest offender was the wild yam scam. Women were told that progesterone comes from yams, and they assumed that wild yam extract would restore their body's progesterone supply. Women came to my office and told me they were rubbing this yam cream on their arms three times a day.

The truth is, yam cream has absolutely no progesterone in it, and they weren't getting *any* protection. While progesterone comes from a compound that exists in yams, you have to march that compound into the lab to change it into progesterone. The body cannot convert it on its own.

As far as other progesterone creams sold over the counter are concerned, a study investigating these creams was done by Aeron LifeCycles Laboratory in California. The results were distressing for any woman who had spent her money on these creams, and they weren't cheap. Ten of the creams they studied contained either no progesterone at all or levels so small as to be useless.

A woman's need for progesterone when she's taking estrogen is vital. Get a prescription from your doctor so you know you're getting the protection you need.

▪ **Take less Provera.** There is some discussion in the literature of late about using *long-cycle* progesterone. What this means is that instead of taking Provera twelve days a month, you can take it for twelve days every three or four months to avoid the annoyances every month. A number of studies have shown that there is still safety and protection of the lining of the uterus against overgrowth, but more data needs to be accumulated before we can definitely say that this is helpful. Instead of changing to long-cycle Provera, I prefer to change to Prometrium or another progestin called norethindrone acetate. If for some reason you want to stay on Provera, the long-cycle regimen is better than no progesterone at all.

- **Try Crinone.** If you'd prefer not to take progesterone orally, Crinone may be an option for you. It's a form of natural progesterone in a gel that you place in the vagina. Crinone, used at bedtime every other day for twelve days a month, will protect the uterine lining from overgrowth. Since it is absorbed through the vagina and very little gets into the bloodstream, it shouldn't cause the symptoms one often gets from oral progestins, such as breast tenderness, mood swings, bloating, and especially depression, but I have even seen these effects in a few patients on Crinone. As it is, most patients don't like to use a vaginal progesterone gel due to the need for vaginal placement.

- **Try a cyclic combined regimen.** Women whose biggest complaint about HRT was that it gave them a monthly period were thrilled when the drug Prempro was approved by the FDA. Because it combines progesterone with estrogen every day, the promise was that the lining of the uterus wouldn't grow to the point where it would have to be shed each month. A woman could take HRT and not have a period! What a godsend.

While Prempro may work for many women, it continues to be a major cause of referrals to my office. As a specialist, both gynecologists and internists refer me their patients who have problems with hormone replacement therapy. That gives me a biased view, of course, since the complicated patients are the ones I see. But it has also demonstrated to me that many, many women have bleeding problems with Prempro.

What are the problems with Prempro, and why do these women fill my waiting room? Prempro works by never allowing estrogen to be taken without progesterone. That means that even though the estrogen would like to make the lining of the uterus grow, the progestin in the same pill doesn't allow it. So when you're on Prempro, the lining of the uterus stays very, very *thin*. Now, normally when a woman bleeds postmenopausally, we worry about the development of cancer of the uterus. That usually develops in an *overthickened* lining of the uterus. When someone bleeds on Prempro, that worry is minimal. The problem here is that the lining is too thin, not too thick. When the lining is this thin, bleeding can just break through. It's an annoyance and rarely ever precancer.

Bleeding during the first six months on Prempro is not at all unusual. When bleeding occurs after this, it's a problem. Your gynecologist will usually investigate to see if there are any mechanical reasons for the bleeding, such as polyps or fibroids. Usually, however, there are no mechanical problems, and it's just a problem from the Prempro. How can you solve this kind of annoyance? I have often used a regimen called *cyclic combined* in this kind of situation. Cyclic combined therapy, as it was originally developed in France, is the use of estrogen every day along with the use of progesterone only twenty-five days a month. This seems to allow the lining of the uterus to be more stable and avoid the thinning from continuous combined therapy. The best way to do this is to switch from Prempro to a separate estrogen along with a separate natural progesterone so that you can discontinue only the progesterone for five days. A second way to do it, if the patient really wants to remain on the Prempro, is to stop taking it for the first five days of each month. That's a little different from traditional cyclic combined, but it can work. A better option, if you want to remain on a single pill, is to switch to Femhrt, one of the newer continuous combined HRT pills, which tends to cause less bleeding than Prempro because it contains a better and safer progestin called norethindrone acetate (NA). NA, which comes from a kind of testosterone, may, infact, *increase* libido. It also stimulates bone *growth*, adding to the protection against osteoporosis. Other HRT products that contain both an estrogen and a different progestin than Prempro include Ortho Prefest, Activella, and the combination patch called, as you might expect, Combipatch.

What About Herbal Remedies If None of the Pharmaceuticals Work?

When women ask about herbal remedies for PMS or menopause, they are generally talking about the botanicals known as *phytoestrogens* that can be purchased over the counter at drug or health-food stores.

Phytoestrogens are estrogen*like* compounds that are found in plants and legumes. What research has shown, however, is that the majority of women who are taking these remedies never admit it to their doctors at all.

There's no doubt that there are medical professionals out there who know nothing about herbal remedies and don't want to know. But more medical professionals than ever are regularly taking classes and attending lectures on alternative remedies. It's important to let your health-care provider know if you are taking other medications or herbal therapies.

Here's what you should know so that you can take advantage of the best of what's available and bypass what will waste your money and maybe even make your symptoms worse:

- **Medication that comes from plants is hardly big news, so don't be fooled.** Most medications originally came from plants. If you took the plant that contains the active ingredient and ingested the leaf or root, or whatever it is that contains that ingredient, you'd wind up getting all of the other stuff in the leaf and the root as well. Those other things can upset your stomach or give you a headache or cause other problems. What the pharmaceutical industry did was isolate the active ingredient or component and separate it from the potentially annoying components. That way you wound up with a pure drug. There are major concerns about the other components that are in the plant or the root because people can be very seriously allergic to them or suffer side effects from them. When patients say "Oh, I want to take something natural instead of a drug," physicians should remind them that most drugs came from that "natural" base and the drug was then purified from the natural source. I have major frustrations with how the word *natural* is being used/abused. First, while herbs or plants "exist in nature," hence the term *natural*, the plant or *phyto*estrogens in them are not natural to a woman's body, because they're not the estradiol or estrone she normally produces. They are estrogen*like* compounds. Second, Premarin is produced from *pregnant mare's* ur*ine*, which certainly "exists in nature," but few would consider it natural except to the horse. Finally, there is the dispute as to which among the oral or transdermal patch estrogens is the real "natural" estrogen: the ones with estrone or the ones with estradiol. While estradiol is the natural estrogen made by the ovaries *before* menopause, estrone is the natural estrogen made by a woman's body *after* menopause. So herbal doesn't necessarily mean *natural*, and *natural* can mean many things. A better term would be *bio-identical* to the hormones made in a woman's body.

- **When you take herbal medication, you are taking a leap of faith.** When you buy a tomato at the grocery store, what do you do before you eat it? You wash it. You wash it because you don't know what was sprayed on it or where it was grown or what happened to it in transit to your local produce department.

Herbs are sold to manufacturers of the remedies you find at the health-food store as whole plants, plant parts, cut pieces, particles—it's anyone's guess. Did the people picking the herb know what to pick? Were they skilled at knowing the difference between the plant and a weed or something else? What was sprayed on it to keep the bugs away?

Until 1994, the FDA regulated herbal medicines, and if they were marketed as drugs they had to be proven effective in double-blind, placebo-controlled clinical trials, just as all pharmaceuticals must be today. As miracle claims for herbal medicines became rampant—"You'll lose weight while you sleep!"—consumer complaints of fraud grew. The FDA decided to crack down on the industry. That's when there was a showdown between the FDA and consumer groups. The consumer groups were afraid that vitamins might also come under the FDA's control or even require a prescription. The FDA eventually lost. The Dietary Supplement Health and Education Act of 1994 was passed. Now if an herbal remedy doesn't claim to cure anything and is merely sold as a dietary supplement, the FDA has little recourse unless the agency can prove it's unsafe.

What does this mean to you as the consumer? For one, you're going to get most of your information about what an herbal remedy does from the media, your friends, books by herbalists, and the person behind the counter. More importantly, there are *no* government standards to monitor the quality of herbal products sold to manufacturers in the United

States or to monitor what else may be in the bottle that does not appear on the label.

Studies have been done on many of the more popular herbal remedies, especially those touted as cures for menopausal symptoms. You'll find the results of those studies and a discussion of these remedies on the following pages. If you are a frequent buyer of herbal remedies, you may have heard it said that the reason these herbal remedies are not studied is that it is too expensive for an herbal manufacturer to conduct the kind of million-dollar trials that result in getting FDA approval. Interesting, considering that the herbal medication industry is a billion-dollar industry, growing every minute. But would you spend the research money if you didn't have to, weren't required to, and might be proven wrong? In their defense, they may be hesitant to spend this kind of money on a product that they would be unable to patent as the pharmaceutical companies do with the products they develop.

What some people rely on today to determine whether an herbal remedy is safe are the recommendations of Germany's Commission E. In 1978 the German Federal Health Agency created Commission E to develop recommendations on herbs and plant medicines based on clinical trial results, medical association opinions, and other sources. Based on this information, Commission E judges a remedy to be approved or unapproved.

Does that mean that you can rely on this information? Keep in mind that in Germany standardized amounts of the herb and its ingredients are regulated. That's not true in the United States, where sometimes all you can find are crude forms of a particular herb. A study of ginseng a decade ago made headlines when it was found that in the United States many of the products advertised as containing ginseng contained none of the substance at all.

- **You aren't going to beat the costs of pharmaceuticals.** Botanical remedies for perimenopausal and menopausal symptoms are very pricey. It's possible you will pay more for a botanical remedy of estrogen than you would for Premarin, Estratab, Cenestin, or other pharmaceutical estrogens.

Herbal Remedies for the Symptoms of Menopause

Although the strongest plant estrogens are only ½₀₀ as strong as what your body made before menopause, make no mistake—these *are* medications and can be potent.

Black Cohosh (Cimicifuga Racemosa)

WHAT IS IT? Black cohosh is said to be a source of both plant estrogen and progesterone. It's often taken in doses from 40 up to 200 mg per day. It's taken in the form of capsules or drops.

WILL IT WORK? Herbalists maintain that black cohosh has worked for menopausal symptoms such as anxiety, mood swings, hot flashes, night sweats, depression, anxiety, and vaginal dryness. It's also been reported to reduce the symptoms of PMS for some women. It's widely used in Europe for dysmenorrhea, which is pain with menstrual periods. One theory is that it binds to estrogen receptors, which produces a weak estrogenlike effect. Another is that the triterpenes and flavonoids contained in black cohosh act on the pituitary gland to suppress the secretion of luteinizing hormone (LH). High levels of LH can be associated with hot flashes, night sweats, headaches, and vaginal dryness.

Black cohosh is one of the more widely studied herbal remedies for menopause symptoms. In one study of sixty women under age forty who had undergone hysterectomies, half the women were given pharmaceutical estrogen and half were given black cohosh extracts. The two groups had similar results in terms of reduced problematic symptoms.

There are many different brands as well as compounds that contain black cohosh as well as other herbs. Commission E approved it for premenstrual and menstrual discomfort but did not recommend that it be used for more than six months because little is known about long-term effects. The brand of black cohosh most often used in the European studies where results were positive was Remifemin.

WHAT TO WATCH OUT FOR. It has been shown that unopposed estrogen (that is, estrogen alone) over an extended amount of time, whether it's pharmaceutical or herbal, can cause overgrowth of the lining of the uterus, which can lead to hyperplasia and possibly to cancer of the uterus. When doctors prescribe estrogen, they prescribe a progesterone also, to prevent the uterine lining from proliferating. In fact, most women on hormone replacement therapy have a lower risk of cancer of the uterus than women on no hormones at all because of progesterone.

Just because black cohosh is said to be a source of progesterone doesn't mean you don't have to worry about hyperplasia. You don't know what that progesterone *is* or if it's enough. There is still the possibility of hyperplasia occurring over time. Therefore, it should not be taken for more than six months in a row without a progesterone challenge. A *progesterone challenge test (PCT)* means taking progesterone for a number of days to see if the lining of the uterus will bleed in response. If there is no bleeding, that means the lining was still very thin, and there's nothing to shed. If there is bleeding from a PCT, the herb is stimulating the lining enough and a concern about hyperplasia exists.

Overall, if an herb works for you and doesn't increase the endometrial lining as demonstrated by a PCT, it can be very useful in combating the symptoms that can drain your energy as well as your sex life. If you want to use it as a substitute for estrogen, understand that there is as of yet no evidence that it does anything for the prevention of osteoporosis or heart disease.

Red Clover (Trifolium Pratense)

WHAT IS IT? Also known as *cow clover, meadow clover, purple clover,* and *trefoil,* red clover contains isoflavones. Isoflavones are plant estrogenlike substances. They are commonly a part of most people's diets, because they are found in legumes such as lentils, chickpeas, and beans.

Although it was once touted as a tumor and cancer remedy, there has been sudden interest in the last few years about red clover's effectiveness in treating menopausal symptoms.

WILL IT WORK? One extract of red clover that is being marketed actively for menopause symptoms is called Promensil. Promensil has been formulated to deliver 40 mg of four isoflavones in a single tablet to be taken once a day. Novogen, Promensil's manufacturer, claims that in its product each of the four isoflavones is in a standardized amount and ratio. To get the same amount of isoflavones, a woman would have to consume something like eight cups of chickpeas and a cup of soy milk—two thousand calories!

Two placebo-controlled clinical trials have been done on Promensil. The studies involved ninety-eight perimenopausal women. The studies revealed no adverse side effects after three months of treatment. None of the women experienced uterine bleeding over the course of the study, and vaginal ultrasound performed on forty-three women showed no signs of overstimulation. I have had success with Promensil for some patients who did not want to take traditional HRT. It also can be useful during the perimenopausal transition.

The FDA placed red clover (not Promensil) on its list of herbs "Generally Recognized as Safe" for food use, which does not mean that it will work for menopausal symptoms of hot flashes and night sweats but that it probably will cause no harm.

WHAT TO WATCH OUT FOR. There is a difference between an "estrogenic effect" and estrogen. Isoflavones aren't estrogen. They're nonsteroidal estrogenlike compounds—compounds that can occupy the estrogen receptor. It's not the same as the estrogen you make in your body. If it mimics estrogen's effect, it will turn the receptor on. If it's working as an antiestrogen, it will turn the receptor off. Watch for much more data on red clover and Promensil.

What's also very interesting about Promensil is the recent commercial use of Cybill Sheperd as its spokesperson. A number of years ago, few actresses in youth-obsessed Hollywood would consider endorsing any product that had anything to do with menopause because of the fear of losing their livelihood. Cybill Sheperd's commercial attachment to Promensil and her frank discussion of menopause on "Oprah Winfrey" are huge steps toward the normalization of menopause. It's helping more women move into menopause with a positive view.

Vitex (Vitex Agnus Castus)

WHAT IS IT? Also known as chastetree berry, coister pepper, hemp tree, chasteberry, and monk's pepper, the dried berries have been used since ancient times to treat problems such as painful or absent menstrual periods. Vitex has also been recommended as a remedy for hot flashes, headaches, heart palpitations, and vaginal dryness.

WILL IT WORK? It is supposed to work by inhibiting the release of follicle-stimulating hormone and/or increasing luteinizing hormone, depending on which study you read. Germany's Commission E recommends it for symptoms of PMS as well as menopause. In German studies, it appeared that vitex increased progesterone relative to estrogen. In animal studies in Germany, it appeared to inhibit production of the hormone prolactin, which is often blamed for bloating and breast soreness. No reports of dangerous reactions or side effects have been associated with the use of vitex, although some women complain that it upsets their stomachs.

WHAT TO WATCH OUT FOR. If vitex does, in fact, inhibit the release of follicle-stimulating hormone, it may do you good. FSH being elevated is responsible in one way or another for problems like hot flashes and night sweats. If your symptoms are the aggravated forms of PMS that often accompany the transition to menopause, this may help you combat some of those symptoms.

The Combos

At the time this book went to press there were shelves full of products in the women's health section of most health-food stores. Pick up any bottle and see what's in it. Most of these products are combinations of herbs and vitamins, sometimes with ginseng or isoflavones thrown in.

It would certainly seem that getting it all in one capsule rather than having to buy five bottles of pretty expensive stuff would make some sense. But as with multivitamins, you tend to get multiple products but at a lower level of strength. If some substance is working, will you be able to tell which one it is? These are always the questions, and as the baby-boom generation passes menopause, hopefully the demand for real answers and definitive studies will be met.

What to Do When HRT Does Everything You Want It To—*Except* Improve Your Sex Life

Janet, fifty-two, began HRT shortly after her periods stopped at fifty-one. "My hot flashes disappeared, I started sleeping through the night, and overall I felt good. But I had no sex drive at all, which used to be strong.

I felt embarrassed complaining about *that* when HRT was working so well for everything else. Still, it was taking so much clitoral stimulation for me to feel aroused, and I rarely had an orgasm, that I started to think sex just wasn't worth the trouble."

Samantha, fifty-four, would agree. "I met Ron four years ago, and the immediate thought I had the first time we made love was, I can't believe what I've been missing all these years! With my ex-husband it had never been that good. I couldn't believe I had settled all those years for a man who had gone through the same routine, the same way, every time, interested only in satisfying himself. With Ron, I felt like I was having real sex for the first time in my life. We both brought a lot of baggage from our previous marriages into our relationship, but even during the rockiest times, sex pulled us through." Then Samantha reached menopause. Because her mother suffered from osteoporosis and her grandmother had died of heart disease, she instantly requested HRT. "I thought HRT was supposed to be good for your sex life, but my sex life completely bottomed out. I felt no interest. I didn't even have fantasies anymore. It was like someone had turned off a switch."

I suggested to both Samantha and Janet that they add a small dose of testosterone to their HRT. Within two months Janet began to notice a change. She felt more energetic. She didn't feel like hiding when her husband took her in his arms. Although it still took more manual stimulation than it had in the past to become aroused, the quality of her orgasms improved.

Samantha noticed little change until three months later. At first it was very subtle. She began to have dreams about sex. As she continued using testosterone, her feelings of passion returned, and six months later she reported that she and Ron were thinking of getting married.

Janet and Samantha are not alone in their experience with HRT. If you feel as if your hormone replacement therapy rid you of symptoms like hot flashes and vaginal dryness but did nothing for a waning sex drive, it's probably not your imagination. Testosterone is the hormone that fuels both the male and female sex drive, and women produce it mainly in their ovaries. When a woman reaches menopause, even though her ovaries stop producing estrogen, they continue to release testosterone into the bloodstream. Now, suppose she begins to take HRT. Taking estrogen can actually *diminish* the amount of testosterone in a woman's bloodstream. Here's why: When hormones—whether synthetic or produced by the body—are released into the bloodstream, they have two possible fates. A very small amount will remain free and be able to affect cells that are receptive to them. But most of the hormone in the bloodstream will wind up bound to certain proteins that prevent them from having any effect. The main binding protein for estrogen and testosterone is called sex-hormone-binding globulin (SHBG). In fact, testosterone binds even more heartily to SHBG than estrogen. Now, estrogen causes the liver to *increase* its production of SHBG. In effect, when a woman takes estrogen, the increase in SHBG may actually gobble up more of her testosterone, leading to a drop in sex drive and energy.

Even without this chemical process occurring, as a woman ages she produces less testosterone. Studies on younger women who have their ovaries surgically removed or destroyed chemically from chemotherapy have shown that the loss of ovarian testosterone often causes a sudden drop in arousal, fantasies, and desire. In the same women, replacing testosterone caused an increase in sex drive.

Testosterone supplements have also been shown to strengthen bones, increase a woman's sense of well-being, enhance her energy level, and increase cognitive brain function. With these kinds of claims, one might wonder, Why isn't every woman in the world taking it? More and more women are. In fact, in 1999, there were so many prescriptions written for Estratest HS, a pill that combines estrogen and a small dose of testosterone, the pharmaceutical company couldn't produce it fast enough, and drugstores across the United States ran out of it for months.

The questions that follow are the ones I hear most often from women who are already on HRT, have heard about the benefits and drawbacks of testosterone, and are considering adding it to the mix.

"If I want to take testosterone, and I'm already taking a pill for estrogen and one for progesterone, do I have to take yet another pill?"

I recommend a combination pill called Estratest or Estratest HS (half-strength). Most women find that Estratest HS is sufficient. It combines estrogen, specifically Estratab, a plant-based estrogen, with 1.25 mg of methyl testosterone. You *will* still have to take progesterone. In my practice of complicated referral patients, I've found the use of Estratest to be extremely helpful, with excellent results.

Another option is testosterone cream. You rub the cream into the clitoral area on a regular basis. It will be absorbed into the bloodstream, as well as increase the sensitivity of the clitoris itself. These creams are made by compounding pharmacists who can make them with varying concentrations of testosterone. For women who are concerned about taking testosterone orally and are worried about systemic effects, or who have no fatigue and are just looking for some response sexually, creams can be the answer. But be aware that some of the testosterone will be absorbed anyway.

How about a patch? No testosterone patches made specifically for a woman's needs are presently available in the United States. Although women have cut patches intended for men into smaller pieces, this doesn't work well, and I advise against it. My hunch is that testosterone patches for women will soon be available as the demand for them increases.

"I use the patch for estrogen replacement. Do I have to switch to Estratest?"

It's certainly an option. But if you're happy with the patch, you can take an oral pill containing methyl testosterone. Most of my patients who use the patch first try testosterone cream, usually because they don't like to take medication orally.

"I use estrogen cream, and I hate pills. Can I still use testosterone cream? Or will adding cream on top of cream just be one huge mess?"

Women sometimes think that using testosterone cream is going to be like using Monistat or other creams that treat yeast infections and come with rather large applicators. You use a small amount of testosterone cream on the outer part of the vagina around the clitoris. Estrogen creams are inserted inside the vagina. Many of my patients have used both successfully.

"What about testosterone injections?"

They're available in Europe and Canada, but the testosterone injections available in the United States are used to treat prostate cancer. Not a good idea for women looking for a small testosterone boost. There may be more available in the near future.

"My doctor told me that Estratest is not approved by the FDA for treating low libido. Does that make it dangerous?"

It's approved by the FDA for use in treating hot flashes and other menopausal symptoms. The fact that it isn't approved for treating low libido means that Solvay, the pharmaceutical company that manufactures the drug, hasn't gone to the FDA with its research and asked for approval. Therefore, when doctors prescribe it, they are prescribing it "off label." Doctors regularly prescribe drugs approved for one indication to treat something entirely different if research warrants it. There is nothing illegal about this or even controversial. Personally, I don't know any doctor who prescribes Estratest HS strictly for hot flashes.

You will find more answers to questions about testosterone blood tests and potential concerns in the following chapter about libido.

Will testosterone help you? Is it worth the hassle? I had a new patient recently who came in for an annual exam. She had her menopause four years ago and was taking Premarin and Prometrium. When I inquired about her sex drive, she told me, "Nonexistent. I really have no desire at all. We haven't had sex since I had my menopause. Nothing turns me on."

Then I asked, "What about before your menopause?"

"Oh, I never thought it was such a big deal then, either. Actually, sex has never been very exciting for me."

If your sex drive has never amounted to much, it's doubtful that taking Estratest is going to make a difference. It isn't going to solve marriage problems or make you desire a partner you've never had desire for. While any woman can certainly try testosterone, the best candidates for testosterone supplements are women who notice a sharp decline in their libido that coincided with perimenopause or menopause.

When You Suddenly Begin to Have Symptoms Again

Lorraine, fifty-five, came to see me with this complaint: "All of a sudden these hormones don't seem to be working like they used to. I'm having hot flashes. They aren't as bad as they were years ago, but I still can't understand why I'm having them. I don't sleep as well as I've been sleeping over the last two years. And recently I couldn't care less about having sex. Do these pills just stop working in some women?"

If this happens to you, your menopause isn't "getting worse." This type of problem is called *relapse*. Recall that the only hormones in the system that can affect the cells of the body are hormones that are floating freely. Taking estrogen increases the amount of sex-hormone-binding globulin (SHBG) in the body, which both estrogen and testosterone bind to. You end up with less free estrogen as well as less free testosterone. You can begin to have symptoms of relapse because the body feels like it's lower in estrogen, too.

When women start having symptoms of relapse, it's a mistake to take more estrogen. Jennifer, forty-nine, had this experience: "When I first had my menopause, I was taking 0.625 mg of Premarin. After six months I started having night sweats and a lot of trouble falling asleep, so my doctor increased my Premarin to 0.9. That was fine for years. Then, again, I started having problems sleeping, and I had no interest in sex at all. That really bothered me, because there was a new man in my life, and not only was I making him nuts with all my tossing and turning, but when we made love he knew I wasn't with it at all. Once again my doctor increased my Premarin, this time to 1.25 mg. It didn't help my sex drive, and my breasts got really painful. The days when I thought my libido was low were starting to look like wonderful days."

Adding testosterone can take better care of the symptoms of relapse. It *diminishes* the binding protein, thereby increasing the amount of free hormone in your body so you're back on track again with more free estrogen and free testosterone. Instead of increasing the estrogen, you wind up getting more bang for your buck, or estrogen effect, staying at the *same* level without having to increase the estrogen dose.

Another way to treat relapse is to change from oral estrogen to a patch. Because the patch delivers estrogen directly to the bloodstream without going through the liver, the binding protein is not increased as it is with oral estrogen until the patch has been used for a few years.

What to Do If HRT Works—but You Come Face-to-Face with Emotional Issues of Menopause

HRT may make you feel great physically, but unfortunately it doesn't help the emotional issues that menopause tends to kick up. Menopause is saying good-bye to childbearing years. Both you and your partner may feel ambivalent about this, even if you've never particularly wanted to have more children. "I stopped having regular periods at forty-four," Katherine, mother of three, recalls. "No sooner did I find out that I probably couldn't get pregnant than my husband started this campaign about wanting to have another child. There was the nasty implication of 'I can and you can't.' Then he started talking to me about using donor eggs. I argued with him that he was just looking for something new in his life and could probably find it in better ways than for us to have a fourth child, but he wouldn't let up. For the first time I thought seriously about divorce."

While there definitely are men who realize they missed out on much of the child raising as they pursued their careers and suddenly want to have a midlife baby, Katherine's husband's issues went deeper. "We ended up in therapy because our fights were so bitter over this. The counselor hit the nail on the head about this sudden baby lust. My husband's father was dying, and the counselor thought this was as significant as the fact that I was reaching menopause. 'You can't regain a father by becoming a father,' she told my husband. We spent a lot of time talking about wanting what we couldn't have, something the therapist said was very natural."

And you may have other fears. One woman told me, "The really troubling thought for me was, Will I still be able to hold my man? It wasn't just insecurity, either. How many times have I seen couples around me married twenty years and then divorced—and the ex-husband goes off to father a child at fifty-two!"

Most people are familiar with the twenty-years-and-then-divorced syndrome. There's even a forum of people on America Online who regularly post comments and experiences with this. It's one of the busiest bulletin boards on the site.

Caroline, fifty-two, was almost a victim of the syndrome herself, and she has this story to tell: "I felt a loss of confidence when I hit menopause. There was no such stage my husband was going through, and I got very insecure. It didn't help that so many of the wives of my husband's friends from work were second wives and a good deal younger than me. My mistake was that I never got any help or support for what I was feeling. I never talked to my doctor, a psychologist, a marriage counselor, or other women who had gone through this. The more insecure I got, the more my husband got annoyed with me. I'd say things like, 'Do you still think I'm pretty?' Or 'If you had to do it over again, would you still marry me?' I'd get mad at him for talking to another woman at a party. I think, looking back, that I gave him the idea that I wasn't good enough, because I didn't feel I was. We separated. We were definitely on our way to a divorce when my lawyer suggested a support group for divorce recovery. These women talked about how you can't get confidence from another person. You can't convince other people that you're vital, interesting, and exciting if *you* don't believe it. You have to do things that build your confidence. I signed up for a screenwriting class, something I'd always wanted to do, and I got so involved in it I felt excited to get up each day for the first time in years. When the instructor said my writing showed talent and a real understanding of dialogue, it changed my whole outlook.

"I had lunch with my husband. He could see something had changed in me. Suddenly I wasn't so frightened about what was going to happen to me after the divorce. Instead of thinking that a divorce was the worst thing that could happen, I started seeing some possibilities. I was even having fantasies of moving to Los Angeles. Being on my own was starting to feel better and better. In the end it was my husband who finally convinced me to give our marriage another try."

Changing jobs or careers, taking courses, meeting new people, embarking on a new fitness program, traveling alone for the first time—

these can all be enormous confidence boosters at any age. Some partners are just not that helpful or loving around the whole issue of menopause or fluctuating hormones, because it threatens their own feelings about the changes they see each day in the mirror. Or your partner may not understand how much reassurance you need. "My wife can't say that I ever said anything to hurt her feelings when she went through the change and had such a hard time," admits Dan, sixty-five. "Her complaint is that I didn't say anything positive, either. I didn't know how much she needed it. Well, to be more honest, I knew she was going to the gym every day and really making an effort to look better. She would have liked some encouragement from me. But I was in the middle of a career crisis. I realized that the younger people in the firm weren't taking me seriously. My opinion wasn't being sought. The good cases were going to younger attorneys. Suddenly I was being treated like the 'old guy.' It made me so angry I hated going to work every day. They weren't going to fire me—they knew it would cost them a fortune. They were just going to ignore me and hope I'd retire. My wife's problems just made me feel even older. When another man, one of our good friends, began to take her to lunch and listen to her, she almost began to fall in love with him. She told me later that even though I might not have intentionally wanted to hurt her, getting a little positive feedback from him made no feedback from me look pretty bad."

It's always interesting to me how many people tell me they met their soul mate in midlife. It's not that it's taken so long to find a true soul mate. It's that they've been living with someone for twenty years, they know absolutely every negative thing about them, and their interests have changed or diverged over the years. Then they find someone who shares an interest they have. This person respects them and gives them positive feedback. That feels like a soul mate, even if this is a person they never would have considered a decade ago.

Countless women I've seen in my practice have told me a story similar to this: "He never wanted to go to museums. He hated the theater. So I never went. I turned fifty and said, 'Forget it. Life is too short. I'm going to go by myself. He can stay home.'"

Once empowered to pursue those interests, it's inevitable that they meet other people with the same interests. Often they meet a man with the same interests, and the seeds leading to a love affair are sown.

If this scenario sounds all too familiar to you, try talking about your feelings. Tell your partner, as positively as you can, that you love his compliments, his interest, and his attention, and you miss it. But don't go to the same dry well over and over again looking for water if he doesn't respond. Sometimes your partner is indifferent and your relationship needs serious work. Sometimes the real truth is, he needs reassurance, you need reassurance, and neither of you has the emotional energy to reassure the other person because your own needs have become so great. None of us like to think of ourselves as particularly needy, but at every transition in our lives it's natural to need extra support. The hormonal changes of perimenopause and menopause make women feel more vulnerable emotionally at the point where they often feel physically vulnerable for the first time.

See a counselor; talk to someone you trust. Find a doctor who specializes in menopause. If it's hard for you to admit what you're feeling face-to-face in a group, join an Internet support group. Two excellent ones are Power Surge (www.power-surge.com) and HotFlash! (www.pinksunrise.com). Try the keyword "Baby Boomers" on America Online, and you're bound to see questions, problems, and solutions you can identify with.

Some women, happily, do not feel a lack of confidence at this time but a growth in self-esteem. "There really is something to getting older and wiser," says Leann, sixty. "I don't second-guess myself because I know exactly what I want. I feel free to be exactly the person I am, without having to please everyone else. When it comes to sex, I feel deserving of the time and attention I need. I'm also more of the aggressor these days. I'm more likely to wake up in the morning, reach for him, and say 'Hey, don't go anywhere so fast,' and start making love to him."

Still, other women may feel like Karen, sixty-two, who believes menopause gave her very conflicting feelings about her sexuality. "In the years while we were raising the twins, it was always so hectic that sex definitely went on the back burner. Then they went off to school, and we were alone, looking at each other, saying 'Now what do we talk about?' I once asked my mother if she and my father had sex as they grew older. She said, 'No, and we didn't miss it. Your father and I were wonderful companions. That was much more important.' In truth, I had mixed feelings about trying to reconnect sexually with my husband. Sex had never been that wonderful, and menopause seemed like a good place to quit."

These secrets can cause more havoc in the bedroom than any bad experience with menopause. A woman might have been conditioned to think that sex should end at a certain age. She can experience guilt or shame about continuing her sex life past menopause, especially if she also feels that sex is essentially about reproduction.

Although the concept of menopause and what it means has undergone tremendous change in the last decade, the idea that it means the beginning of being old or that it means being less sexually desirable dies hard. When Julie, forty-six, found that her missed periods weren't a sign of illness but menopause, she was shocked. "It's like anything else. You always think 'It will never happen to me.' I didn't tell my husband. I didn't want him to think I was no longer sexually desirable. But I realized eventually that I didn't really know what he would think. I was the one who believed that menopause made women less desirable to men. When I told him, he said, 'You mean I never have to hear about PMS again or run out and buy you Tampax? Let's go celebrate!'"

You stop the downward cycle of emotions by taking steps to feel more in control of your life. For some women, counseling or speaking with friends is the first step. For others, HRT is a beginning. When that doesn't seem to help, they feel even more out of control. But failure to feel relief from symptoms of menopause often has more to do with not finding the right friend or professional to guide you and help you find a treatment that works for you. Sharing the secrets, whether with a partner or a professional, makes them less alarming and easier to solve. You can be fabulous and forty, fifty, sixty, and beyond. The only question is, are you ready to move forward? If not, why not? Are you ready to see yourself as a person of value, who is accomplished, deserving, and sexually desirable? What prevents you? What could help you? Who can help you? What do you need? Ask these questions, and you start a quest for what can make the coming years an adventure rather than a regret.

6

THE SECRET

"Libido? Where Did It Go?"

 Making Love the Way You Used To

"My husband really thinks he's the cat's meow. When we had sex last night, he rolled over on his back after he finished, stared up at the ceiling, and said, 'I am Spartacus!' I thought, I'm glad this is doing something for him, because it's not doing a damn thing for me. I just don't seem to want sex anymore. Where has my desire gone?"

"Mornings used to be very special for my wife and me. Now when I get up in the morning, I just don't have that same urge to have sex."

"He's fifty-five, new in my life, and a very exciting man. I really want to marry this guy. The problem is I think our sex life is great, but he keeps saying things like 'I wish you had known me twenty years ago.' I don't understand. We make love, and I can't tell that anything is missing. He seems disappointed because he isn't what he used to be. What is it with him? What in the world does he want?"

"I just need more intensity these days than I ever needed before to be in the mood for sex. My wife gets upset about this and calls me the once-a-month man."

> "Rich and I planned a weekend away from our kids, our phones, and my parents, who were driving me crazy. At the last minute my sister told me that she didn't mind taking our eight-year-old for the weekend but that her husband was giving her major grief about taking the baby for the weekend. I told Rich that we'd have to take the baby with us. He said, 'You know if we take her and she sleeps in the same room, we aren't going to be able to make love. We'll wake her up.' I almost laughed out loud. 'Rich, when was the last time you heard me scream in ecstasy?'"

There *are* changes in midlife sex. But what do the changes mean? If you've always had a healthy appetite for sex and suddenly you'd just as soon visit the dentist as make love, is something wrong in your relationship?

There's no question about it: twenty years of marriage can lead to familiarity and boredom, which can cause a lack of libido. But so can two years of marriage. They say that when sex is good, it's 20 percent of the marriage, but when it's bad, it's 80 percent.

And what if you're single and you've found "the right" person in midlife? Thousands of people do. You want to have the best sex ever. Can you turn back the hands of time? What if it feels like something is missing?

This chapter is about libido, or sex drive. Libido, very simply, is the desire for sexual activity or fantasies of sexual activity. Libido is affected by many factors, including hormones, social and psychological factors, work, children, parents, and more. In this chapter you'll learn:

- how to quickly rule out physical factors, such as hormonal changes
- what to do if you've never gained back your libido following surgery or menopause
- how to know if it's depression or unexpressed anger that's undermining your sex drive or his
- what to do about bad sex in good relationships—why it happens, why you needn't accept it, and what you can do to revive your sex life
- how to talk to your partner in a way that will excite him about new possibilities rather than demoralize him with the problem

When You Lose That Loving Feeling: What's Normal, What's Not?

Almost every woman has at one time wondered, How often is normal? You may hear twice a week, twice a month, or some other number. The truth is, no one has the answer to this because no one can really quantify it. Even researchers who claim to have studied this question at length admit that, since they weren't hiding under the beds of their study participants with a clipboard, they had to rely on self-reported information.

Think about this for a moment. A researcher phones you and asks you how many times this month you've had sex. Even if you are convinced this call is legitimate, would you be truthful? *Could* you be accurate? Quick: Name the dates of the last three times you had sex.

There's also the old joke about the researcher who called and asked, "How often do you have intercourse?"

"Infrequently," the man replied.

"Is that *one* word or *two*?" the researcher asked.

Even if you can recall every time you've made love in the last month, do you trust that every person who answers this question is honest and accurate? This is the kind of information most studies that attempt to quantify how often the typical couple has sex have to rely on.

Therapists point out that many couples don't even have a steady pattern. They go without sex for a long period of time, then they have a lot of it for a while, then they have it once a month. Some couples have very little sex, feel very emotionally connected, and that's fine. There are couples who have a great deal of sex and feel little emotional connection. They rate their sex lives as unsatisfactory. And then there are those couples who *do* have a regular pattern, such as every Saturday night or twice a week without fail unless one of them is sick.

Although hearing your best friend tell you that she has sex with the man she's been married to for twenty years five times a week may make you think, Hey, what's wrong with us? the truth is, probably nothing. Forget the notion of "normal" for a minute since there's no real way to measure that. The only way to judge whether your libido (or his, for that matter) is a problem is *if it's a problem for you or a problem for you two as a couple.* If you're having sex once a month or less or lately not at all, and he's not complaining, and neither are you, this may be normal for you.

When to worry? Use the following as guidelines:

- You've always enjoyed sex—in fact, your lusty, take-no-prisoners prowess in bed is something you've been proud of most of your life. Now you can't seem to muster up any sexual feeling at all. Vacations don't do it, a dozen roses don't do it, kisses on your neck that used to drive you wild don't do it. Your partner might not be complaining, but *you* are.
- Your partner wants much more sex than you do, and it's causing an unhappy, never quite resolved battle between you. You are either defending your sex drive or worrying about it. Therapists term this "desire discrepancy." You term it "pushing."
- You want more sex than your partner does. She'll make love to you, you'll both enjoy it, and she'll say, 'We should do this more often.' But weeks pass, and whenever you initiate, she's not interested.
- You're definitely into sex and fantasy and eroticism—just not with your partner. You're very interested in new techniques, new positions—in fact the key word here is *new*. The trouble is, he's not new.

These problems respond to very different solutions. The first two may very well be a signal that something physical is amiss. In the section that follows, you'll learn how to rule out the type of physical problems that can affect libido and discover the best medical treatments.

The next two probably signal trouble in the relationship, although there may be physical issues. In the second half of this chapter, you'll learn how to cope with boredom, different sexual paces, and emotional factors that can affect libido.

Ruling Out Medical Causes for Her

Let's take a closer look at the *female* libido at midlife. Women in midlife often report less intense peaks at orgasm—and a longer time getting there. But libido or desire is different from orgasm. If your libido suddenly disappears, the problem may be a physical one. Consider the following likely possibilities:

Generalized or Systemic Illness

When was the last time you had a complete medical checkup? Any chronic systemic illness can affect your desire to have sex. I don't mean to scare you by suggesting this. Anything that drives your energy level down (such as simple allergies or low blood sugar) can take away from your ability to desire sexual activity. If you treat the problem, your sex drive may return.

Your Medicine Cabinet

Hundreds of medications list change in libido as a possible side effect. These include high blood pressure medications, antihistamines, antidepressants, fluid pills, heart medications, and antibiotics. This doesn't mean that everybody who takes these drugs will lose their sex drive, but it's certainly worth a talk with your physician about what you're taking and what might be contributing to a sudden change.

Alcohol

While a glass of wine at dinner may enhance your meal and be good for your heart, three or four is like sending ether to the brain. Alcohol in large quantities is a depressant. And a few glasses of alcohol at dinner as a prelude to an evening of sex may add up to a feeling of being too tired even to lift your head off the pillow. Anyone who drinks regularly and is now noticing libido problems should try taking a twenty-one-day hiatus from all alcoholic beverages and see if that improves matters.

The Birth-Control Pill

Birth-control pills are used by more than seventy-five million women in the United States. Women in their thirties, forties, and fifties are often not using them for pregnancy prevention alone but to ease their peri-menopausal symptoms as discussed in Chapter 4.

Whether birth-control pills enhance or inhibit sex drive is still a subject of debate. Knowing you can't get pregnant can ease tension and be a plus for your sex drive. However, many women experience a decline in libido while they're on the pill. It may have to do with the fact that the pills put a stop to ovulation and cycle changes. Why would this affect libido? The strong surge of hormones, especially LH, that stimulates ovulation causes a sharp increase in testosterone. That makes many women feel amorous and may be nature's way of continuing the species. Since women have hidden ovulation—they don't show any outward signs that they're ovulating like an ape in the wild, for example, with a red rump she shows to the world—nature has a vested interest in increasing a human female's sex drive at ovulation to help continue the species. When you don't ovulate, that hormonally infused spark of desire doesn't happen.

The second effect the birth-control pill has on libido has to do with the fact that all birth-control pills decrease testosterone levels in the bloodstream throughout the month. This can be a good side effect, and it's why most birth-control pills diminish acne. But it can also work against libido. Although we tend to think of testosterone as a male hormone, females produce it too, and it fuels sexual desire in both men and women. Less testosterone often means less libido. It doesn't happen with every woman on the pill, but many do experience this.

If you're just starting to take the birth-control pill, and you find you have a decrease in libido, the first thing to do is wait a few months. The problem may resolve on its own. However, if it doesn't improve, ask your doctor to prescribe a different pill. There are many kinds of birth-control pills. There are *monophasic* pills where you take the same pill for three weeks and *triphasic* pills where you take three phases of pills over a three-week period. Changing from one kind to another may help. Both monophasic pills and triphasic pills are available with different levels of estrogen and different kinds of progesterone. Only as a last resort do I tell patients to stop taking the pill, because we can generally find one that works without diminishing libido. See Chapter 4 for more on the pill and libido.

Antidepressant Medication

Clinical depression is nearly twice as prevalent in women as in men. In one study, researchers found that almost 30 percent of subjects (most of them women) evaluated for low sex drive had undiagnosed depression.

Depression can be treated through medication or psychotherapy or a combination of both. Medication can sometimes increase libido by decreasing depression. I have known patients who notice an increase in desire, pleasurable sexual thoughts, and fantasy. Some antidepressants even have the side effect of improving premature ejaculation in men. However, many antidepressants, especially the SSRIs (selective serotonin reuptake inhibitors), which include Prozac, Zoloft, and Paxil, can lower the sex drive or make it difficult to achieve orgasm. In fact, studies have shown anywhere from 33 percent to 96 percent of people taking SSRIs report some reduction in sexual desire. The link between loss of libido and SSRIs and why this happens is still under study. Antidepressant medications have been implicated not only in decreased libido but also erectile dysfunction, vaginal dryness, delayed orgasm, and lack of orgasm.

One option is to try a weekend "drug holiday," where you discontinue the drug for a couple of days. This is strongly discouraged by psychopharmacologists because it can interfere with the drug's antidepressant effect. Don't try this without discussing it first with your doctor. Another option is to consider switching antidepressants. Wellbutrin, Serzone, Cipramil, and Remeron all claim to be less harmful to the libido, but results are mixed.

With any medication you take, you have to look at the cost/benefit ratio. Obviously if an antidepressant helps a depression that has made your life miserable, that may outweigh any other side effect.

Will Hormones Help?

You may find that life after menopause has been a boon to your sex drive. You aren't worried about getting pregnant, and the hormonal happenings often coincide with a time when you have fewer all-consuming responsibilities and more time to relax and play. You may even notice an increase in sexual aggressiveness after menopause, where you are more likely to initiate sex rather than being a passive receiver. One study, A Mid-life Women's Health Survey, conducted through Penn State University, found that of their 505 participants ages thirty-five to fifty-five, only 25 percent said they were less interested in sex now than in their younger years. In addition, many women say that they feel more deserving of a good sex life now than ever before. "I'm much more adventurous sexually now," one patient recently told me. "After twenty-five years together, I figure, why be coy?" But there is no shortage of gynecologists who will testify to the fact that many women who reach menopause report a drop in sexual desire.

If you've had your menopause, vaginal dryness, dyspareunia (pain with intercourse), fatigue, or other symptoms caused by the loss of estrogen can drain the life out of what used to be a satisfying sexual relationship. If you're physically uncomfortable, you obviously aren't going to desire sex.

Although taking estrogen will relieve these symptoms, there is no data that says more estrogen will specifically increase sex drive or libido. The reason estrogen therapy often restores sexual desire is usually its ability to relieve nuisance symptoms like hot flashes, vaginal dryness, fatigue, and forgetfulness and to maintain vaginal blood flow. Carolyn, fifty-three, whose sex life improved dramatically once she began taking estrogen, says, "I didn't have hot flashes, headaches, or any of that, but I definitely had insomnia and mood swings that I didn't relate to menopause at first. I was tired and real short with my husband, and nasty fights seemed to spring up out of nowhere. That's why neither of us ever felt like making love."

Estrogen has been shown to even out those moods as well as improve a woman's sleep. Still, you may find as one woman did, "I'm on HRT, I'm exercising, I feel pretty good, my husband looks as handsome to me as ever—and my libido is still in the toilet." The answer many of these women will receive from their doctors comes in the form of testosterone.

Testosterone: A Passion Pill?

It puts the hair on his chest, the depth in his voice, the muscles in his arms. Why are thousands of women suddenly interested in what testosterone can do for them? Prescriptions of EstratestHS, a pill that combines estrogen and testosterone, are being filled at the rate of over two million a year in the United States.

The reason is that although we tend to think of testosterone as a male hormone, this hormone fuels the libido of both men *and* women. A woman's testosterone is produced mainly in her ovaries, with a smaller amount produced by her adrenal glands, which are small glands located on top of the kidneys. The level women produce is only about one-twentieth of the amount men make. Yet a woman's body has testosterone receptors in the brain, in her nipples and clitoris, and her skin—all of which make her sensitive to sexual stimulation.

During her twenties and thirties, a woman's body actually makes more testosterone than estrogen. When a woman's ovarian function begins to decline in midlife, the amount of testosterone she produces declines as well. Between the ages of twenty and forty, it is estimated that the amount of testosterone declines by half. However, even when she has her menopause and her ovaries stop producing estrogen, they continue to release testosterone into the bloodstream. There are more and more studies that have been showing the relationship between testosterone and libido, but a clear example of what actually happens in women whose ovaries are removed during hysterectomy gives the best evidence.

When a woman's ovaries are removed, there is a sudden drop in testosterone. For this reason, a woman may suffer a dramatic loss of sex drive following an oophorectomy, which will be discussed more fully in the next section. What happens at menopause with testosterone, however, is more complicated. Bear with a little science for a moment to learn why your doctor might recommend you take testosterone to increase your sex drive.

For testosterone to work, it has to flow freely through the body. The trouble is, there are also two proteins in the female body—albumin and sex-hormone-binding globulin (SHBG) that bind testosterone, making it powerless. Normally, 98 percent of testosterone is bound, and only 1–2 percent is free for use. Think of a great lover with his hands tied behind his back—he's there, but with his hands bound up, he's of little use to you. More SHBG means less free testosterone and vice versa. So *free* (unbound) testosterone is what's important.

Remember that the first change we see during the perimenopausal transition is an increase in FSH that overstimulates the ovaries. This increases both estrogen and testosterone levels. However, in late perimenopause, the ovaries are less able to produce estrogen. But they can still produce more testosterone in response to overstimulation. Therefore, during the perimenopausal transition, women may notice an *increase* in libido or an increase in energy and aggressiveness because of this transient increase in testosterone production by the ovary.

After a few more years, there is a natural, age-related, gradual decline in testosterone production by the ovaries as well. That's when women may begin to see a decrease in libido and a decrease in energy. When you take traditional hormone replacement therapy, you may not correct this. In fact it may complicate the situation because estrogen *increases* SHBG, which binds more testosterone and can make the problem worse, so you get a further diminishment of the libido by adding hormone replacement therapy. After a while, this becomes noticeable. Your doctor may suggest adding testosterone to your hormone replacement therapy. Testosterone *decreases* SHBG, which then allows more free testosterone and estrogen.

How do you add more testosterone to your body? You can do this by switching from estrogen and progesterone to estrogen, testosterone, and progesterone. The best way to do this is by taking a combination of estrogen and testosterone in pill form. Because testosterone itself cannot be absorbed through the gastrointestinal tract, methyl testosterone is used instead. Estratest is simply Estratab, a well-known estrogen, plus methyl testosterone. EstratestHS (half strength) is .625 mg of Estratab plus 1.25 mg of methyl testosterone, while Estratest is double that amount. I usually start my patients on EstratestHS, with the philosophy of starting out with the lowest dose possible to see if it provides the desired effect. Some women find they need the higher dose. Others will do well alternating between the two. Others will do well alternating between EstratestHS and Estratab. In other words, if the testosterone in the half-strength tablet causes insomnia, anxiety, or some other side effect, it can be cut back to every other day and Estratab can be used in between. I've even had patients who take it every third day. The important thing to remember is that, as with any kind of hormone replacement therapy, one size does not fit all, and a tremendous number of combinations and options are available. Individualizing therapy is the key.

Another option is testosterone cream. The cream is rubbed into the clitoral area on a regular basis and works in two ways. First, it can increase the sensitivity of the clitoris itself, which is important for arousal and orgasm. Second, because of absorption into the bloodstream, it can affect libido.

A lot of women ask, "Well, doesn't it make sense then to use just the cream?" But everyone absorbs medication through the skin a little differently. Some women just don't like creams. Pills will give you more uniform blood levels. Sometimes women use both.

Testosterone replacement is still considered somewhat controversial and often misunderstood. Here are the questions women most frequently ask me:

"Should I have a blood test to see if my testosterone levels are low?"

To me, the drawing of a testosterone blood level may very well be unnecessary. Sometimes the results come out normal. Even if a woman's level is normal but she has signs and symptoms of decreased libido, she may still have a very good response to testosterone. What I use is the woman's *bioassay*. A bioassay is simply the biology of her body. She tells me, for example, that her libido has decreased. That's enough information for me to suggest a trial of testosterone after a full consultation reveals no psychological or relationship factors.

A woman may want a blood test because what she really wants to know is "Is the loss of my sex drive physical? Or is my marriage the problem?" There are better ways of knowing than a blood test for testosterone levels. There's a good chance the problem is physical if (1) the loss of your sex drive came on rapidly or coincided with a physical change in your body, such as menopause, a new drug treatment, or surgery; (2) tissues that were responsive to sexual touch, such as your clitoris and nipples, feel "deadened"; (3) it's not that you've lost interest in having sex with your partner but that you've lost interest in sex, period.

"Will testosterone make me grow body hair or look more like a man or even make my voice lower?"

Not at the low doses typically prescribed. Generally, when women have gotten these symptoms, they were taking testosterone in doses far larger than their body normally made. A very interesting study was done by Elizabeth Barrett Connor looking at different levels of estrogen plus testosterone compared to estrogen alone. There was no difference over two years in the amount of hair growth in either of the groups. In fact it's *menopause* that has the potential to cause growth of facial hair and loss of scalp hair, not so much hormone replacement therapy, with or without testosterone.

"Can every woman take testosterone?"

Certain women have very low HDL, the good cholesterol. One important study has shown that, while the greatest predictor of heart attack risk in men is elevated LDL, in women the greatest predictor is low HDL. A low level of HDL, therefore, can increase a woman's risk of heart attack. Testosterone can lower HDL by a small percentage, so those women with levels below forty should probably not take it. However, most women have normal or elevated HDLs, so taking testosterone will not make a significant difference. This is something your doctor should look at prior to prescribing it.

"Does testosterone have other side effects I should know about?"

Some women notice that they feel "hyper" or somewhat more aggressive. Some have trouble sleeping. This can be prevented by lowering the daily dose or alternating estrogen/testosterone combination with estrogen alone. Lowering the dose can also help if you notice some acne as a side effect, which is seen in a small percentage of women.

"How fast does it work?"

Be patient. It takes a while. Usually when you take estrogen as part of hormone therapy replacement, you notice a change within days to weeks. The change that you notice from testosterone may take weeks to months. There are many patients for whom I've prescribed testosterone who felt little effect after the first two months but in the third or fourth month began to feel a change. You need to give it time. Ultimately the change can be dramatic. Gradually you notice an increase in your energy level and sense of well-being. This is when women often notice an increase in their libido, their arousal capability, and their sexual fantasies. After I added testosterone to Barbara's unsuccessful HRT, she returned six months later to exclaim, "I love my hormones, and my hormones love me!"

I've had two patients with chronic fatigue syndrome who found that their symptoms completely went away using testosterone. So it's possible that their diagnosis of chronic fatigue syndrome wasn't really chronic fatigue but menopausal lack of testosterone.

"Why do some women use special testosterone made at compounding pharmacies?"

What's being referred to here are oral testosterones and creams that are not made by pharmaceutical companies. They are compounded or put together by pharmacists. They can be taken under the tongue or as a pill or capsule or as a cream rubbed into the skin. The problem with this kind of preparation is the lack of uniformity. When compounding pharmacists make a drug, you can't be entirely sure that the dose you're taking right now is the same as the dose you took yesterday. However, if that's the only game in town because the dose in EstratestHS is too high, then a compounding pharmacy can make up a preparation that's a lower dose and better tolerated. These pharmacies can be an important resource for these and other preparations.

"What about DHEA?"

DHEA can be converted into testosterone in the body. It is available over the counter as a food additive. A recent study demonstrated that 25 mg of DHEA twice a day significantly increased libido in women who were complaining about diminished sex drive. More about DHEA in Chapter 9.

When You Don't Recover Your Sex Drive After You Recover from a Hysterectomy

Make no mistake: there can be *great* sex after a hysterectomy. There are women who have told me that hysterectomy was the best thing that ever happened to their sex lives. If the hysterectomy relieves problems like chronic bleeding, pain, large fibroids that cause pain with sex, or the threat of cancer, relief of these nuisances and anxieties may make you feel like you're a whole new woman. Also, knowing you can't get pregnant and you don't have to use birth-control methods can be a real plus.

Then there are stories like Lisa's: "I was bleeding at all different times of the month, bloated, exhausted, and crampy all of the time. My doctor tried everything, but nothing worked, and finally I got so sick of it I told him, 'I want a hysterectomy. I have other things to worry about than my vagina and my bleeding.'

"Eight weeks after surgery I was recovered enough to do my morning mile walks. My energy was almost where it had been before, and the operation was a success. But when my husband and I made love, I had difficulty achieving an orgasm. We waited another month. When I realized time wasn't making things better, and my ability to have an orgasm had changed, I wanted to know why."

To determine what was causing Lisa's problem, she first had to understand what was removed during her hysterectomy. It is surprising how many women do not know exactly what was removed during pelvic surgery and what this might mean to their sexuality. Was it the uterus? The cervix? One or both ovaries?

Women speak of having had a hysterectomy, a total hysterectomy, or a complete hysterectomy. All of these words mean the same thing: removal of the uterus. But some women use the term *complete hysterectomy* thinking that it means the removal of the ovaries as well. *Bilateral oophorectomy* is the medical term for removal of the ovaries, which is separate and apart from a hysterectomy, although it may occur during the same surgery. Other terms you may hear are:

- TAH—*total abdominal hysterectomy* means removing the uterus through an opening in the abdomen. Be aware that the uterus includes the cervix.
- BSO—*bilateral salpingo-oophorectomy* means removing the tubes and ovaries.
- VH—*vaginal hysterectomy* usually means the uterus with the cervix is removed via the vagina, but the ovaries are left behind.
- Supracervical hysterectomy—removal of most of the uterus while leaving the cervix behind.

It's imperative that women understand exactly what was removed during pelvic surgery, because the absence of different organs may be the key to understanding and solving sexual problems.

Suppose a woman's uterus is the only organ that is removed. How might this affect her sexuality? There may be no change at all, because the ovaries are still functioning just as they did before surgery. Most of the vagina and the clitoris have likely not been affected by the surgery either. But researchers estimate that up to a third of women who have had hysterectomies notice *some* changes in their sexual function. During sexual arousal, blood rushes to the pelvic area. This makes sense because, when you eat, the body rushes blood to the stomach. When you're thinking and working hard, the body rushes blood to the brain. When you're exercising, the body rushes blood to the muscles. When you're having sex, the body rushes blood to the sex organs. The uterine muscle fills with blood, enlarging and increasing its size. As arousal continues, the uterus actually elevates in the pelvis, which causes the vagina to lengthen and open.

During orgasm, the uterus can contract. In some women, part of the pleasure they feel during orgasm comes from the contractions of the uterus. The contractions also have a job to do—to force the blood out of the genital area and back into the general system. Without the uterus, there are obviously no uterine contractions. Most women won't notice the difference, but others will. Some women also like the feeling of the penis thrusting up to the cervix. (Others may actually find that uncomfortable—it's a matter of personal taste.) In any case, without the cervix, that sensation, too, is missing.

More clitoral stimulation or deep thrusting against the deepest part of the vagina may be all that is needed to substitute for these sensations. Stimulation of what's known as the G spot (*Grafenberg spot*), a sensitive area in the roof of the vagina thought to contain prostatelike tissue, is a good substitute. The location of the G spot varies slightly from one woman to another, but it's generally about one to two inches from the opening of the vagina on the anterior wall or roof (the wall toward the front of your body). If you and your partner want to explore G-spot sensation, use lubrication and experiment with different amounts of pressure and stimulation. Try lying on your back. Your partner can insert his (or, for that matter, her) finger and massage up toward the ceiling. Or if that doesn't work well, try lying on your stomach. Have your partner insert his fingers inside you from behind, about an inch inside, and press gently down toward the bed.

When the ovaries are removed, a different set of issues come into play. Of the many hysterectomies performed annually in the United States, more than half are done on women under forty-five. If the ovaries are also removed, the sudden withdrawal of estrogen from the loss of the ovaries throws these women instantly into menopause, and they can experience "hormonal shock." It can bring on all the symptoms pretty rapidly, including hot flashes and thinning and drying of the vaginal and urethral tissues. This can obviously create a change in sex drive. Also, testosterone levels plummet after the ovaries are removed, which can lessen one's sex drive.

The study of female arousal and the impact of hormones is really in its infancy, but growing research is one reason why routine removal of the ovaries during hysterectomy has become a matter of controversy in this country. In the past, many doctors felt if a woman was older than fifty and she was having her uterus removed she didn't need her ovaries for childbearing anyway, so what was the point in keeping them? When I did my medical training three decades ago, the message I got was that any doctor who did a hysterectomy on a woman who was forty or older and left the ovaries in was doing something tantamount to malpractice. The reason for this mind-set was the horrible outcome of ovarian cancer in women. In those days, by the time ovarian cancer was found, it had often spread, becoming a deadly disease. Today we have devices such as ultrasound and blood tests that can find ovarian cancer in its very early stages, when it is more likely to be curable. This gives women a choice when they are considering pelvic surgery. Also, we know that post-menopausal ovaries still produce testosterone, and we are learning more every day about how this hormone affects the feeling of well-being, energy level, libido, and sexual function. This is why more and more women who have real indications for hysterectomy, such as big fibroids or severe pelvic relaxation or even early uterine cancer, are interested in the option of keeping their ovaries.

To safeguard your sex life when you're considering having a hysterectomy, you need to ask your doctor these important questions:

"Do I really need a hysterectomy? Can these problems be solved with birth-control pills or other medical and less invasive therapies?"

For example, Lupron is a shot you can get every few months to treat fibroids, heavy bleeding, or pelvic pain. A myomectomy is a surgical procedure where only the fibroids are removed, leaving the uterus in place. Hysteroscopy is another procedure where fibroids are removed from the lining of the uterus through a telescope without removing the uterus itself. The key here is that surgery should always be the last resort—after medical therapy has been tried and failed. There are certainly instances when hysterectomy may be absolutely indicated when there is cancer of the uterus, cervix, fallopian tubes, or ovaries or severe bleeding or pain.

"Can I keep my ovaries?"

If it's not cancer or perhaps endometriosis, why not? If you are willing to monitor them with regular follow-up visits to your gynecologist, you may find that it's worth the extra effort. Be aware that leaving in the ovaries after hysterectomy does not guarantee continuing normal function. Just removing the uterus still decreases the blood supply to the ovaries by about 30 percent. Once again, as with anything, you must weigh the risks and the benefits with your physician. Don't fail to get a second opinion on this, even if your doctor is the best doctor in the city.

It never hurts to learn more from another source. It may even help reassure you that you *need* the surgery. I believe that this reassurance alone can enhance your postoperative healing and help you recover more quickly.

"Can I keep my cervix?"

The cervix is the lower part of the uterus. It is located at the apex or deepest part of the vagina. It is, in fact, connected to the top of the vagina. There are lots of nerves as well as important blood vessels that travel from the inside of the abdomen to the cervix and to the top of the vagina at the same time. So more researchers are beginning to think that when you remove the cervix you are removing some of that blood and nerve supply to the top of the vagina. Now that we know the vagina rises up into the abdomen during orgasm, it's possible in some women that removing this nerve supply might indeed affect their orgasms.

If it's feasible—if the disorder for which you are having a hysterectomy is the kind of disease that could allow you to keep your cervix—this is a discussion you should have with your gynecologist, because of the concern about possible change in your orgasmic capability after the cervix is removed. More gynecologists are now doing supracervical hysterectomies, where they leave the cervix and remove the rest of the uterus. These hysterectomies weren't done as often in the past because of the risk of cervical cancer. But now that so many women have regular Pap smears and proper follow-up, cancer of the cervix is rare, and keeping the cervix is a safer option.

"What can be done during and after the surgery to avoid hormonal shock?"

When a premenopausal woman's ovaries are removed, estrogen, progesterone, and testosterone are suddenly withdrawn from her system. She can enter into a state of "hormonal shock." This is a sudden and abrupt loss of hormones as opposed to the slow and gradual loss that takes place over a natural menopausal transition. The body has lots of time to adjust to a gradual loss but is often unable to deal with the sudden drop after surgery. A woman's estrogen levels prior to surgery at ten o'clock in the morning might be normal, and at 2:40, after her ovaries are removed, her estrogen levels drop precipitously. Hormonal shock can result in not only terrible hot flashes, lethargy, and depression but also a sudden loss of sex drive.

These drastic changes to the body can have far-reaching effects, but a little planning can soften the blow or allow more gradual changes. If your doctor places an estrogen patch on your body just prior to surgery, the whole roller-coaster ride can be prevented. Testosterone can be added later.

When Undergoing Fertility Treatment Causes Dwindling Desire

By necessity, fertility therapy requires sex on demand, and the doctor's recommendation is to do a lot of it. But, as one woman who had undergone treatment for months put it, "After all that scheduled sex, I felt like saying 'Come here, Donor Boy, and make your deposit already so that I can go to sleep.'" When sex becomes a job, it is often the source of loss of libido, erectile dysfunction, and vaginal dryness.

If your arousal is disappearing as you try to achieve pregnancy, keep two things in mind. First, there is a window of opportunity for having intercourse when you're fertile, and it isn't as narrow as you may think. He does not have to run home from work the moment you realize that the time is here. Nor should you have sex several times a day. You want his sperm count to be high enough. Once or twice in three days is fine.

"The whole thing was a sexual turnoff," one woman recalls. "Even from the beginning it was ridiculous. He had to come in this jar so we could get a sample of his sperm tested. It was six-thirty in the morning; he had to be out of the house in an hour. I was told to get the sample to the lab by eight, and I was trying to help him every way I knew how. Nothing was happening. Of course, I got nervous, he got mad, and I started resenting him, thinking, He doesn't really want a baby. Finally it happened. I got in a cab to rush to the doctor's office, and there was a huge traffic jam. I wanted to shout, 'Step on it, you idiot, I've got my husband's semen here!' It was just like the movie *Forget Paris*. Looking back, it wasn't that kind of split-second emergency, but we got everything wrong because we were just so worried about doing it all perfectly so I could get pregnant."

The truth is, treat any man like the Sperminator, and he can get a good case of what therapists call "demand resistance." That can equal no erection when you need it most. In fact, this woman's husband complained, "She expected me to drop everything and come running home and be turned on. I can't function like that."

What saved the day for this couple? Counseling with a fertility expert, who had been there herself. "My husband hated the first two counselors we saw. I thought, Forget counseling; it just doesn't work. The third one was the charm. Keep searching—it's worth it. She didn't buy my victim act. That made me mad at first, but then I saw how I was always making him feel like he was the problem, and he was starting to think, Maybe with some other woman, it wouldn't be so much of a problem. She made me understand how treating him like a machine was going to hurt more than it helped. She helped him understand how I felt every time I saw a woman with a baby carriage on the street. She reassured us that we were normal. Next she hooked us up with some other couples we could talk to and laugh with about the whole fertility experience. We still get together with those couples—and our kids are in preschool."

When a History of Sexual Abuse Causes Lack of Libido

Researchers say that one-fifth of women have suffered some form of sexual abuse in childhood or from a spouse or partner. Some of these women never regain their natural sex drive without therapy. For others, a sexual experience can cause flashbacks to the earlier abuse, causing their desire for sex to plummet. Is this a medical problem? It can become one. I've seen quite a few patients who developed vaginismus as a result of sexual abuse and were even unable to undergo a pelvic exam. This needs to be treated medically with gradual vaginal dilation, necessitating an immense amount of trust in the physician. However, the most successful therapy used today in treating the fallout from sexual abuse begins with psychotherapy that encourages the patient not to forget or minimize the experience but to explore it fully and intensely so that the feelings can be felt and then released. Medical and sex therapy are usually not effective until after this process has taken place.

His Drooping Libido:
Is There Such a Thing as Manopause?

Roxanne, fifty-six, admits, "I've been using testosterone cream for over a year, with great results. But I'm beginning to think *he's* the one who needs testosterone. For the last six months I'm the one who always initiates, and he's the one with the headache. Do men have *manopause?*"

A debatable subject. There's no question that as a man ages he is going to notice some decreased interest in sex and some difficulty sustaining the kind of erection he had in his youth. In fact, 50 percent of men over the age of fifty have some degree of erectile dysfunction. But male "changes" are not due to an abrupt loss of sex hormones. His testosterone might taper off, but he doesn't lose it or, in most cases, need to replace it, except in certain medical instances or testicular failure. He doesn't lose his reproductive capacity. Men have fathered children very late in life.

He may no longer get aroused just from seeing a naked woman or fantasizing. He needs more manual stimulation. Performance anxiety can also be a problem as a man begins to see that there's a difference in how he's able to perform. He may worry each time about whether he's going to be able to get and maintain an erection. Chapter 9 reviews this in more detail.

Just as you may feel some discomfort and worry about the changes in your body, he has his own special set of worries. The things that can cause a woman's libido to disappear can do the same damage to the male's sex drive. These include but are not limited to medications, alcohol or drugs, poor physical health, depression, stress, and fatigue. He is also as prone to questioning and reassessing his life up until now as you are. If this process leaves him with self-doubt, he may well not feel the same sexual self-assurance he has in the past. His children are leaving home, too. He is also likely to be concerned with the finances of retire-ment, his aging parents, his unfinished dreams. He may turn to experi-mentation—physical, intellectual, spiritual, and, of course, sexual—in an effort to reassure himself that he is desirable or to try to regain his old sense of energy and virility.

In many ways, women today are much more assertive about find-ing solutions at this point in their lives. Since Gail Sheehy made menopause an event rather than a shame with her book *The Silent Pas-sage*, increasing numbers of women will go to their doctors, complain about a lack of libido quite frankly, and ask for treatment. When Oprah Winfrey did a show on testosterone cream, the show's 800 number rang off the hook with women calling from all over the world, wondering where they could buy it.

For a man, however, to go to a doctor and admit he's no longer func-tioning as he used to is still a major hang-up. His self-worth is often tied to his sexuality—his sense of being a man and being able to function as a man. The countless sites on the Internet where men can download a prescription for Viagra without ever seeing a doctor face-to-face attest to this. These sites are closed down regularly. Dispensing drugs without ever seeing the patient obviously poses a health hazard. Still, demand encourages supply, and new sites spring up faster than any regulatory commissions can cope with them.

A more common solution for men than searching the Internet for Viagra is denial: "I don't have a problem; I'm still in my prime; my life is boring; this marriage is stifling; these kids are driving me crazy; I need something stimulating—something that will excite me."

A patient recently asked me, "So, does that mean he's going to go out and do something exciting, like buy a motorcycle or take up moun-tain climbing or something?"

I said, "Well, let's cross our fingers and hope so!" What was going through both our minds was the fact that some men take their feelings of vulnerability into the arms of another woman, often a younger woman, to regain a sense of control and masculinity. (More on this in Chapter 8.) Given that reality, many women would prefer to see him zip off to his legal practice on a Harley.

What About the Jaded Man Who's Been There and Done That?

Here's the trickier part of midlife sex. You haven't been with your partner for twenty-five years. It's only been twenty-five days. Perhaps you're like Karen, fifty-three. "He lost his wife to cancer. I lost my husband to mutual boredom. I met him at a restaurant opening I was covering as a journalist, and we talked until two-thirty in the morning. We began seeing each other three times a week. We were both pretty wary at first, but then we realized something was really happening here. Finally we went to bed. It didn't rock the world, but I was certainly into it. And we've been sleeping together twice a week since then.

"The trouble is, he makes these offhand comments about sex sometimes. He doesn't get specific—if he did, I'd be able to talk to him about it. But it's like he had some really incredibly hot thing going with his wife, and now she's gone, and no woman will ever measure up. It's doing a real number on my self-esteem."

Patricia, forty-eight, is dating a man who is a lot more blunt. "He goes on and on about how he did this kinky thing with this one and had an incredible night with that one, and then there were these twins in college he met at a bar and took home. He thinks this is supposed to turn me on or something. I've been pretty blunt about saying, 'Hey, if you think I'm going to do *that* with you, forget it. I'm not in the circus.' I wonder sometimes why he bothers to make love to me at all if all these past thrills were so incredible for him."

Here's something to consider before you conclude that the sex you have together can never be as great as his past:

- **Try not to take it personally.** The sexual conquests of his twenties may really not have been that great, except that they remind him of what it felt like to be young, when everything was ahead of him.

You want to say "Give me a break already with your tales of sleeping with every cheerleader in your class. I don't see Miss Cheerleader of the class of '69 working five days a week to put your daughter through college."

Instead try "I miss those days, too."

He may be telling you these stories because he needs reassurance and doesn't think it's manly to come right out and ask for it. If you can muster it, say something like "I'll bet you were pretty hot. I can almost imagine you then. Show me what it was like."

■ **Don't compete.** No one can compete with a fantasy. If you find yourself with a man who is constantly talking about the sexual things he did with other women in his past, consider this: he didn't end up with any of those women. He's with *you*. Why did he do all those wild sexual things with this woman when he's pretty straightforward in bed with you? Men admit that it can take a tremendous amount of stimulation to "get off" when there's no feeling in the relationship, no emotional connection at all. Perhaps with that other woman, sex was all they had.

Bad Sex in Good Relationships: What to Do If the Sex Died While the Love Lasted

There's an old story that goes like this: Two men are sitting at a bar, having a couple of beers, when the first man gets up to leave. "Stay for a few more," the second man says.

"Can't," the first guy admits. "It's not worth the hassle when I get home late. I mean, I park half a block away so she won't hear the car, I turn the key in the door softly, I take off my shoes and go up the stairs not making a sound, I sneak into the bedroom, but no matter what time it is, my wife jumps out of bed, turns on the light, and starts screaming: 'Out drinking again, you sonofabitch?!'"

"You're doing it all wrong," says the second guy. "Do what I do. I pull into the driveway honking the horn. I slam the front door as hard

as I can. I turn on all the lights and make as much noise as I can coming up the stairs. Then I throw open the bedroom door and yell, 'Hi!
Anyone want sex?' Not a sound out of her."

Funny, because it rings true in so many marriages, but if sex has
become about as exciting as brushing your teeth and a reason to fake
sleep, it's no laughing matter. "I feel like he's a brother to me. A wonderful brother, but I don't feel anything for him sexually," muses Tracy,
forty-four. "I just miss that feeling I used to have when he'd call and say
he was coming over. I'd be practically bumping into the furniture. We'd
make love three or four times in a night. I *do* love him, but it scares me
to think that I'm going to go through the rest of my life and never feel
that kind of passion again."

The trouble is what Tracy was feeling then probably wasn't even
passion. Those types of feelings are generally not passion but a mutual
kind of paranoia. That queasy feeling, the excitement of wondering—
Will he call? Do I turn him on?—often comes from insecurity. Am I
good enough? Does he like me? So much of attraction and excitement
at the beginning of a relationship is based on not knowing each other.
Once you've shared a life together, had babies together, and shared a
bathroom, he walks across the room naked, and you probably feel,
Who cares? That doesn't mean the marriage isn't a solid one or that
there will never be passion.

Still, many people are disappointed when they can't re-create those
early thrilling feelings. We don't really have many examples of how to
keep a twenty-five-plus-year marriage alive sexually. At the turn of the
century, a forty-seven-year-old male was considered old. Now we can live
into our eighties quite easily, and many people are living far beyond that.
We're still marrying at a fairly early age—an average of twenty-five in
America. If you marry at twenty-five and die at seventy-five, that's fifty
years of being with the same sexual partner. People could go from one
partner to another to rekindle that youthful high, but there are more positive ways to deal with this than trading in your partner every ten years
for a new model.

R for Reviving Passion

While serial monogamy is certainly a way to get back that newness, it's not the answer for most people. Couples might not be able to get the fire back, but they can get what I call *sparkles*—little boosts of kindling that are different, fun, and exciting. Jake, fifty-four, married for twenty-two years, realized this recently at a friend's barbecue. "My wife met me there, and she walked into the yard in a black tube dress. I was really frustrated with her at first. Everyone was in swimsuits or khakis, and she hadn't taken the time to go home and change after having lunch with one of her friends. I was embarrassed. Then I realized that my friends weren't staring at her because she was overdressed. The dress hugged her from her thighs to her breasts, and even the two teenage boys were taking looks. I noticed *women* looking at her, like they wanted to know where she got that dress. I suddenly lost interest in discussing the strategy for my Keogh with two of my buddies. I wanted to sit next to her, to be near her. I couldn't stand it when she got into conversations with other men. I was seeing her the way other people see her. It woke me up. I made love to her that night, all night. When we get bored or tired of each other these days, she says, 'Want me to wear that black tube dress?'"

Jake's experience of suddenly seeing his wife through new eyes is not at all unusual. So often one hears, "The best thing that happened to my marriage was when she left me, or we separated, or she got a job." Passion is often fueled by a feeling of separateness, of not really knowing how the other person will react or what would be accepted or rejected or who else was interested in him or her. It's further fueled by the feeling "This person could do fine without me."

In other words, there's mystery. Most of us know that when we somehow throw our partners a little off base, when we make them a bit jealous, when we make them chase us a little, it doesn't matter if we've been married two years or thirty-two years—it works.

The problem is, a sense of mystery can't be set up or faked. As one woman remembers, "I felt like I was losing his interest, so I tried to make him jealous by telling him about this man at work or that man I met at a lecture and how interested they were in me. You know what I got? A yawn. It was really humiliating."

Partners who know each other well sense when they're being manipulated. You can't lie about how stimulating you are to other people if it really isn't true, if there's an edge of accusation to your voice, or if you're merely doing it to get a jealous reaction. Why not really become interesting, instead, to the person who's *most* important—yourself! The real secret to creating a little more mystery in your marriage starts not with your partner but with you. Reviving midlife sexuality is not about one technique or one weekend away or one romantic dinner. It's a process. Here's how to begin.

How to Have Sex That Sparkles

Think About What's Erotic to You

Some of us feel ashamed of what turns us on, because it seems odd or in opposition to our values, our religion, our upbringing, or even our view of how one should *act* in "adulthood." Lara was a case in point. "I never told my husband what I was like in college with my steady, who I more or less lived with for four years. We once made it in his car at 10:00 A.M. in a McDonald's parking lot! When we'd drive somewhere on the highway, I'd do things to him in the car, and when truckers would drive by, and we knew they could see down into the car from their cabs, it excited us even more. We did all sorts of things that were wild. Once we were staying at a hotel in another city, and he told me to answer the door in a robe, with nothing on under it, when the pizza delivery guy rang. He wanted me to sort of let my robe fall open while I was paying the bill. He wanted to watch the guy's face. Stuff like that."

It's hard for Lara to admit that her mild exhibitionism wasn't just kid stuff. Thoughts of having sex out in the open where she might be caught still eroticized her. The idea of doing that kind of thing with her rather staid, conservative husband went against her view of herself as an adult, a wife, a weekend soccer mom.

Sharon, fifty-six, had similar feelings. "I think both of us are bored, even though it's not something we come out and say. But the other day we were in a video store, and we gravitated over to the porno section. I hadn't seen one of those films in years, and he was definitely into the idea, but there were teenagers all over the store—we thought we'd die if one of our son's friends saw what we were renting—so my husband finally just grabbed one, paid, and we were out on the sidewalk laughing hysterically. It was like the first time you go into a drugstore and buy Tampax or condoms or whatever."

It was a promising start to an interesting evening. But it proved to be more enlightening than Sharon had ever imagined. "The film turned out to be strictly anal sex. Over and over again. We kind of looked at each other, and then my husband started to laugh, and he said, 'That's really disgusting! Want to turn it off?' I laughed back and said, 'Yeah, gross.' Part of me was repelled, but part of me was drawn and wanted to see what happened. That part of me was saying 'We've never done that. What would it be like?'"

Sharon never admitted that she found the film erotic, and her husband never spoke about it either, each following the other's lead.

Lara and Sharon have choices other than denying their erotic thoughts or taking them to some other person. They can take some small risks. They can begin to share some of those thoughts with their partners. Lara doesn't need to bulldoze him with a blow-by-blow experience of her college days where truckers honked their horns as she gave her boyfriend oral sex in the car. She might begin by saying "I had a dream the other night, and we were doing this" and gauge his reaction. Sharon doesn't have to say "Let's try anal sex," although that's an option that might yield a grateful and excited husband. She doesn't have to say anything more vulnerable than "I thought about that film the next day. I was sorry we didn't watch a little more of it, just to see. Did you have mixed feelings, too?" Regardless of how their partners react, both women can still use these erotic memories as part of their fantasies.

When you divulge your erotic thoughts to your partner, you'll generally get interest instead of rejection. If you get rejection, that doesn't mean your thoughts are wrong or that you can't use them to stimulate your own eroticism.

To fully explore your eroticism, try not to judge it, analyze it, or feel compelled to play it out right away. Just explore it. See where it leads. Get used to the contradictions, the sudden feelings of embarrassment. Give yourself permission to be honest with yourself. Don't feel ashamed if you have erotic desires your partner can't share. It's what makes you separate, an individual, and sometimes can even present a challenge to your partner. That's important after all the togetherness of raising a family and entwining your lives in so many ways. Chances are the more you are willing to accept yourself, the more you will begin to see midlife sex as an opportunity rather than a liability.

We often can't separate how we feel *sexually* from how we feel about ourselves generally. Ask yourself:

- Do I feel alive and passionate in any area of my life?
- Am I passionate about my work?
- Am I enthusiastic about my children?
- Am I excited by my friends and the things we talk about together?
- Am I continuing to grow and change and have exciting, interesting experiences in my daily life?

Some of us have lost our own internal passion in a massive and repetitive list of things to do. It's going to take a lot more than buying sexy lingerie or making a date for sex with your partner to bring up feelings of passion if a part of you feels almost dead inside.

People don't get bored if they are truly living every moment to the fullest. You can accomplish this. Many men and women look back at midlife as exactly the time they were comfortable enough within themselves to make the effort this requires. Now's the time to reassess. What is missing in your life? What steps do you need to take to get back a sense of "aliveness"? Which people can help you? Which people will hinder you? What more would you like to learn or explore?

Don't Forget That the Most Important Sexual Organ Is the Brain

Good clear communication absolutely enhances sex. When sex therapist Paula Harper, L.C.S.W., treats couples having sexual problems, the first thing she does is get them talking. "I have each person look within and report his or her version of the relationship."

Harper asks the couple to explore and discuss issues such as:

- how I think our relationship is
- how I think our relationship should be

- what I wanted and what I feel I have
- how we fight
- how we communicate
- the life I would love to have
- what's missing and what's really good

"At the same time," Harper explains, "I ask them to back up and basically replicate their dating behavior in terms of touch. Initially there is no sexual touch. I want them to get away from their performance issues and all the pressure of that and back up and learn about pleasure."

You don't need a therapist to explore those questions for yourself, although one might be helpful in guiding your discussion and making sure each of you has an opportunity to speak. You can answer these questions in writing, in a journal. If you each have the willingness to listen to the other's view in a spirit of exploration without blame, your thoughts may lead to greater intimacy.

Try Some Sexual Subtlety

Baby boomers are a very sexual generation. They grew up with "free love," X-rated movies they could rent at home, sex stores, erotic magazines, Victoria's Secret, and four-letter words. In fact, some of us feel that these things have been banged into our heads for so long that what would really spark things up sexually is some *subtlety*.

Richard, forty-nine, admits, "I enjoy my wife's body but what turns me on these days isn't so much watching her walk around naked but when she's dressed! The other day she was wearing a simple white linen blouse with just the top two buttons open, no makeup, and her hair was swept back in a ponytail. She was in the garden, and each time she leaned over I could see a little of the lace from the top of her bra. It started really turning me on."

Renee, forty-eight, says, "I was brushing my hair in the mirror and all of a sudden I noticed him watching me. He said, 'Don't stop. Keep doing that.' At first I thought, What the hell is he talking about? Then I just started brushing slowly, my eyes half closed, just concentrating on the feel of the brush and the softness of my hair. Believe it or not, we ended up having more sensual sex that night than we'd had in years."

Gene, fifty-six, remembers, "We were out to dinner for her birthday, and she was eating lobster. She kept licking her fingers and running her tongue over her lips, and when she saw I was watching, she did it even slower, and it was sexy as hell."

Kiss More

Many married couples hardly kiss at all anymore. Try taking time in kissing, not only the mouth but the ears, the neck, and all over the body. Spend fifteen minutes doing nothing but kissing, with no other sexual touching allowed. Kissing is a very sensual art. Don't forget licking. Try feeding your partner strawberries, or a fruit that is drippy, and licking and kissing it off.

Have Sex Where, When, and How You're Not Supposed To

You don't have to have sex in the kitchen sink or in your car in broad daylight. And sex doesn't have to mean intercourse all the time. This is what got the sparkle back for several couples:

> *"She and I ran upstairs for a quickie when my mother-in-law was in the house watching television. No real foreplay, no tricky positions, but it was incredible."*

> *"We did it at a friend's home during a party, in their bathroom while they were serving dessert."*

> *"We were on the terrace, making love on a lawn chair forty floors up. It was pretty dark, but anyone in the high-rise across the way who had a telescope still could have caught us, even though we were under a blanket."*

> *"She pulls down her top in the elevator and then pretends like she isn't going to pull it back up when the doors start to open."*

> *"I gave him a hand job under a blanket on an airplane—and he was in the middle seat!"*

> *"Never mind an airplane. Making love in the changing room at Bloomingdale's was one of the most exciting things we've done in years."*

"I went out to dinner and wore a short dress with thigh-high stockings and no panties. When I put his hand on my leg and pushed it up, and he suddenly realized what he was feeling, wow!"

"I removed my shoe under the table in a restaurant, and I started using my foot to arouse him."

"I was stroking him, and I let my fingers travel down farther, and I brushed them across his anal area so quickly, barely touching, that I knew he couldn't tell if I'd meant to do it at all. A few moments later I did it again, still pretending like I didn't notice what I'd touched. He didn't say a word either, but he started to moan, and I knew I was driving him crazy."

What to Do When Anger Dampens Sexual Desire

"There is absolutely nothing seductive about having my husband say 'Let's do it,' and considering that enough foreplay. I feel like I'm his tranquilizer, something he 'does' so he can fall asleep. But he rolls his eyes when I tell him that. How can I get him to listen?"

"I've tried foreplay, fiveplay, sixplay—my wife just doesn't like sex, and it's very frustrating."

If you listen closely to the preceding statements, you can almost hear the anger and frustration. Nothing is a bigger sexual turnoff than repressed anger. It can cause erectile dysfunction, failure to lubricate, lack of orgasm—even if you're willing to get into bed in the first place.

"I was so upset about the way he seemed to favor his child with his first wife over ours that I wasn't willing to invest much energy in sex," admits Brooke, forty-five. "I thought, Maybe this relationship isn't going to work out if we can't resolve this. Maybe I'm going to leave him. Why worry about sex?" After counseling, when Brooke and her husband dealt squarely with his guilt over his first divorce and the child he seldom saw and her feelings that he was rejecting his new family, Brooke felt much less ambivalent about investing herself in improving the relationship.

Sometimes sexual problems in couples are really emotional power plays. One woman who complained about a lack of interest in her partner said this about her marriage: "He's too controlling. It's his way or the highway. When I make a decision about even the simplest thing, like where to take our dry cleaning, he has an opinion about it. I've argued with him about it dozens of times, and he says he's just trying to help me." Unconsciously this woman began to withhold sex as an indirect way of saying "You think I'm not enough? Well, I'll show you that *you're* not enough."

What is the antidote to using sex as a battleground? Letting go of secret resentments and letting your partner know what you're feeling are a beginning. But how do you communicate about things like sexual boredom that have become serious issues without causing even more anger? Here are some suggestions.

Be Direct

One man complained, "She started teasing me in front of our friends about how we hadn't made love in a month. Then she said, 'Only kidding,' but by that time I not only didn't want to make love to her; I didn't even want to speak to her."

Little indirect hints like "Amanda told me her husband made love to her for eight hours the other day! Isn't he incredible?" are going to land flat and probably make him defensive. After all, what is he supposed to say? "Gee, I'll ask Amanda's husband how he does it and come back here with my notes"? Not in this lifetime.

Talk About You, Not Your Partner

Instead of "You always make love to me the same way," try "I love when we do it differently." Instead of a blunt "Aren't you bored? Don't you ever fantasize about being with someone else? I do!" try "I think it would be fun if we made this more intense. Want to try something new?" Rather than say "Why don't you ever give me oral sex anymore?" say "I love when you give me oral sex. Let me tell you how good it feels." Use *I* more than *you* and *we*, and you'll gradually break down the barriers.

Remember That There Is a Difference Between Being Honest and Being Blunt

"I've been lying most of my marriage about whether or not I've had an orgasm and about how wonderful he is in bed," says Karen, who just reached her fiftieth birthday. "There's something about turning fifty that made me feel deserving of better sex. But how do you tell someone that for the past ten years most of what you've told him about that has been a lie?"

The question is: What will you gain by telling him? What do you lose? Honesty can be an intimacy builder in relationships. But a shakedown, where you tell him that you've been faking orgasms for twenty years and you think of him as a slug who sits in front of a computer all day long, isn't going to jar him into a fit of passion. You don't always have to be brutally honest to communicate your needs to your partner.

Keep Your Sense of Humor

The new techniques you read about, the positions, the toys—let's face it, you might not always be able to carry them off, and some of them are bound to bomb, even outrageously. Three cases in point:

> "I read this book about how to give a man a hand job, written by a gay man, so I wanted to try it. There was this up-and-over technique—it sounded great, and my husband was game. So I'm trying it, with a lot of Astroglide, and nothing is happening. Being the academic I am, I actually went and got the book. I brought it to bed and turned to the page, and tried to follow the diagram, like it was a recipe book. He started laughing, and then he lost it completely. He finally said, 'Honey, close the book. This is ridiculous. Just do what you always do.'"

> "We went to one of those sex stores. We bought some toys. She left them out on my desk, as a joke, with a funny note. The problem was I was out to dinner with a friend from work, and I brought him back to see the new software program I'd installed on my computer. Here were these things sitting there on my mouse pad. Was I ever the talk of the office the next day. I almost died."

"Making love on the kitchen counter didn't exactly turn out to be incredible. I kept thinking, This is supposed to be exciting, but it feels stupid. And my back hurt for two days."

These are extremes, but the take-home lesson is: keep a sense of humor and a sense of perspective. No one new technique is going to turn it all around immediately. And it can take time to find something new that you both really enjoy.

Let Your Partner in on the Fact That You're into Trying New Things

If you don't, you run the risk of having your partner think, Where is he getting this? Where did he learn that? Is he having an affair?

Accept That Great Sex Often Comes in Waves, Even for the Most Adventurous Couples

There are going to be times of quickies and sex-just-to-have-sex and same old, same old. As one woman put it, "Right now it's more of a priority to me to go watch my son play soccer or to get a decent meal on the table or to help my daughter write her research paper. I have no time for myself, let alone for sex. These are crucial responsibilities to me. I know when my kids are teenagers they probably won't want me near them. Is it wrong to let sex wait?"

Make it wait forever? That may leave you both so estranged that you no longer look to each other for stimulation. You may have to leave sex on the back burner while you deal with other pressing concerns. Most of us do it. Your relationship can survive it if you both communicate it. In that case, let it be quality instead of quantity. Make the sexual experiences you do have together count.

Finally, don't forget the sexual/marital problem equation. Marital problems can cause sexual problems, and sexual problems can cause marital problems. All of these are interrelated and sometimes the solution comes from figuring out which came first.

7

"Sex Is OK as Long as the Lights Are Out and I'm Wearing a T-Shirt!"

 How to Overcome a Negative Body Image When You're Making Love

WHEN YOU LOOK in the mirror, are your first thoughts about what you'd like to change? Are you annoyed with yourself because you easily meet most goals in your life except the ones that have to do with your weight and exercise? If your partner says, "You look as sexy to me as ever," do you think, Hmmm, I wonder what he [or she] really wants this time? If you had to take your clothes off tonight in front of a new sexual partner, would you make sure the lights were off?

If so, you share the feelings of many people today, and it's a blueprint for sexual turnoff. Take Tonya, a thirty-eight-year-old office manager, for example. She never lost the weight she gained when she was pregnant with her second child. Getting to the gym regularly with two preschoolers and a part-time job is next to impossible. "My husband says he'd rather have two great kids than a wife with a flat stomach. But I hate the way my stomach looks. Sometimes when we make love, he pulls me over, on top of him. He thinks this should excite me like it used to, but my stomach just hangs there, and it makes me sick. I look the best these days lying flat on my back. Even then I could take most sex—and leave it!"

Your body image is how you see your body—not necessarily how others see it or how it really looks. Men suffer body image problems, too. "I'm wearing a T-shirt to bed these days," one man told me. "All this travel with no time for the gym put fifteen extra pounds around my waist. I don't need her to see that. Maybe it wouldn't bother her, but it bothers *me*."

My nurses will tell you that the worst moment for many patients is stepping on that "medical scale" and having their official weight recorded on a chart. But a few extra pounds isn't the only contributor to a bout of body image blues. Louise, forty-five, says, "The other day I heard a construction worker whistle and make a crude remark, and I turned around to give him a dirty look. That's when I realized the whistle was meant for the twenty-year-old with the pierced nose walking behind me! My anger turned to disappointment. It's hard to realize that men no longer whistle and stare at me, even though I once found it annoying."

Dave, forty-nine, admits his hair loss has knocked his confidence to the ground. He's experimented with hairpieces and has considered surgical hair replacement. "I look in the mirror and I see an old man and think, Where did *you* come from? I'm glad I'm not on the dating scene. It's hard enough to watch my wife of fifteen years lust after Brad Pitt."

A negative body image can drain the joy out of many aspects of your life, but it can be especially damaging to your sex life. It's difficult to abandon yourself to pleasure when you're obsessed with sagging breasts or sucking in a potbelly.

It's a scientifically proven fact that you don't have to be skinny or have perfect breasts or an unlined face to have a great orgasm. In your heart of hearts, you probably know this. So why are you turning off the lights, hiding under the sheets, and losing the visual stimulation of watching your partner respond to you? Why isn't sex something you look forward to, as you used to?

Body image and the ability to achieve sexual release are often closely related. In this chapter, you'll learn:

- how to assess your current body image and what it may mean sexually
- the latest research about the effect of body image on sexual feelings
- the truth about weight gain as we age—what's due to metabolism, and what's an excuse
- why women's bodies normally change from the pear shape to the apple shape as they age and what metabolism and the hormonal change of menopause have to do with this change
- whether cosmetic surgery will make either of you happier in bed
- what body image therapy can offer you and what any man or woman who is motivated can do to improve sexual self-confidence

Test Your Body Image

Psychology Today conducted a national survey on body image in 1996. Of 4,000 responses, 3,452 came from women and 548 from men. These were some of the interesting results:

- 89 percent of women would like to lose weight
- 56 percent of women said they were dissatisfied with their overall appearance
- 63 percent of men were dissatisfied with their abdomens
- 15 percent of women and 11 percent of men would sacrifice five years of their life to be the weight they want to be

Do you have the body image "elephant" in your bedroom? To find out, answer each of the following questions with the following scores: Give yourself 0 points if you *never* feel this way, 1 for *rarely*, 2 for *sometimes*, 3 for *often*, 4 for *almost always*.

1. When people say I look good, I think they are just being nice.
2. There are several activities I want to try, but I won't do any of them until I lose weight.

3. I don't like to eat in front of other people because I'm heavy and I know they'll be judging every spoonful.

4. I'd feel very embarrassed to have my partner see my penis/vagina during sex with the lights on.

5. I hate anyone to see me the way I look when I first wake up in the morning.

6. I look at people who are young and get depressed.

7. When I go to the doctor and step on the scale, I feel embarrassed that anyone else knows what I "officially" weigh.

8. I don't like to dance; I think my body looks awkward.

9. I hate having my picture taken, because I almost always hate the results.

10. It makes me feel insecure that my partner never compliments my body or makes me feel sexy.

11. I'm worried that my partner is turned off sexually by the way I look.

12. When I look in the mirror, I often concentrate on what I don't like instead of what I do.

13. When I'm on the beach in a bathing suit, I spend more time worrying about how I look than enjoying myself, and I'd never walk around without a cover-up or T-shirt.

14. I feel I have to look fit to go to a health club and exercise with other people.

15. I'd want to cancel a vacation to a tropical island if I didn't diet to my optimal weight in time.

16. If my partner walks in when I'm showering, I feel annoyed and want to quickly grab a towel.

17. I've stopped spending time with friends who look so much better than I do because I get so frustrated.

18. I'm uncomfortable with oral sex unless I've bathed right before it because I worry about odor.

19. There are certain parts of my body that my partner hasn't seen recently or ever—and I don't want him [or her] to see.

20. When we're making love and my partner says "I love your body," I think it's a ploy to get me in the mood.

21. I prefer the lights off during sex.

22. I don't like activities where I sweat, because I'm embarrassed about how I look when I get "messed up."
23. There are certain colors or patterns I won't wear because I think they draw attention to parts of my body I find unappealing.
24. If I ever left my partner, I think I'd have to lose ten or twenty more pounds even to get back into the dating scene, because no one decent would be attracted to me.
25. I pull the sheets or blanket over me when I'm making love.
26. There are sexual positions I just won't do because of the way I think I'll look.
27. I feel upset when my partner makes a positive comment about someone who is younger or better looking than I am.
28. I'm embarrassed about the way I look when I'm having an orgasm.
29. My partner gets annoyed when I ask how I look, and he feels that no matter how big the compliment, it never satisfies me.
30. During sex I find myself distracted with worries about how I look to my partner.

Scoring

0–25: Your answers indicate a positive body image. You feel comfortable with your body. When you look in the mirror, you take any flaws you see in stride. If sex becomes a problem, the last thing you'll blame is your body.

26–50: Your answers indicate a normal or average body image. Chances are you wish you could love your body without reservation, even though you can accept yourself, flaws and all. This chapter can help you feel even better about your body or help you understand your partner's body image issues.

51–75: There are definitely times you feel frustrated with the way you look, and although it doesn't stop you from having sex, chances are you have a small, somewhat distracting "elephant" in the bedroom. This chapter can help you find some medical answers, as well as a new approach to thinking about your body that will ease your mind.

76 or higher: Chances are your feelings about your body are often upsetting to you. This negative image of yourself may stop you from enjoying many of the pleasures of romance and sex. You may be holding back a great deal of yourself, waiting until you change your body to enjoy your life. There's no reason these painful self-doubts need to continue. This chapter will help you find medical answers as well as body image therapy for those "I'm not good enough the way I am" feelings.

The Real Secrets in the Bedroom

You may think at this point, It's no secret to me that I really hate some things about my body. In fact, it's usually no secret to your partner either, especially if you've been a couple for a while:

> *"Of course I know she hates every new line she gets in her face. She's spent a fortune on 'revitalizing' creams at the department store. I love her, but I'd cut my tongue out before I'd ever say 'Honey, you look tired.' That can make her nuts for a week."*

> *"I don't care that he's gained some weight, but he looked at himself on the video we took of our vacation and said, 'That's it. I've got to lose fifteen pounds. I look like a tub of lard.' I thought, Oh, no! Is he going to become a vegan again? Or drive us all nuts by going on some weird diet?"*

Those are really not secrets. If it isn't the growing potbelly or the cellulite on our thighs, what are we really hiding? The real secrets in the bedroom can become such thoughts as the following, and the long list illustrates what a major problem this is:

Hers

> *"Why does he get so angry when I ask, 'Do you still think I'm as sexy as I used to be?' Do I really look that bad? There's this man*

at work who always flirts with me. He doesn't know how tempting it's becoming."

"What if he finds out that sometimes I make myself throw up after a big meal, and that it's happening more and more often?"

"I wonder if he still thinks of me as sexual since I had breast cancer surgery."

"He forbids me to have plastic surgery. Is there a way I can go somewhere, have my eyelids done, and come back without his finding out?"

"We're both on Weight Watchers, and he's absolutely obsessive. What if he finds out I've become a real closet eater?"

"I tell him I love his 'love handles.' The truth is, ugh!"

"We've dated a month, and I know he's going to want to make love the next time we're together. What excuse can I make so he doesn't stay over and see what I really look like naked in daylight?"

"My hair down there is getting gray! It's so embarrassing that I've been pushing him away when he wants to give me oral sex. I wonder if it's dangerous to dye it."

"He's so heavy that when he gets on top of me and makes love, the next day my thighs feel like I've been horseback riding for a week. Talk about grin and bear it!"

"My ex always complained that I wasn't 'tight' enough. Will he notice, too?"

"He thinks I should be turned on in spite of his unibrow and the fact that he comes to bed smelling like a cowboy. Why do men think they can come to bed like such slobs, but their wives will go into raptures over the sight of an erection?"

"Is it my imagination, or since he's gained thirty pounds, is his penis really smaller?"

His

"Why doesn't she understand that it doesn't make a damn bit of difference if she's ten pounds overweight? I love her. Her constant talk about dieting and weight and the clothes she buys to try to look younger is a real turnoff. It's like my crazy, narcissistic mother."

"Ever since she had her breast cancer surgery I'm frightened of touching her breasts."

"These young women at work come and sit in my office and chat, and they want my advice, and they respect me as an older adviser. But I don't think one of them would want to have sex with me. It's a shock to realize younger women suddenly see you as a middle-aged man, not even someone to consider. No one knows how much this bothers me."

"She really has put on a lot of weight. It really is hard to get turned on."

"Of course I look at the bodies of younger women. What man doesn't? But what the hell, I also realize I probably couldn't last half as long as I used to if I was with one of them."

"She doesn't realize that the more she tells me about how fat her thighs are, the more I think, Well, you know what? Never thought about it, but you're right! Now she's got me focusing on them."

"I fantasize about being larger and filling my wife, and it bothers me that it will never happen. When I see her not respond, I think it's because I'm not big enough."

"My wife looks old, to tell the truth. They say men age better than women . . . do I look that old?"

"She says she's on a diet, but that's baloney. She's really let herself go. It's hard to admire someone who can't admire herself enough to at least exercise a little. The only reason I'm staying is I don't know how she'll provide for herself without me. I've even thought about having an affair with someone at work."

"She wants plastic surgery. It scares me. What if she looks worse? Will I still be able to perform when the idea of her having fat suctioned out of her body turns me off so much?"

"She's thin and wouldn't miss an exercise class. But she's obsessed. Sometimes I think I'd be happier with someone fifteen pounds overweight who lets herself relax once in a while."

The Weight Debate

It's no surprise that researchers easily find a statistical correlation between body weight and body image. Grow up with Barbie and Ken and GI Joe as your role models, and even though today's outcry against unrealistic advertising makes sense, it can still be hard to swallow emotionally. These were our childhood images of what we were going to grow up and look like. We never saw Ken lose his hair, GI Joe unable to button his fatigues over his potbelly, or Barbie's breasts sagging after her pregnancy.

This is what medical science knows about weight gain: The majority of adults gain ten pounds every decade. Nearly 55 percent of the U.S. adult population is overweight according to the National Institutes of Health. The $50-billion-a-year diet industry is a dismal failure at getting America to take the weight off and keep it off. In truth, medical science is just beginning to shed some light on the complex problems of weight gain as we age. The diet experts argue over whether one should reduce fat and raise carbohydrates or try to eliminate almost all carbohydrates and eat as much protein as you like, and the jury is still out. In the meantime, more than half of us are overweight. Twenty percent of Americans qualify as "obese," which is defined medically as thirty pounds overweight.

But not all of us feel diminished and angry at ourselves over our body proportions or let it get in the way of our sex life. I have met many patients who are absolutely overweight by anyone's scale. A patient who recently came in for her annual exam comes to mind. She was forty-nine and weighed 265 pounds. She said, "I know you'll think I'm crazy, but the other day I bought one of those pregnancy tests at the drugstore.

It came out negative, but I just want to know, how reliable are they? You told me last time that I'm close to menopause. That's probably *it*. But I met this incredible man. We've been doing it twice a day, and I haven't had a period for three months! He's insatiable and I *love* it."

I assured her the tests were reliable. I offered to do another one if that would ease her mind. Then we talked about her cholesterol levels, which weren't good. When I asked her if she was getting much exercise, she said, "Does having all this sex count?"

Her earthy humor and self-confidence brought a smile to my entire office staff as she told jokes about sex and gossiped about her new man. I was still thinking about her when I met my next patient, Beth, who was about 5′4″ and 135 pounds. When I asked her, along with my general questions about her cycle and her health, "Are you having any problems with intercourse?" her voice was bitter.

"Oh, come on, you're kidding. Look at me," she said. "Who would want to have sex with me? I look terrible. I can't lose weight no matter what I do. I want to leave my husband, but with the way I look, how could I ever take my clothes off in front of another man? I don't want to live alone for the rest of my life."

It's clear to me that body image isn't based solely on body size. I've met patients who are thin, fit, or even skinny. They point to their thighs or their stomach and say, "I don't like *this*, and I've been taking aerobic classes for five years for *that*. My personal trainer has helped me with *this*, but I'm so disgusted with *that*!"

Then there are those patients who are clearly overweight. They are absolutely aware of whatever fat there may be on their hips, thighs, stomach, or upper body. Still, they *feel* sexy. They feel comfortable in and with their bodies.

Unconditional self-acceptance of fat thighs and thinning hair is difficult in a culture that reveres self-improvement. For our honeymoon, my wife and I went to Brazil. On the beach at Ipanema we saw women in little string bikinis and men in tiny swim trunks, and frankly, many had round stomachs and waistlines hanging over. The Brazilians had a different snapshot of beauty. It was obvious in their media, in their magazines, and most of all on their beaches. If you have a body that meets American standards of beauty—flat stomach, skinny thighs, what one of my patients calls the "antiseptic look"—you start to feel emaciated on Ipanema. It was amazing to me how quickly one could adjust a lifelong vision of beauty after a week or two in those surroundings.

While I can't tell patients that it is good for their health to be overweight, I truly admire those who are comfortable with their bodies and so accepting of themselves. I have the same question most baby boomers have: "What do *you* know that the rest of us need to know?"

From the Pear to the Apple, or What Happened to My Waistline?

In the *Psychology Today* survey on body image in 1996 that I mentioned earlier, 71 percent of the women who were dissatisfied with their bodies were specifically dissatisfied with their abdomens. While many women berate themselves for their growing waistlines, the extra pounds around the middle may be the result of their own personal biology, not their habits.

A patient of mine, Kathy, fifty-two, is a case in point. "I've spent my whole life hating my 'thunder thighs,' but the other day I was in a dressing room and I caught sight of myself and thought, You know, they don't look half bad. But whose stomach is this?! I always had a flat stomach. I'm getting a potbelly! I can't find jeans I can button that aren't baggy everywhere else."

It's not her imagination. As women age, and especially after menopause, the distribution of weight changes. Hips and thighs—the cause of the pear shape many women deplore in their youth—tend to narrow as these parts of the body lose some of their fat tissue. But the shoulders, upper back, and stomach become thicker. The change from a pear shape to an apple shape in middle age is a biological fact.

If you haven't been exercising, there's the added chance that your abdominal muscles have also grown weaker. "I can't just suck my stomach in when I walk across a room like I used to," admitted one woman. "I can barely do twenty crunches when I used to do a hundred, because I don't do them anymore. My lower back just can't take it."

What about HRT and weight? Does it make women put on the pounds? Research says no. In fact, postmenopausal women on HRT tend to gain less weight than those who don't take it. However, hormone replacement therapy doesn't seem to help rid women of this new "tire" around the waist. In fact, in some women it can make matters worse by causing fluid retention. A five-pound difference on the scale due solely to water retention is not unusual.

Men have always sported the apple shape, but as a man ages, twenty minutes on the StairMaster no longer keeps it in check. There's growing evidence that the bigger the "apple," the more risk of a heart attack. This is true for both men and women.

What can you do?

1. Believe it or not, the key to reducing bloating and fluid retention is drinking more water, not less. Water is the best diuretic. Aim for at least six glasses a day.

2. Add weight training to your exercise regimen. The key to weight loss for both sexes appears to be building more muscle. The reasoning goes like this: We lose muscle mass as we grow older, beginning as young as age twenty-five. Besides the strength you lose, your metabolism—the rate at which your body burns fat—slows down. It's been estimated that, in midlife, metabolism drops 2 percent a year. That means that if you change nothing about the way you eat or exercise, gaining weight is inevitable, and it will gravitate to your upper body whether you are male or female. If you rely solely on aerobic exercise, you may find that you lose weight but that potbelly is still there. You've merely become a smaller "apple." Only resistance training can change the body's shape.

It's a myth that weight training won't help you burn fat. When you gain muscle, your body requires more energy to maintain that new muscle. However, the mistake many people make is not exercising with enough intensity to actually build muscle. If you can easily do twelve reps without feeling fatigue in the muscle group you're working, you aren't working hard enough to see results in terms of your metabolism. You have to damage your muscle fibers slightly as you work so that they rebuild more strongly and firmly. A good personal trainer or videotapes featuring an expert in weight training can fully explain how this works and how you can use weights safely. Strength training can also have a positive effect on PMS, libido, and depression. It can also increase your good HDL and help you sleep better.

3. What about aerobic training? It's definitely good for your heart as well as burning fat. Do your aerobic training first thing in the morning and on an empty stomach. Bill Phillips, founder and editor in chief of *Muscle Media* magazine, explains why in his book *Body for Life* (Harper-Collins, 1999): "Doing intense aerobic exercise on an empty stomach first thing in the morning is more effective in burning fat than a full hour of aerobic exercise performed later in the day after you've eaten a few meals. You see, after an overnight fast, blood-sugar levels are low, as are carbohydrate reserves. Exercising before you eat causes the body to dip right into stored fat to come up with the energy required to make it through whatever rude awakening you've subjected it to." In fact, you can lose three times as much fat doing this before you eat than if you do it later in the day.

4. If you decide to diet, do it for yourself, not for anyone else. Marcia Germainne Hutchinson, Ed.D., in her book *Love the Body You Have*, writes, "I cannot emphasize enough how important it is to accept yourself as you are, especially if you are overweight. It is hard enough to be overweight in this culture without, in addition, abusing yourself. Accepting overweight is not the same thing as resigning yourself to it. In the process of learning to accept the body you have, you develop a stronger sense of yourself, with a clarity about how you truly want your body to be. Not what your mother wants, or your lover or society. It will be what you want. If you diet to satisfy someone else and if you have the slightest trace of rebelliousness, it will come to the fore complete with anger, resentment, and the desire to sabotage your more carefully laid plans."

Because so many people are all-or-nothing thinkers when it comes to dieting ("I'm either on a diet or I've had a chocolate chip cookie and blew the diet, so why bother?"), the latest technique therapists are using is damage control. Instead of setting a goal such as "I'm going to lose thirty pounds" on a diet that probably won't be sustained for long, the client is asked, "What are you 100 percent willing to do? Give up the bagel and cream cheese in the morning? Substitute a turkey sandwich for your usual lunch twice a week? Walk around the block?" It doesn't matter how small the goal, as long as the person feels 100 percent sure he or she can carry it out. New goals are set when other goals have been achieved, and the most important goal is to avoid if-I-can't-do-it-all-I-won't-do-anything thinking. It's not an idea without merit, when you consider that dropping even 5 to 10 percent of his or her body weight will measurably improve the health of a person who is thirty pounds or more overweight.

The Diet Medications: Can They Help?

New help in the battle of the bulge appears to be coming from a prescription medication called Xenical. It promotes weight loss by blocking the absorption of 30 percent of a person's fat intake. However, it is recommended only for people who have a body mass index (BMI) of 30 or more. For example, a 5'5" woman would have to weigh 180 pounds to have a BMI of 30. A man who is 5'10" would have to weigh at least 210.

While Xenical has been proven to help the overweight lose weight, it doesn't happen overnight. It generally takes over six months to lose fifteen to twenty pounds, and diet and exercise are still necessary. Taking vitamin supplements is also necessary, because your body will not absorb vitamins A, D, E, and K as well, since these vitamins are fat soluble.

Is it safe? It's approved by the FDA, and more than two million people across the world have used it. Xenical does not appear to produce long-term side effects.

As far as over-the-counter remedies for weight loss go, such as fat burners or diet pills, I can't recommend them. The diet pills are high in caffeine, and there is no evidence that fat burners burn fat.

Plastic Surgery: Better Body Image Through Science?

The notion that we just have to accept what we can't change about our bodies as we age is becoming passé as we find that surgical procedures such as liposuction, breast augmentation, face-lifts, laser treatments, penile augmentation, and more can change just about everything. If your body image has been hampering your sex life, chances are plastic surgery may have crossed your mind. While it's beyond the scope of this book to detail those surgeries or to advise you on them, many of my patients and their partners have had plastic surgery. While the outer change is almost always obvious, what about the inner changes? In other words, when it was all over, did it change the way they felt about their bodies? Did it make them happier? Did it do anything positive for their sex life or their relationships? This is what I've been told:

"My husband told me I could have new living room furniture or the breast augmentation I wanted. The choice was easy! After nursing three children, I had nothing left but sagging pouches. I love my new breasts. I feel like I've finally done something just for me. They feel totally natural. I definitely feel sexier."

Janice, forty-four, breast augmentation

"They tell you that you have to be realistic about plastic surgery, but I wonder if anyone really can be. When they take those bandages off, it's hard not to hope for a transformation. My surgeon told me that there was only so much he could lift, but I insisted that I wanted to go ahead, that I was being realistic. Eight weeks after the surgery, I was disappointed. I looked like a more rested version of myself, but for all that discomfort, I don't think it was worth it."

Samantha, fifty-six, brow lift

"I heard jokes about my big nose all through school. But a nose job in those days seemed to be strictly a girl thing. I'd never even met a guy who considered it. But I was a mess of allergies, sinus and breathing problems, and I found out that, given my symptoms, a rhinoplasty to correct a deviated septum would even be covered by my insurance. I did it. All I can say is it totally changed my life. I had been this shy guy, afraid to approach women. Now I had confidence. Although I had to be careful playing sports for many years, and it didn't make me Robert Redford, I'm definitely a better looking guy. It's a positive change that never goes away."

Steven, forty-seven, rhinoplasty (at age twenty-four)

"In June of 1998 I had liposuction in three places on each of my thighs. It took me more than two weeks to recover to the point where I could walk without pain or sit without feeling like I was sitting on knives. I was so black and blue that I looked and felt like I had been hit by a truck. My doctor agreed that I was having a hard time of it but he could only say that everyone reacts differently.

"Anyway, a month down the line, I could sit comfortably again. Two months later, the scars were almost invisible. No more saddle-bags. But I still had cellulite and my thighs didn't look like the ones you see in the swimsuit issue of Sports Illustrated *by a long shot. The change was better when I was dressed than undressed.*

"Six months later, the doctor said I was healed and these were the final results. A year later, I have two extra inches around my waist! It's like the fat had to go somewhere — and don't think I don't watch what I eat and exercise daily, because I do. My husband saw the black and blue and the scars after the surgery and it really turned him off. He won't admit it but our sex life was pretty non-existent for a while. He thought the whole procedure was creepy. I still don't like to walk in front of him naked, and I'm 5'4" and 126 pounds. This may sound strange after everything I've said, but I still would do it again. I didn't get 'best' but I got 'better.'"

Mindy, forty-four, liposuction

"When I came to pick up my sister after her eyelid surgery, I almost burst into tears. 'I already looked. It's not so bad,' she assured me, even though she had been told not to look in the mirror. But I thought she looked terrible. She slept at my house for three days. Four weeks later she looked good. Six weeks later she looked great. I knew then that I was going to have my eyes done, too. The surgeon was so good that no one even suspects what I did. People just say, 'You look great. Have you lost weight? Did you just get back from a vacation?' They try to figure out what my secret is. I feel more attractive, more open to going out and meeting men. It's the best thing I ever did since my divorce!"

Cara, thirty-eight, eyelid surgery

"My wife didn't laugh like I was afraid she would when I told her I was thinking of liposuction to get rid of my 'love handles.' She encouraged me. What did it do for my self-image or confidence? I realize that I have to come to terms with the fact that no matter what I do, I'm not going to have the body I had when I was twenty-one."

Karl, forty-eight, liposuction

"I don't think I'm the first woman to ever get a face-lift and then realize that there were more problems in her marriage than her double chin. I have mixed emotions about what I did. For one, I really like the way I look now. But on the other hand, I realize that my husband is never going to give me the kind of attention or emotion I've always wanted. I guess the best thing is that I used to think it was something wrong with me, and now I realize it's something wrong with us."

Teresa, fifty-six, face-lift and eyelid surgery

"I was very depressed right before my face-lift. I think for many people like me, there's a sadness that it needs to be done. There's a sadness that we live in a society that makes people feel that we need to do this because it worships youth and perfection so much. I think you have to be prepared for those feelings."

Mara, sixty-one, face-lift

"I think having plastic surgery is empowering. I felt more confidence just knowing I could take some control, hold back the hands of time a little. I used to look in the mirror and see my father's face. I had the bags under my eyes removed and now I just see me. I'm a little bolder, less full of regrets, more concerned with making the next years the best years."

Ron, fifty-one, eye surgery

What's the take-home lesson from these people's experiences? Changing the body doesn't necessarily change the body image or make sex better. If you decide to pursue plastic surgery, give a few minutes to considering the following:

Don't be surprised if you feel some disappointment afterward. When we make a big change in life, most of all in our physical bodies, most of us have a few wild hopes. For example, who hasn't thought that losing ten pounds would make them more attractive and happier, rather than just thinner and healthier? Enjoy the fantasy and recognize it for what it is. Learn what you can about what your real hopes and wishes are so you can move forward after your surgery toward other changes you wish to see in your life.

If your surgery is successful but ends up kicking up major issues between you and your partner, don't be surprised. You're in an intimate union, but in *this* you go it alone, as one patient told me. "The nurses at the surgi-center were so nice, so warm. They encouraged my husband to walk me right into the OR. When I came home, though, he looked at all the black and blue and was terrified and almost helpless. In fact, I felt like I had to take care of him when I really needed to be taken care of."

You've had a very significant experience, a change that you notice in more detail than probably anyone else except your surgeon. You've gone through something both highly physical and highly emotional. Your partner can be feeling just about anything, including glad, disgusted, envious, angry, frustrated, insecure, embarrassed, frightened, thrilled, or afraid to touch you. It's an emotional time for both of you. Wait until you are healed and have your energy back before you confront your partner with your disappointment with his or her reactions. Talk to other people who have been through the experience of plastic surgery. As one of my patients told me, "I was so angry that my husband kept harping on the money I had spent. It wasn't like we couldn't afford it. But a close friend who knew someone who had just gone through the same thing took me out to dinner. We talked for hours. She said, 'He's talking money, but he's probably scared. Will he lose you? Have you changed? It took six months before my husband and I could start talking about real issues.'"

Does Size Still Matter?

Penile augmentation, a concept first introduced in Asia and Africa centuries ago, is part of a new wave of surgical procedures directed toward midlife men. Why would a man who has lived forty or more years with what nature provided suddenly opt for such surgery? Body image, self-esteem, and ego enhancement are three reasons. By midlife a man may feel "I've never been happy with my size; it's always embarrassed me. Now I have the money, and medical science has the techniques to do something about it."

In 1990, penile *widening*, known as the *circumferential augmentation penile enhancement procedure* (CAPE), was widely reported by the media. Fat tissue, obtained from elsewhere in the body by liposuction, was used to augment penile width. While the procedure made a few entrepreneurial surgeons millionaires, it also caused disastrous complications for thousands of men who had their penises "enhanced."

The widening procedure most likely to be used today is dermal fat graft technique (DFG). During surgery, the first three layers of skin, epidermis, dermis, and fat, are taken from two sites on the patient. The harvested pieces are the same length as the patient's penis in its erect state and grafted on. The graft scars are hidden in natural body lines, and the gain in width is usually ¾ to 2 inches.

While DFGs can successfully widen the penis, enhancement phalloplasty surgery can also be performed to lengthen it. The way it works is this: Approximately one-third to one-half of the penis is inside the body. It's attached to the undersurface of the pubic bone. The surgeon cuts these attachments so more of the penis appears outside of the body. Afterward, the patient is instructed to use penile weights or a stretching or vacuum device to prevent shortening due to scarring. The net gain is usually 1 to 2½ inches.

The best instant lengthener for the average midlife male is actually losing weight. For every thirty-five pounds a man loses, he may gain as much as one inch. Thinning of the pubic fat pad will make the penis longer. Men should be warned of one important fact: none of these techniques will automatically make you a better lover.

Breast Cancer and Body Image

Men and women often react to a diagnosis of cancer with depression and loss of libido. But women really have a unique situation with breast cancer. It's cancer of a sexual organ that can't really be compared to cancer of the prostate gland, which is not thought of as a sexual organ, or testicular cancer, which is hidden in the scrotal sac.

With all the advances in diagnosis and treatment, the good news is that breast cancer is becoming a chronic disease because women are living so much longer after diagnosis. However, that also means more worry. Has it spread? Will it come back? Why was I susceptible in the first place? Those worries can definitely affect one's libido just because they are so draining. There may be less sensation in the breast area, regardless of whether you've had a lumpectomy, mastectomy, or postoperative implant. Chemotherapy and medication can also take their toll. Chemotherapy can bring on premature menopause and a host of annoyances, such as vaginal dryness, with it. Yet women who have had breast cancer are reluctant to put estrogen in their systems and therefore often live with the postmenopausal symptoms for years.

Depending on the type of surgery she has had, breast cancer can definitely affect her body image. It's not necessarily appearance—reconstructive surgery can do marvelous things—but the way one feels about it. Obviously what the mirror shows and what we see in our minds can be two very different things.

A woman may react with depression and avoidance of sex. Her partner, unfortunately, may be only too happy to avoid sex, because he's afraid. He may wonder, Will I hurt her breast if I touch it? Am I going to catch something from her?" The answer to both questions is no, but unless the man asks the questions of an understanding doctor who can explain all of this to him, he may never know.

In my opinion, we need to train more professionals to talk to women and their partners about breast cancer and sexuality. Support from someone who is experienced not only with breast cancer but with the issues it causes in the families of its victims can make all the difference.

Help from the Body Image Therapists

Many of us are tired of walking around saying "I hate the way I look. If I could just find the right clothes, the right hairstyle, the right aerobics instructor, the right *whatever*, I'd look different and then I'd like myself."

Can you change your body image without changing your body? Psychology professor Thomas Cash of Old Dominion University is one of the highly respected specialists in the area of body image therapy. He believes the answer is a resounding yes. "One of the assumptions that many people have is 'The only way I could ever like my body is to change my body.' But what we've found in clinical trials is that with body image therapy, people can really make substantial gains in how they feel about their looks."

Dr. Cash's eight-step program is outlined in his book *The Body Image Workbook* (New Harbinger, 1997). Part of the program involves challenging ten "appearance assumptions" that may underlie a person's discontent with his or her body. These include assumptions such as "Physically attractive people have it all"; "If I could look just as I wish, my life would be much happier"; and "The first thing that people will notice about me is what's wrong with my appearance." He points out that physically attractive people often don't have it all. "Beauty often breeds envy and jealousy. It's a weak foundation for self-esteem. The more people put all their eggs in the 'beauty basket,' the more vulnerable is their self-worth."

Dr. Cash's research has demonstrated in women that body image is often related to sexual dissatisfaction. A recent study he conducted along with Dr. Jill Hangen compared fifty women who were highly self-conscious about their body's appearance during sex and fifty women who weren't. Body-conscious women reported that they had orgasms on an average of only 42 percent of their lovemaking occasions—versus an average of 73 percent of the time for less physically self-conscious women.

Body image therapists routinely hear three specific complaints about what happens when that negative image sneaks into the bedroom:

"During sex, I'm so distracted thinking about how I look to my lover that it interferes with my enjoyment."

"I don't want to have sex at all because of the way I look."

"It's hard to feel sexy and desirable because my partner never compliments me [or because he insults me]."

For these feelings, body image therapists have solid advice.

What You Can Do If You're Distracted Thinking About How You Look When You're Making Love

"We're in the middle of it, and he says, 'That's too hot.' He's not talk-ing about me. He's talking about the blanket I keep pulling over us."

Famed sex researchers Masters and Johnson first referred to wor-rying about how you look in the midst of sex as "spectatoring." Body ther-apists refer to killing the lights, pulling up the blankets, and shielding your stomach from view as "hiding." It means that you watch yourself while making love instead of availing yourself of the pleasure. The trou-ble is, while trying to distract your partner by sucking in your gut, you can become too distracted to experience the pleasure of true intimacy. At the very least, you give up the pleasure of watching your partner's response since hiding you means you're hiding both of you.

Sex therapist Paula J. Harper, L.C.S.W., doesn't feel such behavior means there's something really wrong with you. "Realize that to some extent everybody does that. Every client I've had does that. Your partner is probably worried about his or her own body. You can bet that there are things your partner would prefer you not notice."

Hiding at its very essence may be a way you try to please your part-ner: *I know she'd be totally grossed out if she saw how flabby I'm getting. I'll turn out the lights.* It's a strategy doomed to backfire. What excites sexual partners most is watching their partner's excitement. How excited can you be when you're worried about covering your stretch marks?

How can you stop spectatoring so that you can give and receive more sexual intimacy?

■ **Recognize that if you've been with a partner for a while, chances are he or she has seen whatever it is you're hiding anyway—and doesn't care.** If your partner hasn't remarked on it, don't think it's because he or she hasn't seen it. Your partner probably knows it's a hot button for you. He knows she's sensitive about the size of her rear, for example, so he just kind of avoids mentioning it. He plays the game with her because he loves her and doesn't want her to be uncomfortable. She notices his "love handles." She encourages him to pass on dessert every time they go out to eat, although she'll say "I'm tired, let's go," rather than "Keep eating that chocolate mousse, buddy, and you're not going to be able to get your body through the front door." Most people in long-term relationships can immediately list five things that their partner dislikes about his or her own body. Try it. If you know his, he knows yours. You can count on that.

■ **Exchange *idealistic* for *realistic*.** Much of our angst about our bodies comes from idealistic media-driven conceptions of how we "should" look, not how most of us really *do* look. For example, it's estimated that only 2 percent of women can ever attain the degree of thinness of the models pictured in women's magazines, not because of their appetites but because of their *genes*. Yet many women become miserable trying.

Here's an exercise: Find an old family photo album. Wedding albums are best because so many family members are together and looking their best. Look at your ancestors. Notice the body shapes that tend to repeat from one generation to the next. Should you really blame yourself for that little paunch when every person in previous generations had the same thing?

I had one patient, Kathy, forty-five, who had struggled with her weight most of her life and, as a result, had a very negative body image. She told me she was adopted at birth, and a year later her adoptive parents had another child. "I was the fat one in the family. I ate the same meals my sister ate, but I was the one who gained. I knew about diets before dieting was in fashion. I did it all, from juice fasts to eating chocolate three times a day to see if I could desensitize myself to it! I even took up biking, miles a day, but the only place I really looked thinner was my chest. I was a size-six top on a size-twelve bottom. If I went ten miles, I thought I should go twenty."

Kathy met a man and married, and he encouraged her to feel sexy and desirable in spite of her bulky thighs. "But he couldn't look me in the eye and tell me I had great legs, either. I mean, what is *is*."

The story might have continued her entire life except that in her thirties, natural curiosity and a desire to know her medical history drove her to begin a search for her birth mother. Within a year, she had found her. She also found four sisters. "Every one of them has the same body shape I do. I'm the thinnest one of all!"

It wasn't a lack of willpower or a penchant for chocolate but genetics that had given Kathy a tendency to carry her weight in her lower body. Today she has stopped punishing herself for her body's flaws and is concentrating on looking the best she can within realistic limits.

- **Set your own standards.** There are so many perfectionistic societal standards that women are subjected to when it comes to their bodies that it's no wonder so many suffer from poor body images. These standards are illustrated on the cover of every major women's magazine. For example, women are supposed to go through pregnancy and the trauma of delivery and have a flat stomach six weeks later. They are supposed to prepare dinners, snacks, and lavish desserts for their families but never to overindulge or let their waistlines grow. They are supposed to find hours in the midst of all their obligations to exercise so they don't get flabby and appear less sexy. What's implied is that if a woman doesn't do this, she'll lose her lover. Yet I can guarantee that there aren't crowds of young, thin, perfect women waiting in line for your husband.

Men feel the pressure, too. He's supposed to retain his flat stomach and muscular chest and arms. He should have a full head of hair into his seventies, graying slightly at the temples. He should be at least six feet tall, broad shouldered, and well-endowed sexually. One man told me, "I used to find porno movies exciting, but the other night when the woman I've been seeing suggested we watch one for fun, I thought it was depressing. It was frustrating to watch those young guys and the way they are hung, banging away for a half hour straight even though I knew it wasn't reality. I've been told I'm a good lover, but I've never had a woman scream the way they do in those movies. The whole thing was depressing. I kept thinking, I hope this isn't what she expects from me, because those days are gone."

If you can identify with this, keep in mind that what's really sexy is an adventurous, willing lover who is not afraid to let his or her partner know he or she is turned on. Dr. Cash says, "Societal standards can't harm you unless you buy into them. You don't have to allow your sense of self-worth to be determined by voices not of your own choosing. If you hold ideals that are more moderate and realistic, and stop beating yourself over the head with unreasonable yardsticks, your more favorable body image will promote acceptance."

▪ **Give what you like about your body equal time.** Do you have beautiful hair? A great smile? Wonderful eyes? When you look in the mirror, give those parts of yourself equal time. Combat the nasty self-talk that goes, "You look fat; you look old; you look awful" with "I might have a few lines around my eyes, but I love the color of my hair" or "I've got some extra pounds around my waist, but I look great in this suit." If you can't find anything nice to say, consider that it may not be your body's fault. Some of us have grown up surrounded by so much negativity in our families that we think that giving ourselves a compliment is conceited or just plain wrong. If you have trouble giving yourself a compliment about your body, begin with other positive statements and work from there.

▪ **Shift your focus to your own pleasure during sex instead of your partner's.** Try a few sessions of extended touching and kissing where you just focus on what you're feeling without moving on to intercourse. This is the number-one treatment recommended by sex therapists for people who are having arousal difficulties. Once people abandon themselves to sexual pleasure, they generally stop thinking about lumps and bumps.

▪ **Realize that having thinner thighs or a flat stomach wouldn't necessarily make sex better.** "What makes sex better," explains sex therapist Paula Harper, "is having a really wonderful, emotional connection and being able to communicate about your needs. If partners feel so comfortable emotionally that they can redirect each other in order to get their needs met, that's what makes sex great. Remember, the point of sex is pleasure."

What to Do If You're Avoiding Sex Completely Because of the Way You Look

Picture this: You're enjoying a wonderful meal with your partner and celebrating the day you met. You relish every mouthful, including the dessert the two of you share. You have to loosen your belt and unbutton the top of your pants, and you both laugh when you do it. You go dancing, get turned on holding your partner close, and end the evening with a romantic bubble bath and sex.

Now picture this: Same occasion, same meal. Only as you eat the wonderful meal, you feel ashamed because you're so far off your diet you might as well quit. The waistline of your pants cuts into you so badly you have to unbutton them, and you do it so your partner won't notice. When you dance with your partner, all you notice is the other people on the dance floor who look thinner or better than you imagine you do. When your partner suggests a romantic bubble bath, you say, "After that meal, all I can think of is sleep." But you don't sleep. You spend the next two hours thinking how disgusted you are with yourself. You know your partner went to bed angry, but you can handle the anger more than you can the exposure of making love. You'll make it up to your partner later, when you lose ten pounds.

Dr. Cash refers to situations like this as "beauty bondage"—feeling you can't do something because of your looks. His advice? "Talk back to 'I can't do it' by asking 'How *can* I do it? What would make it easier to do?' Face the fact that other people who are far from perfect physical specimens engage in the same activities that you deny yourself."

Your partner might be more accepting of your body than you could ever imagine. One of the statements I hear most often from men is "Why can't she understand that it doesn't really matter that she's gained ten pounds? I love her anyway."

Kara, thirty-nine, made up a variety of work-related excuses for why she couldn't stay overnight at her lover's house. The truth? She couldn't cope with the thought of his seeing what she looked like in the morning. The unconscious fantasy in these situations is often "If he never knows what I look like at my worst, I'll be able to keep him around forever." The pressure comes from convincing yourself that you know exactly what the other person will think when you really have no evidence on which to base it.

One night Kara accidentally fell asleep at her boyfriend's apartment. She awoke the next morning to find him smiling down at her. She squirmed away and pulled the blankets up over her head, embarrassed. He said, "Hey, come on, you look adorable."

Breaking through beauty bondage is a one-step-at-a-time process. If having the lights on embarrasses you, what about lighting a candle? If you become self-conscious when your partner begins taking off your clothes, what can you do to distract yourself from your negative thoughts? If you can't make love at all, what, beyond changing your body, would be a first step in feeling more desirable?

Body image therapists can teach you the techniques of mirror desensitization, where you can learn slowly and patiently to look at your body in the mirror without feeling distress. That's often the first major step for those who avoid sex completely over fears of how they look. How do you find a good therapist? Unfortunately, there isn't a registry of body image therapists. Because your goal is to change your thinking rather than your body, cognitive behavior therapists are a good resource. Those who specialize in eating disorders may be especially helpful because they treat body image issues on a daily basis. The Association for Advancement of Behavior Therapy maintains a referral service that can help you find a therapist in your area (see the Appendix).

What to Do About Critical Partners Who Make You Feel You're Undesirable No Matter What You Do

Theodora, forty-four, got so tired of the energy she expended trying to smooth away the lines around her eyes that she had laser surgery. The lines are gone, but now she sees that her eyelids are sagging. "I want to go back and have my eyelids done. Then the other night my husband said, 'I think you wasted your money with the first surgery.' You can't imagine how bad I felt."

Did she assume what he meant was that, in spite of her surgery, she still wasn't appealing? Here's the truth: "I never understood what she was talking about. I thought she looked great the way she was, and I just don't see a big difference."

Dr. Cash says, "If a person has a negative body image, they are often sure that their partners evaluate them just as negatively. But, in fact, when you look at the partner's actual evaluation, as we have during research, the partner is usually a lot more positive. Generally a partner's attitudes are much more favorable than individuals believe that they are."

What if you know for a fact that your partner's opinion of your body isn't favorable? In fact, what if annoying, teasing comments are hurting your feelings? Dr. Cash advises, "Say 'It is very difficult for me to accept my own body myself. When you make these comments, even though you say you're teasing, it hurts. It makes me not want to have sex with you. It doesn't matter if you're kidding or not. Do you want me to lose a little weight? So do I. But you need to learn to accept that my waist might be one inch larger than we'd both prefer, just as I need to learn to accept it. So I'm asking you, if you care about me, kidding or not kidding, please don't make any of these remarks anymore.' "

If your partner continues to make insulting remarks after a strong statement like that, you have several decisions to make. Do you wish to stay in a verbally abusive relationship? Is your partner angry at you for other reasons? Can the two of you talk it through? Would counseling help?

What about the partner who doesn't criticize but doesn't compliment you very often either? Take a look at what you do when you do get a compliment. Some people automatically put themselves down: "You like this dress? I think it makes my hips look enormous." Or they criticize their partner: "That's the first compliment you've given me in ten years!" Or they refuse to just accept the compliment and move on: "Do you really like this suit? Do you think it fits in the shoulders? What about this tie? Do you think the blue one would be better?"

If you want compliments, learn how to receive them. Let the other person know you appreciate the compliment. Try saying "Every once in a while you tell me I'm sexy. I love it when you say that. It makes me feel so good. Let's both try to do that more for each other and take time to notice the good stuff."

If, however, you're in a relationship where you're feeling less and less desirable, or less motivated to make yourself appealing, it may be time to look even deeper.

Help from the Intimacy Experts

Therapists Mitch Meyerson and Laurie Ashner (who also happens to be coauthor of this book), in their book *When Parents Love Too Much* (Hazelden), wrote: "Some of us find ourselves in an intimate relationship that allows us to be comforted without being vulnerable, to take without giving, and to feel intimate without the risk of being abandoned. This relationship is with *food*."

They point out that a constant focus on food, dieting, weight, and body image can be used to avoid feelings or conflicts in a relationship. A roller coaster of overeating, feeling anxious, moody, and deprived, and "blowing the diet" can unconsciously be a way to fend off intimacy. They write, "When we're constantly absorbed with food, our weight, our diets, our sudden loss of control, we don't ask, Am I happy with my life? Is this what I really want? Am I still in love with my husband? Does he love me? Is what I feel still important to him? If I share what I'm feeling, will he listen? We prefer not to think about these things, because thinking about them would bring feelings we don't want to have. Instead we eat."

Jamie, forty-one, for example, became completely absorbed with food and dieting when the emptiness of her marriage became intolerable. Her husband, Bill, took a new position at this company where travel was required. Although they had both agreed that it was a great career move, Jamie was unprepared for how often Bill would be away. "I'd be hurt when he'd call and say 'Listen, I'm going to stay overnight because I'm exhausted and fly home tomorrow.' Sometimes I took it out on him in bed. I'd clench my fists and say 'I am not going to respond no matter what he does.' He didn't even notice. Or I'd meet him at the door in a new outfit and hug him and press myself against him. He'd get aggravated. 'Don't you know I just got off a nine-hour flight?'"

While Jamie had struggled with her weight before her marriage, now she really began to gain. One night she found herself in the kitchen eating an entire cheesecake. "My stomach was full, but I felt like I could never get enough." She started to binge compulsively every time she felt hurt or taken for granted. "I'd start a diet every Monday and give it up by Wednesday. He was physically disgusted by me. I was afraid to complain about his traveling because I was scared that it would be the last straw for him. It took counseling to learn to deal with my feelings directly. Until then I stuffed them and just numbed out."

Obsessions with food, dieting, and our weight are sometimes convenient ways to keep our minds engaged and unavailable for dealing with feelings. They can also be a way to accomplish the following:

- avoid conflict
- relieve anxiety
- nurture ourselves
- punish ourselves in response to guilt
- quiet restless dissatisfaction
- avoid maturity

What Jamie found was that dealing with intimate feelings can be painful. But it's a lot more valuable (and interesting!) than an obsession with weight, dieting, and your body. If you feel you might be using food, dieting, or an obsession with your body image to escape other problems, here are some suggestions to help you.

Ask yourself what you're using food to avoid. One man told me that he always ate too much when he and his wife went out to dinner on Saturday nights. It used to be their night to make love, but he felt so stuffed he couldn't do it. "Now I realize I did it on purpose. I didn't want to have sex with my wife, and it was the only excuse I knew would get me off the hook." Once you know what you're avoiding, you can decide to deal with it directly. For this man, the next step was to figure out what he was going to do with a relationship where he no longer wanted to be intimate.

Some of us will express all sorts of angry feelings about what we ate, how we blew our diets, how other people eat like horses and never gain weight. But we won't express angry feelings about two-minute foreplay, a spouse who acts like sex is servitude, or a relationship so devoid of intimacy that food is the only excitement in our lives. Some of us can't get enough food because what we're really hungry for is love, appreciation, or acknowledgment. As one woman put it, "Ice cream is an inner hug."

If you're having difficulty expressing your feelings or working on the real issues in your relationship, assertiveness training courses and seminars where communication skills are taught can be enormously helpful. If you're not sure what your feelings really are, therapy can help you clarify them.

Body image is probably one of the largest sources of secrets in the bedroom. Although body image is an individual thing, it takes two partners to get beyond the sexual issues it causes. One look or one little statement from a lover can really set you off if you have body image problems and knock your sexuality right to the ground.

Everything that has been discussed in this chapter underlines the fact that the main sexual organ is the brain. What you think about how you appear to your partner ultimately has a major effect on your sexuality. The real solution to ridding the bedroom of the body image secret isn't complaining about your body to your partner. It's learning to accept yourself and support each other.

8

THE SECRET

"He Seems More Interested in Having Hot Chat on the Internet than Being with Me, His Willing Wife."

 Understanding Sexual, Intellectual, Emotional, and Cyber Affairs—Why They Happen and What to Do If It Happens to You

"I can't believe I let myself get into this. I've always thought that women who do this are evil and destructive. I know it's the wrong thing to do, but damn it, I'm fifty-two, and I've finally found the man I've been looking for. The problem is, he's married."

"I'm forty-six, and she's twenty-eight, but we have so much in common. I know this affair is wrong, but I've been bored at home for ten years."

"He was an ex-boyfriend. I was just curious to see what it would be like to be with him again. It was strictly a physical thing. I felt guilty for months."

"It's just incredible. We bounce ideas off each other, and it's the biggest turn-on. It's like we're making love without touching each

other. It's a whole different level of intimacy that I've never experi-enced before, and we've never even held hands."

"I'm thinking of meeting him, and I can't believe I'd even consider it. We met on-line. We've been chatting for six months. He's on his way back from Europe, and we're going to have dinner during his stopover. My best friend tells me I'm crazy."

Whether an affair just happens or it's planned and actively sought, feeling attractive, desired, less bored, and more excited are well-documented reasons why affairs continue. The baby boom generation—a very sexual generation—has more challenges to monogamy as they enter the third millennium than any prior generation has ever had. Today people find they no longer have to touch someone to feel stimulated, aroused, or even in love. For example, one patient told me about her husband, "He has never met her, he has no idea what she looks like, but he tells me, after eighteen years, that he has found his soul mate on the Internet. I said, 'Did you ever think that this person you're corresponding with could very well be a man?'"

The new millennium brings a host of opportunities for sexual affairs as well as affairs that are strictly emotional or intellectual. What can you do if this is *your* secret in the bedroom? In this chapter you'll learn:

- five frequent reasons men and women have affairs that are unique to midlife
- what emotional, intellectual, or cyber affairs are really like
- the pros and cons of confessing your affair
- how the aftermath of a midlife affair can end up being a positive force—not a divorce or the end of a relationship, but a resetting of one's sights that will carry the relationship onward in a way that is stronger and more emotionally honest

Is Monogamy Impossible?

There are social scientists who argue that now that our life expectancy has reached the eighties, monogamy with one lifelong partner is unrealistic. Thirty or more years with one sexual partner can seem to some like a jail sentence rather than an intimate union.

Others suggest that there may be a biological imperative for people to wander—at least for the male of many species. That argument grows out of the fact that it was the male's evolutionary obligation to spread his seed into as many different females as possible, thereby guaranteeing that his genes would populate the next generation. The most "successful" males were the ones who produced the most offspring. Around the time of ovulation, when she was most fertile, a female would demonstrate to the males in the vicinity that the time was right with some obvious behavioral or physical signal. A male, usually the strongest or most dominant one, would oblige by depositing his sperm; then he would wander off to find another receptive female. Meanwhile, after the event, the original female lost her receptivity to other males.

As we evolved from primate species, we wound up having fewer babies and a much longer gestation. When you had fifteen babies at a time, individual survival didn't mean as much. With only one baby at a time, a long gestation, and years until the baby could be independent, child survival necessitated more than just the mother. If there was some way to keep the father around, it would help guarantee the presence of food and protection. Nature found a way. Hidden ovulation evolved. Without any obvious signal from the female, the male wouldn't know when she was ovulating and couldn't be sure that his sperm was going to impregnate her. Some other male could come along and have sex with the same female, and the first male might end up raising the other male's offspring, a waste of energy and effort since it was not his own genetic material he was raising. Hidden ovulation meant that he had to hang around so he wasn't cuckolded into bringing up someone else's genes. Since he had to hang around to be sure, a pair bond was formed. The presence of both a mother and a father became vital to a child's survival to adulthood. Suddenly we had monogamy.

Now, if you will allow a huge jump, it's possible, some anthropologists say, that part of the reason men have affairs is this biological imperative buried deep in their genes. The interesting thing, however, is that no pair of social scientists who have studied infidelity can come up with the same percentage of men and women who actually engage in it. Studies have reported that anywhere from 20 percent to 60 percent of married people have affairs. What, beyond evolutionary biology, could drive close to half of married people into someone else's arms?

The Secrets in the Bedroom

Almost every affair begins with a need. It's usually a need that isn't being met or can't be met in the marriage:

> *"I want someone who excites me, but I don't want to leave my kids or break up the family, because otherwise we're really very happy."*

> *"I didn't marry the person I had the best sex with, and I can't stop missing it."*

> *"I wonder if I can still attract younger women [men]."*

> *"The sex is as good as it always was, but I just don't want to go to my grave with the thought that this was the only person I ever slept with."*

> *"I don't want to live alone; before I can leave him [or her] I need to know someone else is there for me."*

> *"I want to be with someone who will spoil me, buy me things, take me to expensive places, and never worry about the bill. My whole marriage has been the two of us battling for economic survival, and I am so tired of working so hard and never getting anywhere."*

One unfortunate fact about affairs is that even when they are discovered, many partners never share what the need was or tell the *real* secret in the bedroom. From these we hear of the need for sex, a need to feel young, the need to experience more than one person, the need for excitement, the fear of loneliness, the need for sexual variety, and the need to feel spoiled. But there are deeper secrets.

Deeper Secrets Behind Sexual Affairs

Some of the biggest secrets in the bedroom are the ones we keep from ourselves. Here are some of the often unconscious reasons men and women become involved in a sexual affair.

To Help You Stay in Your Marriage or to Try to Save Your Marriage

Perhaps the most confounding fact research has come up with about midlife affairs is that people often use them not to seek a way *out* of their marriages but to find a way to stay *in*. As one man put it, "We share so much history. We brought up kids together. We know the best and worst about each other. But it's almost like we know each other too well. This other woman gives me excitement, newness, the unexpected. I'm much more content with both of them. I don't think either one alone would be as good."

There is clinical research showing that both men and women who have affairs as a way to ease themselves out of a committed relationship leave their marriages within the first six months of the affair. If you believe that your lover will eventually leave his or her marriage to be with you after the two of you have been involved for over a year, think again. If the statistics hold true, you've lost that possibility. Ongoing affairs appear to be about supplementing the marriage. I recall one year when I had a patient come in to see me. While we were speaking, I could tell that something was bothering her. I asked her, "Is there something else you want to talk about?" But she declined. At the end of the exam, I assured her that everything was normal and once again said, "Are you sure there's nothing else you want to talk about?" She said, "No, no, there isn't." As I was about to leave the room, she stopped me and said, "I'm having an affair." She spoke about how it had happened, and I just listened to her because she needed to tell someone. "I love my husband. I love the life we have together, and I'd never want to change that part of it. Since I started having an affair, our relationship is better. We still have occasional sex, but it's a caring type of lovemaking, not really passionate. I need more. My affair gives me that passion and just makes everything more complete. I have absolutely everything I've ever wanted. I've never been more content in my life."

Then there's the Madonna-whore syndrome, first described by Freud, in which a man feels that after marriage or childbirth it's inappropriate to have sex with his wife. She has become the Madonna in his mind and seems too pure for sexual activity. The only way he can feel turned on is with someone else.

A sexual affair may have obvious consequences. Aside from being intimate with another person, there is the challenge of trying to balance the two relationships if you're intent on keeping both of them going. One of the problems with that balance is, first of all, the lying and the deceit. The other is the ability to perform with your spouse.

Gary, forty-eight, recalls, "I had just come home from an afternoon with my lover. When I got there, my wife was at the door, with a glass of wine in hand, a fire going in the fireplace, and thoughts of making love that evening. I couldn't perform, even if I had wanted to. So I tried to make excuses. She was hurt, and I knew it, but there was no way I could do anything at all."

Gwen, forty-six, admits, "It became more and more difficult to make love to my husband. When we did, it didn't compare at all to the passion I had with my lover. Maybe my husband and I could have worked to repair our sexual relationship that had become so unsatisfying, but I couldn't respond after making love constantly with my lover."

Wendy, forty-seven, related, "I only saw my lover every two weeks or so, but when my husband made advances, his touch, his kiss, his mannerisms didn't compare at all to my lover's, and I found them almost repulsive. I didn't even want my husband to touch me—in spite of the fact that, in counseling, one of my major complaints was his lack of touching and attention. Now that it was there, I couldn't even force myself to accept it. It was so foreign to me. I felt terrible for him."

Darren, sixty-three, recalls this about his affair: "When I'd get in arguments with my wife, I was saying to myself, I have someone else; I don't have to put up with this. Each argument became a reason to leave. Where normally we'd have a dispute and work it out, there was no desire on my part to work it out. When the affair ended, my wife and I had so many issues, I almost lost her, too."

If the bottom ever falls out of this triangle, and the spouse learns about the affair, he or she may react the way one of my patients, Deana, did. "That son of a bitch! So *this* is why he never wanted to make love! I thought there was something wrong with me. I was worried that there was something wrong with him. I was going to doctors and therapists, for God's sake. How could he do this to me when he knew what it was the whole time?"

The one-night stand might somehow be understood or at least forgiven. This ongoing "supplementation of the marriage" that made your partner worry about his or her sexuality or your health can become a real deal breaker. I've seen it toss away twenty or more years of a good marriage in one confession. In using an affair to try to save and maintain a marriage, it can also blow up in your face.

To Prove That the Sexual Dysfunction You're Experiencing Isn't Your Fault but Your Partner's

A man confides to his doctor, "I can't make love to my wife the way I used to, but it doesn't happen with this new woman. I haven't been this hard in ten years. I don't need any Viagra. The only thing wrong with me is that I'm bored with the sameness I've lived with for twenty years."

The same thing can drive a woman into an affair. One of my patients told me: "I never got turned on by my husband. I read about orgasms, listened to my friends talk about them, but it never happened to me. Then I met my lover. Shortly after we began the relationship, I had my first orgasm. It was like I was losing my virginity all over again. I lay there, looking at the ceiling. My God! So this is what it really is. My sex life has never been the same since. With this other man, it's wonderful. I just needed someone who would help me learn about my own sexuality. The only worry I have is, if this ever ends, will I need to keep looking for another man? Will I ever be able to teach my husband how to stimulate me?"

To Make the Other Person Leave *You* So You Don't Have to Be the One to Say Good-Bye

Tom, fifty-one, has a master's in economics, is a university professor, and one would think a man with brains enough not to get involved with a student. Yet he did, and when his wife found out about it, he swore the affair would end. Deeply troubled by his own behavior, he went into therapy, where he explored the reasons for his lapse in judgment and the problems in his unhappy marriage. He vowed to his wife that he would never do anything like that again. She went away for the weekend to visit her parents with their children. He met a student in a bar and took her back to his house, where they had sex. His wife found out that another woman had been in her home from a neighbor who couldn't wait to tell her the moment she pulled into the driveway. "I wasn't really attracted to this woman at all," he told his therapist. "Am I a sexual addict or something?"

What he learned in therapy was that his real addiction was avoiding hard decisions. If he provoked his wife enough, the decision to end the marriage would seem like hers, not his. The secret in the bedroom? "I tell her I want to change and work things out, but I'm deeply ambivalent. I can't stay, and I can't leave. I wish something would make up my mind for me one way or the other."

There are people who constantly test their relationships by doing the worst they are capable of. Unconsciously, they can't accept that they are capable of being loved and desired. They are so sure that they are going to be rejected eventually that they make sure they behave in a way that ensures they'll be rejected first. The secret in the bedroom is "How bad can I be before you'll leave me the way everyone else has?"

To Answer the Question "Who Am I Now?"

When Karl, forty-five, came up to Audra at their high school reunion and said, "Didn't you used to be Audra Frank?" even she had to smile. There was little left of the somewhat overweight, shy Audra Frank who had roamed the halls of high school feeling lost and alone. In her place was a woman to whom the years have done a favor. She looked better than she ever had in her life. Yet she never expected Karl, of all people, to notice. "He was the guy every girl wanted. I would have given any-thing for him to even speak to me, let alone date me, in high school. Here he was acting like I was the most interesting woman he'd ever met."

He gave her his business card, with his cell phone number writ-ten on the back. She kept it for two weeks before she called. "I would have sworn on the Bible that day that my only plan was to meet with him and talk about old times. It wasn't true. I knew we'd end up in bed, and we did."

For weeks she felt guilty and terrified. What if her husband found out? It was agonizing. She tore up Karl's business card.

Three months later she was at a new restaurant with her friends, and the wait was long. A man sitting at the bar entertained all of them but showed special interest in Audra. After dinner, when they were leav-ing, she told her friends that her husband was picking her up but instead returned to the bar alone. The gentleman was still there. He coaxed her into trying her first martini. She sipped and coughed and laughed and then drank it down.

She slept with him that night. Physically she had never had such a stimulating experience. Emotionally she was confused and terrified. Her husband was in Europe. Her kids were waiting for her to kiss them good night. The baby-sitter was angry that she was home four hours later than she said she would be. She spent a week picking up the emotional pieces of the puzzle that was her "real life." What had made her risk everything she cared about for a man who didn't even seem so special to her after they had made love?

In therapy Audra came face-to-face with the truth. She had never had the experience of being admired, sought after, or sexually desired when she was younger. She had married the first man who showed her attention. But that quest to be popular and desired had never left her. Today she could attract the type of men who wouldn't give her a glance two decades ago. How could she resist?

The knowledge that you can attract men or women who would never give you a second glance years ago is a more powerful ego trip than many of us want to admit. It's the reason behind the "trophy wife," and now that women are becoming more economically independent, they have their trophies, too. In midlife, as people adjust to aging, career and family changes, they become especially vulnerable to affairs because of the need to show who they are now and demonstrate to others what they are capable of.

To Figure Out "Where Have I Been, Where Am I Going, and Who Am I Going With?"

Closely related to "Who am I now?" is "Is this all there is?" Whether we say it aloud or we merely think it when we reach midlife, we eventually have these questions. Louise DeSalvo, in her book *Adultery* (Beacon Press, 1999), writes, "I see adultery as the soul's desire to be something other than staid and stable and the heart's desire to yield to ecstasy." At midlife most of us begin to assess everything that's been staid and stable: your relationships with your spouse, children, parents, boss, and community. Having an affair may be an attempt to help us answer those questions about where we've been and where we're going.

Some people are shocked by the kind of sexual experimentation this search for answers can lead to. Julie, forty-eight, found herself in bed one day with her best friend, Carole. "We shared a bottle of Merlot at a conference we were at. We were laughing and talking about all the men we'd known and all the crazy experiences we'd had. We went up to my hotel room. In the middle of all the giggling and laughing, it got to a point where we found ourselves unbuttoning each other's blouses. We then found ourselves in bed together, kissing and touching. It was a wonderful sensation. It taught me more about my own sexuality than I had expected. Later, we couldn't believe what we'd done. We blamed it on a two-cocktail lunch. Still, I know I wanted to find out what it would be like with another woman, and so did she. And we're still great friends."

One man's need for experimentation led to an affair with a much younger woman: "I was trying to prove to myself that I was still young and desirable. I was tickled to be forty-eight and have a twenty-two-year-old woman interested and willing. But it was purely sexual. After she put on her clothes and redid her makeup, I stared at her because she was really beautiful. But I ended up thinking, Who is this woman? Why does she come here? Why does she stay? What's she doing with me? It did cross my mind that she might be experimenting, too, just to see what it would be like to be with an older man.

"Finally I realized, this is not really where it is, and this is not where I am. It dawned on me that I'm not 'getting old.' I may be getting older, but that's OK; it's normal to do that. It suddenly wasn't so important to know a young woman would sleep with me. I knew I would be able to navigate better what was ahead in my life with my partner. It was almost like I was on a trip and then I came back. I no longer had to prove anything to anybody, including myself. Slowly, once again, my marriage became the focus. I look back at that affair now and realize it was more of an education than anything else."

To Escape Reality

In her book *Adultery*, Louise DeSalvo sums up why affairs are so enticing:

"In my adultery story, there is love, there is sex, there is passion, there is food, there is drink, there is pleasure, there is languor. There are naps, there is conversation, there is understanding, there is mutual admiration, there is reading (in bed, in the afternoons, propped up on pink satin pillows). There is even art and music. . . . There is time enough to satisfy the body, the soul, the mind, and the spirit.

"In my adultery story, there is no cooking, no dishwashing, no fights, no one ignoring you (reading the newspaper, looking at television, listening to the radio when you want to share a feeling or an idea). There are no raised voices, no bitterness, no rancor, no sorrow, no leaking toilets or sinks, no lousy landlords, no obnoxious neighbors, no work, no bills, no boring or bad sex, no children present. Most assuredly, there are no pets. . . .

"In my fantasy of adultery (in everyone's fantasy of adultery) there is no real life. Which, I've come to realize through the years, is precisely what drives people to commit adultery. Because in everybody's fantasy of what adultery will be like, there is no real life."

Should You Tell the Secret?

If you're having an affair, should you tell? There's not simply a right or wrong thing to do. I've seen people decide they're going to tell their mate about an affair and it had nothing to do with salvaging the marriage or being honest. They wanted to unburden themselves by making a confession. In effect they were saying, "OK, now it's not my problem anymore; it's yours. Deal with it." But I've also seen people who tell, even though it's excruciatingly difficult and painful. In the end, it enhances the relationship. There's a new understanding and a new level of honesty in the relationship. They ask, "How did we get here?" and work together to figure out how to overcome and get beyond the affair.

Sometimes there is even a powerful urge to share with your mate exactly what's happening between you and the person with whom you're having the affair. You've found your soul mate. It's something so important happening in your life that you want to share it with your partner because he or she is one of the most important people in your life. You may look at your spouse and think, I want to tell you about this, because it's teaching me about myself, and it's incredible that I'm feeling this way. I want to share it with you because we've spent so much of our lives together. In fact, your relationship may have gone in a direction where you feel more like brother and sister than husband and wife. However, the hurt factor for sharing such a secret can be huge.

If you want to tell, most therapists advise that you carefully consider your motives. Here are some of the *worst* reasons to tell:

- **To alleviate guilt.** If your partner is furious about your affair, if he or she makes you miserable because of it, you may feel less guilty about what you've done because you're being punished for it. But hurting your partner to assuage your guilt is selfish at best.
- **For revenge.** Sometimes you tell to get back at your partner, but when you punish the other person with an affair, you are bound to cause hurt and anger for both of you. However, *your* hurt and anger—the unhappiness that drove you to this brink in the first place—will seldom get dealt with. Your partner will probably be less willing to listen to your feelings now that you've hurt his.

You both can be caught in an endless cycle of revenge. Unless telling is going to help the relationship continue or end (if that's your desire), there's no positive purpose in telling for revenge.

- **To try to manipulate your partner into showing you more appreciation.** Perhaps you intended your affair to make a statement: *I'm still attractive, and you should treat me better.* Some partners might respond positively to knowing someone else wanted you. Some will just be devastated, angry, or disgusted. It's hard to know which type your partner will be. Research indicates that women are more likely to forgive men for an affair, while men are less likely to forgive women. Men are likely to feel humiliated and emasculated. The real question however is, do you want to stay in a relationship where you have to resort to manipulation to get someone to recognize your value?

Before you tell, ask yourself these questions: What are the costs and what are the benefits? Will this ultimately be helpful or not? What are my true intentions in revealing this information? Will this be irreparable? Could I resolve this guilt by talking to a therapist or friend?

When the Secret's Out

Many couples survive an affair even though it's the worst crisis a marriage can face. Here are some suggestions.

Get Help

Therapy can be enormously helpful in easing the pain and getting both partners to begin communicating honestly. You might think, But I'm in this affair, and I don't want to bring it out yet. How can I go into therapy while this is happening? Wouldn't that somehow be unfair?

Don't deny yourself the help and support of therapy just because you are having an affair you don't want to divulge yet. People having affairs do it all the time. Sometimes they tell the secret, and sometimes they don't. But therapy is about learning to communicate and to deal with real issues. When you go into therapy with your partner, there will probably be a time when the therapist suggests that you both meet with her or him individually. That's when many people confess an affair. It's to your benefit to let the therapist know the facts, but it's not a requirement. You can still be helped enormously, even if you never confide it.

Confidentiality between client and therapist means that she or he will not confide the fact that you're having an affair to your partner or anyone else. Will the therapist judge you or think less of you, or bond with your partner if you tell? My colleagues who are therapists usually suspect that at least one member of a troubled couple is having an affair anyway, since it happens so often. They generally see an affair as just one more symptom, not a cause. You aren't going to be "punished" for "confessing" or get a moral guilt trip. The same is true of confiding in your doctor. Believe me, he or she has heard it before.

If You're the Partner Who Had the Affair, Be Willing to Make Amends

That may mean expressing regret over and over again, even when you begin to resent repeating it. Realize that it may take considerable time for your spouse to trust you again. Resist blaming your spouse for the affair or getting into details about the sex that took place. Realize how unhappy you've made your partner and express remorse for the hurt the affair has caused.

If Your Spouse Has Had an Affair, Resist Concluding That the Affair Is 100 Percent the Other Person's Fault

In fact, therapists say that when couples come to therapy and tell the same story about what went wrong, they have the best chance of having their marriage survive.

Think about what might have gone wrong in your marriage and how that may have led to the affair. Ask yourself, "Do you still love him? Can you ever trust him again? Can you live with this? Can you build on this in your relationship?" The decision you make will chart the rest of your life together.

Nonsexual Affairs

For some people, the secret in the bedroom is that the hunger that draws them outside the relationship isn't a sexual but an emotional need. As one woman put it, "I want to flirt, I want him to flirt back, I want to know he wants me. But I don't really want to have sex with him. I just want to know that I'm being noticed and that I'm desired."

Without ever touching, two people can find themselves in a relationship of such intensity that they can think of little else, often knowing that they will never, ever go to bed together. Three common types of nonsexual affairs are the intellectual affair, the emotional affair, and the Internet affair. Let's look at them more closely.

The Intellectual Affair

When Jerry, fifty-five, thinks about the "other woman," he's thinking of a woman he has never done more than kiss on the cheek—and probably never will. But some of the most thrilling moments in his life have been at her side. They are both responsible for generating new business for the midsize advertising agency they work for. They plan, research, and pitch new clients together. Their firm is an upstart, a mosquito bite on the large, muscled backs of the large firms in their city. When they win an account away from a larger firm, it often makes columns in the newspapers. He knows he couldn't do it without her. "I had a good team, but we rarely won an account when we went up against more established firms. She transferred into the division six months ago, and everything changed. I felt this instant connection. Our instincts about clients were the same, and we fed off each other's ideas. She brought a lot to the table, and we made a killer team."

He thinks about her more than he likes to admit. There are moments when Jerry even thinks it's love. "When she was sent to another division for six weeks when a vice president went on pregnancy leave, I hated it. I actually felt jealous. I miss her if we don't talk for a few days."

She also knows things his wife doesn't know. "I pretty much lost my spot as the center of the universe in our house when we had our first child. After the third child, she stopped asking me what I do all day, and

I stopped trying to tell her. Today I doubt she even has a clue about what I do. But she doesn't like me being so close to a woman at work. She complains, 'Why did you tell *her* you were invited to lecture at the university and not *me*? Don't you think I'd want to know that? Why does she know things I don't know?' I think, For one, she'll be interested in the speech, not just the lecture fee. For another, I enjoy bouncing ideas off her in a way I never have with anyone else. But in truth, sometimes after I've told this woman, there's almost no need for it to come out again. I'm not trying to keep anything from my wife, but it's like when it's already been said, there's no reason to say it again."

Marie, thirty-six, would hear this story and agree. Her intellectual affair is with her music teacher. "We can talk about music for hours. There have been moments when I'm playing the guitar and he's accompanying me, or we're writing a song together, that I feel happier than I ever have with any other man. It's a total turn-on, without the sex."

Does she ever think about leaving her husband and seeing where things could lead with this other man? "I don't let my mind go there. Well, not often. There was one time we were out together listening to a new band. We went for coffee afterward, and I didn't want to go home, and neither did he. There was another night after we wrote a song together and we were full of adrenaline and it was midnight. When he hugged me good-bye, it took every bit of self-control I had not to *really* kiss him. But it's not about sex. As much as I care about him, as much as he adds to my life, he loves his wife and I love my husband. I don't think either of us would want to cross that line, have some cheap affair that would have a beginning, middle, and end, and not be able to keep doing what we do together."

The intellectual affair is like a marriage in some ways. The "offspring" you have are the projects you do together or the conversations you have. You conceive an idea, watch it take form, and create something that you sense you couldn't have done as well on your own. You have memories together that your spouse can't share. If the intellectual affair continues over time, you even begin to have history together. Rather than sexual stimulation, you have intellectual stimulation.

Intellectual lovers aren't necessarily good *to* you — they're good *for* you. One woman put it this way: "He never remembered my birthday.

He certainly never sent me flowers. But he made me feel like the smartest person in the world. He brought out talents in me I never even knew I had." And it *can* have absolutely nothing to do with sex, although you may be attracted to the other person. In fact one patient, an opera singer, told me, "The leading man is almost always gay, but when we're singing together, for those few minutes, we fall in love."

With an intellectual lover, there are moments of thinking and exploring and creating that can be every bit as sensual as an embrace. Even though it's all "in your head," you may find you have the same sense of bonding and optimism and intimacy from sharing your thoughts that two people have after a particularly good night in bed. Couples therapist Mitch Meyerson, L.C.S.W., author of *Six Keys to Creating the Life You Desire* and *When Is Enough, Enough?*, explains: "I call it the *wow factor*. By the time you've been in a relationship awhile, your partner isn't always so fascinated with your skills and talents. He or she knows them, is used to them, admires them, but isn't amazed by them. This new person listens to you talk and says 'Wow! That's fascinating. Tell me more.' It's fresh energy. It's like the honeymoon stage, when you're vitally interested in absolutely everything your partner does and thinks. You get a sense of energy, passion, and excitement from communicating with someone who has that much interest in what you think or do. You don't get it at home. Couples in long-term relationships sometimes forget how much each of them still craves the admiration and attention for their special talents that they used to get from each other."

This is why Meyerson often cautions partners who are jealous of their spouse's intellectual affair to slow down and think it through before they react full force and say "What's it going to be? A therapist or a lawyer?" He says, "When the project is over, the affair often falls apart. The two people involved often have little else to talk about to each other than their work. The wow factor gets lost when they spend more time together and learn all there is to know about the other person's talents. Don't forget that this is often business. Many clients I've had end up fighting about money, commissions, and percentages with their intellectual lovers. The entire collaboration breaks down, and they never even speak again. But until then these 'affairs' can be a wake-up call. Sometimes we look at our spouse and think, What he does at work is amazing, or I can't believe how much people in her company respect her, or I wish she could see the way the kids look at her when she's not watching. But we don't say it, and that's a mistake."

Can intellectual affairs be considered cheating? As long as the passion for the work doesn't become passion for the body, intellectual affairs can go on for years with two people who never even touch. But often a spouse will begin to feel seriously "cheated" of attention. What to do? Some suggestions:

- **Don't try to compete.** If you aren't thrilled by actuarial tables, for instance, learning about them to mollify a spouse who is straying "intellectually" isn't going to work. You can probably fake interest as well as you can fake orgasm—all show and no go. The *other* man or woman is right in the middle of that domain, understands it completely, and is as excited about it as your partner is. If you try to put yourself in the middle, your suggestions might meet with criticism that really hurts. For example, one woman said this about her husband: "He started giving me all of these ideas for my master's thesis because he was jealous of my professor. But his ideas were terrible. Then he got really angry because I wasn't writing them down and using them." Show interest, but don't try to become the expert yourself.
- **Find some other intellectual plane on which you and your spouse can still meet.** If the two of you feel that all you talk about these days is your search for a plumber and your teenager's last algebra test, you are probably craving as much intellectual stimulation as your partner. Develop the areas of your interests that you haven't been pursuing. As one man put it, "When my wife went back to school to study art history, I didn't think this was going to make us our first million. But she got her confidence back. She brought new people and experiences into our lives. I admired her talent, even though I wouldn't know a Monet from a Van Gogh."
- **Try not to put the other man or woman down.** "She lets her kids be raised by housekeepers!" "He's a total loser. I thought you'd have better taste!" That kind of criticism (even if war-

ranted) can backfire and create a stronger bond between the other person and your spouse. Don't forget that you're insulting someone your partner admires and, more important, who admires back, equally. Your criticism can only cause more distance or a more defensive reaction: "He [or she] isn't going to tell me who I can be friends with!"

- **Befriend the "other man" or "other woman."** If you win that person over, you undermine the chances that the affair will move on to a more intimate, sexual affair. Chances are good that the other person isn't going to go after your spouse sexually if he or she truly likes you.
- **Consider this: You fulfill important needs in your partner— that's why he or she stays.** But you can't fulfill every need. Your partner can crave an intellectual soul mate, but that doesn't mean he or she wants to marry such a person. Frequently we have intellectual affairs with the kind of person that realistically we would never marry. That's often why an intellectual affair doesn't go on to become a sexual affair. It's sometimes hard to have your cake and eat it, too. There are people who want someone to stimulate them intellectually and also wait on them hand and foot. These two types of personality traits don't often mesh in the same person.
- **Let it run its course.** The intellectual affair often dies out in the face of emotions or interests outside the workplace that the two "lovers" don't share. When the "project" is over, the excitement is gone. These affairs can be surprisingly shallow:

"We worked together every day for two years, and we were extremely close. Then she left the company. I never got more than a Christmas card once a year."

"I was on the brink of the flu, but when I said, 'Let's call it a day on this project; I'm not feeling great,' he said, 'How about just another half an hour?' I realized then that our relationship really wasn't personal at all, but more about what we could do for each other's careers."

"He was a pediatrician, and we were coauthors who spent hours together laughing and talking. The 'affair' ended the day we handed our manuscript in. We even discussed it once. He said, 'Well, that was business.'"

The Emotional Affair

When Gene and Ellen go on vacation with Rob and Lynne, the places they visit are always new, but some things never change. Gene leaves his wife, Ellen, on the beach and goes out instead with Lynne in a tiny sail-boat after five minutes of instruction from the hotel staff. They capsize and think that's hilarious. In the meantime, his wife, Ellen, and Lynne's husband, Rob, sit on the beach thinking it's a real waste of money to rent a sailboat at sixty bucks an hour and then end up swimming back to shore, the ultimate practical viewpoint. The next winter, when the two couples travel to Vail, Gene and Lynne head for the back bowls after lunch while Ellen and Rob go back to their respective condos for a nap. Gene and Lynne argue about politics deep into the night. Ellen goes to bed bored, while Rob flips channels looking for a basketball game. While Ellen and Rob like each other, Gene and Lynne adore each other. They have often thought, If only I'd met you first! No one is sneaking off to have sex, though. The men are best friends and so are the women!

Sonia, forty-seven, is another case in point. She and her personal fitness coach have a relationship that grows more special every day. "I can tell him things I wouldn't even tell a therapist. We're incredibly close. He's twenty years younger than me, so my husband doesn't see him as a threat, but it's not a sexual thing. He just really listens to me. In some ways he makes it possible for me to stay in my marriage. My husband thinks that if you have any emotions, you should go to bed and stay there until they go away."

To some, these types of emotional affairs may sound very similar to intellectual affairs. The difference is that the intellectual affair has to do with business or work or producing and creating something. Emotional affairs are about wanting sensitivity to your feelings rather than strokes for your intellect. People in emotional affairs can come from two entirely different worlds, such as the woman with the Ph.D. who falls for the construction worker who has two years of college. Or the CEO who falls for the waitress at the coffeehouse where he goes each morning after his workout. This isn't to say construction workers don't have the brains of college professors or that a waitress isn't waiting tables while she finishes her own M.B.A. It doesn't mean they aren't smart, regardless of their respective credentials. It's that credentials don't matter in the emotional affair as much as they do in the intellectual affair. The fact that they live in different financial realities often intrigues the "lovers" and can sometimes give them a sense of power.

I can't tell you how many times patients have told me that they fell prey to an emotional affair at midlife because they met their soul mate accidentally. It's an easy accident to explain. It often happens this way: For years you've skipped the symphony, art museum, tennis game, or something else you enjoy and want to participate in because your partner won't go with you, simply out of lack of interest. One day you decide life is too short to keep denying yourself. You feel literally pushed into doing things by yourself if you ever want to experience them at all. You finally decide you're going to.

You're at the art museum enjoying a painting when another art lover strikes up a conversation with you. You can't believe how much you have in common. You meet again because it's harmless, after all, and you enjoy having a new friend. But the more you get to know each other, the closer you feel. This person *understands* you. You talk about things you've never talked about before with your spouse. You share so many of the same interests.

While you're pursuing your interests, you naturally become exposed to other people who share the same interests. It's only natural to fall into a relationship. If you look at the reason that people marry and what originally attracted them to each other, it's often very different from what attracts people at midlife. In many instances, two people who get married at a young age share similar backgrounds but have very different interests. In contrast, a midlife relationship or affair often begins between two people who share similar interests while coming from very different backgrounds. It's like a more complex wine. The different background gives a complexity to the relationship that often isn't there when you have similar backgrounds. This is why so many emotional affairs may ultimately lead to sexual affairs. Sherry, fifty-four, related to me, "It was a deeper relationship because sex was the *last* thing we had, not the first. We connected mentally before we connected physically."

But sex is still secondary in the emotional affair, if it ever happens at all. The real secrets of the emotional affair are often:

"I'm lonely. . . . I married someone I thought would be good for me, settle me down, and she did, but I'm just so bored."

"I can't talk to my partner without being judged and criticized."

"My partner and I have gone our separate ways over the years. She does her thing, and I do mine. We have little to say to each other."

Sometimes the secret is "I can't believe I married someone who is so different from me. Did we both change? Or was I just too young to know what I really wanted when I got married? Everything that used to turn me on about him is driving me nuts these days."

Why do so many people have those kinds of feelings about the person they married? Often what you're attracted to at the outset of the marriage ends up being what causes you problems later. When you find yourself attracted to somebody, it's often because that person can help you compensate for what you don't have. For example, let's say you're very strong and stable and dependable. Sometimes you think you're too dependable. You don't take any risks, and you don't have much fun. Then you meet someone who's fun loving and a risk taker, and you're strongly attracted. In the beginning, it's great. He's drawing you out of yourself, and you're doing things you never did. He's attracted to you because he needs an anchor and admires your stability and dependability. Each of you is, in some way, what the other person feels is missing. Then you get married. The risk taker is coming home late and gambling your money in the stock market, and you're furious. You're a drag to him because everything has to be on schedule and discussed and analyzed, and he wonders why you just can't loosen up.

Friendship, mutual respect, and a willingness to share another person's interests fuel the emotional affair. These are sometimes the key elements missing in a marriage that's made it to midlife. If you sense your partner has become obsessed by an emotional affair, think about the following before you try to break up the friendship:

- **Just as in the intellectual affair, don't put the other person down.** You'll only increase their bond and appear petty or jealous. Try saying "That's great that you find her so interesting. Let's have her over for a drink" or "I admire people like him. I'm the opposite, I admit it, but I can see what you like about him."
- **Recognize it if the friendship has gone out of your marriage and try to rebuild it.** Therapists recommend this exercise: Each partner makes a list of ten small things he or she wishes the partner would do or say. For example: "I wish she'd listen to me without interrupting." "I wish he'd help with the dishes." "I wish she would watch the Cubs game with me." The partners exchange lists and agree to pick one thing a day to do for the other person. It's amazing how something so simple can restore feelings of goodwill and friendship.
- **Catch yourself the next time you minimize your spouse's feelings.** And it's easy to do!

"Don't be so angry!"

"You shouldn't let this upset you."

"How can you cry over this trashy movie?"

Partners in an emotional affair never say those things. They listen to and explore feelings. They're interested. Although you may honestly be trying to make your partner feel better when you say "Don't feel like that," it's seldom interpreted that way. Try listening to your partner's feelings without giving advice or telling your partner not to feel the way he or she feels.

Cybersex—the Secrets Behind the Internet Affair

It was just past midnight when Carla awoke and realized that her husband wasn't in bed next to her. Curious and a little worried, she went down the stairs where she could see the light on in the den. "My husband was sitting at the computer, so engrossed that he didn't hear me come up behind him. That's when I saw that his robe was open. He was sitting there at the computer, typing with one hand and masturbating with the other. I thought I'd die."

Roger, forty-nine, went to a marriage counselor, alone, with a thirty-two-page computer print-out. It was his wife's "affair" with a man she had met in a chat room on the Internet. "This Bill8672 writes her three times a day," he complained. "She tells me they're just friends. But look at what she writes to him here on page five: 'I feel like you're the only person on earth who understands me.' I told her this is sick. She refuses to stop writing to him."

Far from the sweet romance of the movie *You've Got Mail* is what actually happens to some couples when a partner becomes attached to another person via the Internet. Some of these affairs are emotional or intellectual. Some are purely sexual. They can last minutes, with the partners each going off to the next adventure of hot chat with someone new. Or the two partners can continue to meet on-line for more of the same.

How hot is *hot chat*, the term for sex that takes place on-line? Rexxxxx (that's his on-line name and how he really spells it), author of *Modem Love* (Kensington, 1995) and touted as cyber–Don Juan, told his on-line lovers he was writing a book and recording their "love sessions." He got their OK. Then he published their erotic adventures explicitly in his book, word for word.

I quote Rexxxxx's session with an on-line lover named Maryjo with his permission:

Rexxxxx: You are astride me now.
Maryjo: As I straddle you, our tastes blend in the kiss.
Rexxxxx: I am burying my face in your breasts, kissing one nipple, then the other. Licking and flicking as I do.
Maryjo: Suck my nipples hard. I like that!

Rexxxxx: The kiss is very luxurious as we contemplate the ecstasy that lies ahead. OOOOHHHH!!! IT FEELS SUPERB!!!

Maryjo: Very sensual, the kiss.

Rexxxxx: I suck your nipples and I bite each of them just past the point of pain. I thrust upwards HARD. Although my thrusts are hard and deep and insistent, our kiss is slow and luxurious.

Maryjo: OHHHHH!!! It feels soooo wonderful!

Can you believe this? There are three more pages of that experience—and this was the mild part. There's even a frank discussion later in the book of what constitutes "bad sex" in cyberspace (i.e., "Oops, got to run, my old man just walked in!!")

Hot chat is graphic and explicit because it can be. It's no different from phone sex. People who have phone sex just can't type as fast. With voice-activated computer technology, the poor typists will finally be able to get into cybersex.

One might ask, is this actually cheating? Rexxxxx says he is a happily married man. His book is "Dedicated to my deliciously sexy wife for not murdering me while I was doing this book." As long as he didn't take his adventures out of cyberspace and into real space, she was fine with them, he explains. She even tried cybersex herself but became quickly bored when she was besieged with instant messages like "What RU wearing?" over and over again by men with no sense of grammar or ability to spell.

Some partners truly don't mind or see cybersex as much of a threat to their relationship. "I don't think it's any different than masturbating to a *Playboy* magazine," one woman said. "It's just a fantasy."

Another woman put it this way: "One person types some dirty words. The other person types some back. I mean, how do you spell *loser*? I think that if this is what's missing in my husband's life, I feel sorry for him."

A man told me: "I couldn't type fast enough. My lover left the chat room before we got through foreplay!"

But not every partner handles the cyber affair with such indifference. For one thing, a partner can get so engrossed in the "affair" that whether it's sexual or not, it hurts to know someone else is getting all that attention. And although Rexxxxx claims that his on-line adventures made him a better lover at home because he gained a better understanding of what women really want, some people become absent or indifferent lovers because their needs are being met elsewhere.

What can you do if your partner becomes involved in a cyber affair? Realize that the cyber affair doesn't necessarily mean that your partner is unhappy with you. With all the talk of Internet affairs, some of us simply opt to try one to see what all the fuss is about.

However, if one of you becomes "addicted" to cybersex and the other feels threatened, you have a rather large "elephant" in the bedroom. Therapists recommend that you take a closer look at the reason you or your partner sought this type of thrill. It can "mirror" back to you some key information about yourself and your relationship. This can actually help strengthen your bond. With that in mind, here are some of the reasons people give for engaging in cybersex and the "secrets" behind those reasons.

"It's amazing how easy it is to attract a lover, and no one gets hurt."

Possible secret: "I've never had the experience of attracting an endless array of eager partners who think I'm the hottest thing in the world. I crave being sought after."

"I can do things or say things I'd never be able to say to my partner."

Possible secret: "I haven't had the courage or made the effort to become truly intimate with my partner or let down my guard sexually."

"It's really fun to go on-line and pretend you're a member of the opposite sex."

Possible secret: "I want to know more about what the opposite sex wants, but I don't know how to ask." Or "I want to experiment with homosexuality."

"I'm accepted for myself, not judged by my body."

Possible secret: "I struggle with my body image, and I haven't figured out how to deal with it or find a partner who accepts me the way I am."

"There are no demands on-line. It's just pure fun."

Possible secret: "I feel smothered in most relationships. I have a hard time giving because I feel like people just want more and more." Or "My family makes so many demands on me I never get my own needs met. I haven't learned how to say no without feeling guilty."

"This is prep for my novel" or *"I'm just doing this intellectually, to see what it's all about."*

Possible secret: "There's a little bit of a voyeur inside me, more comfortable watching from a distance without getting too close."

"I feel a connection with this person I've never felt before."

Possible secret: "I am only able to truly be myself when I'm anonymous. I doubt I can be accepted by a lover with all my real doubts and other emotional baggage."

"Cybersex has no limits."

Possible secret: "I want to experiment with things that are a little bit off the map, kinky, or unusual, and fulfill every dream of sexual intimacy I've ever had. I'm afraid that if my lover really knew what I want sexually, he or she would think I'm sick."

"I'm really in love."

Possible secret: "I've created a fantasy and fallen in love with it."

What do you do with a partner who is obsessed with Internet affairs?

▪ **Consider that what your partner might be looking for is to have less demanding sex.** Cybersex doesn't require intimacy, a bath, or even an erection. It's mind to mind. For men and women who have struggled all of their lives with body image, the opportunity to finally be admired just for their inner selves is a nurturing experience. It can be so soothing to the ego that they find themselves on-line, engaged in cybersex, while real life goes on the back burner.

A woman might feel that she finally has the power in sexual relationships when she makes herself available on the Internet. Women are besieged by IMs (instant messages) on AOL, where a man may have to romance a partner with interesting cyberspeak before he asks her to find a "room" with him. Just posting your message with a female name as your E-mail address is enough to make a woman instantly popular in many chat rooms. Men looking for cybersex will respond in droves. You can feel like you're Scarlett O'Hara at the Wilkes's barbecue as the messages pop up on your screen, begging for you to respond.

If your lover is lost in cyberspace, ask yourself if you've been taking the time to be nurturing and appreciative. If you haven't been, why? Are you angry? Do you feel unappreciated? Do you have so many secrets in the bedroom that why you stay together is a mystery to you both?

- **Ask your partner, "How would you feel if I was having a cyber affair?"** Sometimes that can be a real wake-up call for someone who wouldn't want other people talking to his or her spouse in such a manner.

- **Give it time for the novelty to wear off.** It usually does after a month or two. In the same way videocassettes never replaced the movie theater, cybersex will not replace sex.

- **Make a strong statement about what you'll tolerate and what you won't.** For reasons of your own security, you probably won't want your spouse giving out personal information such as a real name, address, phone number. Let your partner know it if you won't tolerate face-to-face contact with an on-line lover and consider it dangerous. Most of all, if you feel that cybersex is something you can't tolerate your partner engaging in, period, then say so. Communicate the ways the two of you can meet each other's needs or regain your intimacy.

Can Anything Good Come Out of an Affair?

Make no mistake: couples can survive an affair. Whether affairs happen because there's some genetic imperative for men to spread their seed or some emotional need that isn't being met, one thing is for sure: you or your partner has probably had *some* kind of affair. It's a fact of life. As you go through the years together, you will be tempted. It doesn't mean you need to divorce. What you do about it can help strengthen your relationship, should you decide to stay together. Or it can help you move on to a new life with somebody else.

At best, an affair will result in a resetting of one's sights that will carry the relationship onward in a way that is stronger and more emotionally honest. At worst, it can rock your marriage and shatter many of the beliefs you have about yourself and/or your partner.

But affairs, emotional, intellectual, or sexual, will always be a turning point if you face the secret, "How did we get here? What were we missing?" If you care enough, the answers can hold the promise of a new beginning.

9

"My Ever-Ready Man Has Turned into the Never-Ever Man. Don't I Turn Him On Anymore?"

 Understanding Aging and Sexual Response— What's Normal and What's Not

AUDREY AND RYAN woke up on the first day of their ski vacation to a sunny day and a mountain covered in fresh, white powder. After skiing all afternoon, they sipped wine in front of the fire at the condo they'd rented.

"We began making love right there on the couch," Audrey recalls, "and it started to be one of our best times. I was definitely turned on, but when I reached to touch him, it was obvious nothing was happening for him. *Nothing* at all. He was embarrassed, especially after nothing I did helped. I thought, Just don't say anything. Don't make an issue out of it. Two days later we tried again, and the same thing happened."

Back home the situation deteriorated. "He started avoiding me. What hurt the most was that I was trying to be so understanding, but he wouldn't even cuddle with me in front of the television anymore. It was like he didn't want to touch me for fear of my responding. There was no one I could talk to about it. Every day I wondered, Why did he turn off to me? Is he having an affair?"

Joan's husband was forty-six when she began to notice a change in her bedroom. "He used to just look at me and get excited. Now I reach for him and I'm turned away, or the whole experience goes wrong in embarrassing ways for him. To put it bluntly, he doesn't get hard. He says, 'Quit talking about it. You're making it worse.'

"He gets dressed and undressed in another room. He won't kiss me or touch me, because he wants to avoid sex completely. He doesn't see what this is doing to me. I feel totally rejected."

It's estimated that 50 percent of men over fifty have *some* degree of erectile dysfunction. When it happens, silence is often the first reaction. She begins to blame herself because she's not turning him on. He, on the other hand, thinks the unthinkable—that there could be something wrong with his masculinity. But there are many options now available for men. There's no reason to give up on sex completely, even if you've gone through a year of very sporadic and problematic sex.

In this chapter you will learn:

- what normal changes you can expect to see in your orgasm over time—for both men and women
- what's classified as erectile dysfunction and what's just a bad night in bed
- what's in your medicine cabinet that might be affecting your or your partner's sexuality
- what drugs can boost male erection and who the ideal candidate for them is
- how you get your man to admit that he has a problem and to accept that it's *his* problem, not yours (that is, it isn't happening because you are not attractive or sexy enough, although it might make him feel more comfortable to believe that)
- what performance anxiety is and how it can have a major effect on the ability of a man (or woman) to function sexually

- how not to fall into the trap of using your partner as a mirror of your own sexual adequacy

Changes in His and Her Orgasm over Time: What's Normal and What's Not?

When I recently asked a patient if she had any sexual issues she wanted to discuss, she looked at me, smiled, and said, "Doc, my orgasms are there. But they're not the Rocky Mountains anymore; they're more like the Blue Ridge Mountains." The attractive forty-seven-year-old woman who made this statement added, "And those mountains are farther away and harder to get to than they used to be." This was really one of the best descriptions I had ever heard of the normal effect aging has on the female orgasm. It isn't always sexual boredom that makes a real toe-clenching, bed-rocking orgasm a rarity as one goes through midlife. Lower peaks and a longer time getting there are normal for both men and women in midlife and beyond.

For him, it may be increasingly rare that he's able to "think an erection." He will probably need you to caress his penis directly to bring him to erection. Once it's achieved, you may have to continue your foreplay to keep him erect, and the erection itself may not be as firm. One woman put it this way: "When we were younger, all I had to do was look at him a certain way and he got hard. There's a certain pleasure, though, in knowing exactly what he needs now. And he lasts so much longer."

Just as there is a gradual decline in a woman's testosterone, there is a normal, age-related decrease in his testosterone that can affect both libido and erection capability. Testosterone levels actually begin to decline in the late twenties or early thirties, so that by the age of sixty-five, over 50 percent of males will have a relatively low testosterone level. This can translate into a longer time needed to obtain an erection, occasional *lack* of ejaculation during intercourse, and a longer refractory or rest period between ejaculations.

He is also likely to experience a decrease in the volume of his ejaculate and fewer and less forceful contractions when he ejaculates. He may still feel sex is quite satisfactory in spite of this. "To me this is actually dream sex," confided Claire, fifty-four. "My husband never liked to do it more than once in an evening. There were many times I knew I could have another orgasm or that I was still turned on an hour later. Now we have these days where we'll make love in the morning. He won't come, and he'll walk around the whole day with anticipation. He'll be grabbing me in public, snuggling up and whispering in my ear when I'm on the phone, and everything we do is leading to that moment when we know we'll be back in bed again. Having him touch me all day, knowing we're going to go and finish what we've started, can be as exciting as hell."

Couples can thrive with the changes of midlife sexuality when they don't take them negatively but see the potential. Just as most of us have eyes that weren't programmed to work for fifty or more years without some help from reading glasses, the sexual organs may not be programmed to work without some extra assistance.

Trouble brews when he doesn't realize those changes are natural and thinks there is something wrong with him or, worse, with her. Or she misinterprets the signs and thinks he doesn't find her attractive and that she doesn't turn him on as much. She has never really taken an active role in lovemaking in the past and resents being coaxed to do so. "I miss how hard he used to get. Sometimes when he comes, he's half soft. I can't even feel it," Cathy, forty-eight, sighs. "It just seems to take a real marathon of stroking and doing whatever else these days for him to have an erection. Once in a while, we've had to use a lot of Astroglide so he can enter me when he's still pretty soft. When he's inside, that will usually do the trick. But what happens when that doesn't work? I wonder, is this what's happening to everyone our age?"

What's Classified as Erectile Dysfunction and What's Just a Bad Night in Bed?

It would be difficult to find a man who reaches midlife without at least one memory of being unable to perform sexually. When is this considered erectile dysfunction? Twice? Three times? A month's worth of trying? The medical community generally defines erectile dysfunction as a consistent problem with erection quality (obtaining or maintaining an erection) that affects satisfactory sexual intercourse or sexual activity for a period of months. It isn't that he needs more time and stimulation but that nothing you or he does allows him to attain or maintain a solid erection over a period of time and it troubles one or both of you.

What's important to understand is that changes in sexual response due to aging are gradual. The changes are usually variations in intensity rather than complete absence of response. The presence of the normal waking erection each morning is reassurance that erectile function can be achieved. A rather *sudden* change usually signals that something is amiss, although neither partner may realize this at first.

Drs. Della and Max Fitz-Gerald of the North Carolina–based Fitz-Gerald Institute have had several decades of experience in treating couples with this problem. "By the time one of the partners in a couple having sexual problems gets to us," explains Dr. Della, "they've gone through a common pattern. She's been with this partner hundreds of times, and suddenly he can't achieve an erection or he loses it in the middle of sex. She doesn't understand it either, so at first she gives him alibis. She tells him that she understands that he is under a lot of stress at work or there are problems with the children or financial difficulties. Those are the best excuses she can think of for what's happening, and usually he buys them. However, it doesn't take long before these alibis wear out. Maybe they take a vacation hoping the problems will go away. Still, it isn't happening in bed. Or a year later they still have this problem. She begins to think, Well, maybe he's not turned on by me. Maybe he's having an affair. Maybe I'm too old; maybe he thinks I'm fat. She begins to get negative and angry.

"Next she begins quietly looking for assistance outside of herself and outside of the relationship. She may speak to the family practitioner, her ob/gyn, or a good friend. Now she mentions it to her partner. Eventually she'll say something like 'Gee, I read an article, and there's help for this kind of problem. My friend Mary Sue told me that someone helped them.' Very often her partner won't be thrilled with her research. He tells her, 'We don't need anybody here to help us work on this; all we have to do is work harder.' He thinks, If I keep a stiff upper lip and keep work-ing at this, everything will eventually be just fine. She's angry, because she knows there is help, but he won't ask for it."

Dr. Max is quick to add the man's viewpoint: "He's angry and frus-trated, so he often begins to withdraw sexual attention. That increases his wife's anger. Now you've got a vicious cycle. What women need to understand is that men have been socialized to take care of their own problems. He's not trying to individually and deliberately harm you and harm the relationship. He is really doing what he thinks is best. A lot of what we do as therapists is to educate and to help the individual defuse the anger that has built up."

Dr. Della adds, "We ask her to go back and talk to her partner about how important the relationship is to *her*, how she wants to have good sex with *him* and wants it to be good for him, because she values him and the relationship. She needs to talk more from that perspective rather than from a blame perspective. A couple can achieve a sense of a fresh start when they begin to believe, 'We can both work together to achieve or recapture the sexual intimacy, the fun, and the play.' What has begun to happen by the time couples come to see us is that both have begun to roll their sleeves up and to *work* at sex rather than to play and have fun with sex. All that pleasure has gone out the door."

If you've been worried, if you've gotten caught in the blame-and-deny game with your mate, how can you start to turn things around? Understanding a little of the science of a man's erection is an excellent place to start realizing why neither of you may be at fault.

It's Not All in His Head

Doctors now estimate that 90 percent of erectile dysfunction has a phys-ical rather than an emotional cause. The good news is that most physi-cal causes can be corrected. To understand why, let's take a look at what actually enables a man to have an erection. The story begins with the main sexual organ in the body, which is the brain, and the need to have adequate testosterone around, preserving maleness. Then sexual stimulation causes a message to be sent from the brain to the penis, where nerves cause the release of a chemical called nitric oxide. This causes the smooth-muscle cells in the blood vessels to relax so the blood vessels dilate, allowing more blood to flow in easily. The blood then fills the two musclelike cavernosus bodies on the inside of the penis, causing them to swell and exert pressure against the veins that normally allow the blood to exit from the penis. This causes the blood to be trapped inside, making the penis wider, longer, and harder.

What all this requires is functioning nerves, healthy cavernosal arteries, as well as veins that are normal enough to keep the blood from exiting. Let's say the carvernosal arteries become blocked by fatty deposits. Urologist E. Douglas Whitehead, who specializes in the treatment of erectile dysfunction, is fond of warning that, just as clogged arteries can cause a heart attack, a man can have a "penis attack." In other words, the arteries cannot open enough to allow increased blood flow into the penis, so either a very weak erection or no erection at all occurs. This is why seeing a doctor is important when erectile dysfunction occurs regularly. A man who is encountering these problems really should have an evaluation, because it can also be a sign that vascular disease is brewing elsewhere in the body, which could eventually lead to a heart attack. Erectile dysfunction can also be a symptom of other problems such as hypertension, spinal cord compression, or pituitary tumor.

Nerve problems can prevent the carrying of the signals from the brain to the penis that say it's time for the blood vessels to open. Diabetes is by far the biggest cause of nerve damage, but multiple sclerosis and Parkinson's disease are also culprits. Nerves can be damaged by radiation therapy, cancer surgery, prostate surgery, or even back surgery. Dr. Irwin Goldstein of Boston University Medical Center adds bicycle riding to the list. He warns that the hard cycle-saddles on sports bikes can reduce blood flow to the penis by 66 percent. Bike riding also puts pressure on the nerves, irritating and compressing them, and that constant irritation can lead to damage. Numbness after a long ride is a symptom that this is occurring. While this type of injury can be reversed, it can take time—time where "bad nights" in bed turn into performance anxiety and then chronic erectile dysfunction.

Vein problems are the least frequent cause of erectile dysfunction, but they certainly can occur. Like a sink with no stopper, it doesn't matter how much blood flows in if there is not enough compression—pressure by the muscle in the penis that's getting engorged—to shut the veins down so the blood won't go out. Failure of the veins to close can be caused by trauma, scarring, or chronic disease.

Erection Robbers in the Medicine Cabinet

If it's not all in his head or his circulatory system, could it be in his medicine cabinet? In fact, 25 percent of problems with erectile dysfunction can be traced to other drug therapy. What's in that cabinet that might be affecting your or your partner's sexuality?

The most commonly prescribed drugs for depression—Paxil, Prozac, and Zoloft—are notorious for reducing sexual functioning and libido. These serotonin reuptake inhibitors (SSRIs) can inhibit erection and ejaculation in men and prevent orgasm in women. While some people will report an improved sex life because these drugs removed their feelings of depression and hopelessness, and some men will experience a reduction in premature ejaculation, estimates are that anywhere between 33 and 66 percent of people find their sex lives affected adversely.

Hundreds of other drugs can affect libido and erection, including blood pressure drugs, antihistamines, antispasmodics used for bowel problems, fluid pills, heart medications, tranquilizers, mood medications, some ulcer medications like Tagamet, and an antifungal agent called Nizoral. Any drug that decreases testosterone or increases estrogen can also affect sexual function. Recreational or illegal drug use, as well as cigarette smoking, can affect erectile function. While alcohol in small amounts can improve erection and increase libido through the lessening of anxiety and dilation of blood vessels, in large amounts it can cause sedation, decreased libido, and erectile dysfunction. While he must weigh the benefits of any drug against the sexual consequences, it's helpful to know that a drug he is taking may be affecting sexual response, so he can explore with his doctor whether any alternatives exist.

When the Problem Is Performance Anxiety

Brian, forty-nine, says, "Any guy who'll tell you that when he fails to get it up with his wife, that's no big deal, and he just passes it off as a bad night in bed—those guys are liars, in my opinion. You worry. No matter what she tells you about how it doesn't matter, you worry. The next time is the worst. I thought, I'm uptight, I need to relax, I'll have a couple of scotches, and then it will be like old times. I fell asleep before I even got her into bed."

Performance anxiety is nothing to minimize. Instead of seeing erectile dysfunction as a medical problem, some men see it as a reflection of their worth as men. That's a lot of pressure on one organ. And even the most enlightened man in the world, who understands that some changes are going to occur in his sexual response as he ages, can still feel alarmed when those changes first occur. The fear "Is it going to work this time?" can be the nail in the coffin. While he may achieve an erection at first, it's all fine and good, until he worries "Am I going to fail in the middle of this?" or "I hope it lasts . . . I hope it lasts," until, in the middle of this mantra, he loses it. Fears often become self-fulfilling.

What helps? An understanding partner who has empathy rather than sympathy. His already shaky ego doesn't need to be further injured by the notion that you feel sorry for him. "Getting the focus off his erection and his orgasm helped us," one woman explained. "I didn't say, 'Hey, it doesn't matter,' because of course it matters. I did say, 'Well, forget that for now, honey, just use your hands.' He started focusing on what was happening to me and BINGO!"

Much more about how women can help their partners who are struggling with erectile difficulties and performance anxiety follows later in this chapter.

The Best "Cure" Is to Start with Prevention

There *are* lifestyle changes that can help many men ward off full-blown erectile dysfunction. Here are some suggestions for them:

- **Kick the smoking habit.** It weakens the heart and the arteries that carry blood to the penis. Two high-tar cigarettes smoked one after another have been shown to reduce blood flow in the penis by about one-third.

- **Lose weight.** Excessive weight is associated with diabetes, high cholesterol, and high blood pressure—all of which can cause vascular problems. Need some added motivation? For every thirty-five pounds a man loses, he may gain as much as one inch in penile length. Why? One-third to one-half of the penis is inside the body. Thinning of the fat pad around the pubic area will make the penis "longer."

- **Strength training can be a very important stimulator of libido in men.** It can also maintain increased blood flow to the muscles, including those of the penis. Yet another benefit of lifting weights is the increase in testosterone that occurs during and after exercise.

- **Choose aerobic exercise other than spinning classes.** Bike riding puts pressure on the nerves to the penis and can cause numbness and erectile dysfunction.

- **If you have diabetes, get as much control over it as you can.** The same goes for high blood pressure. Follow the correct diet scrupulously and monitor your progress carefully.

- **Maintain healthy cholesterol levels, especially HDL and LDL.** Changes in your diet and exercise can help. Exercise and eating more garlic can increase your HDL; weight loss and exercise can diminish your LDL and some of your other lipids. The statin drugs are very useful for lowering your LDL, your triglycerides, and your total cholesterol.

- **Erections are good for erections.** The more often you "use it," the less likely you'll "lose it." I've even written patients a prescription that says "Have sex more frequently." We laugh when I say "You take this home and give it to your husband," but there is no better medical advice.

- **More manual stimulation may be all that is needed.** This can mean manual stimulation for a longer period of time or oral stimulation or helping him place the penis into the vagina.

However, one patient heard this and said, "You're not kidding. My arm gets tired. My neck starts hurting when I go down on him for that long. It's no fun for me." Before you give up, try two things. The first is to put Astroglide or some other lubricant on your hand—you can't use too much for this. Then give him manual stimulation. He should feel slippery in your hands. Try using both hands, one after the other or together. Alternate his hands with yours. For oral sex, read the excellent description in Saul Rosenthal's *Sex Over Forty* (Tarcher, 1987). Experiment with positions where he can move his penis in and out of your mouth rather than your having to move your head up and down.

There are bonuses for making a big effort in trying these types of techniques. A woman may feel closer to a man, knowing she's helping. He may feel closer, more dependent on her in a positive way.

If that's not helpful, there may be a need for a therapeutic answer. Let's take a look at one of the more amazing, dramatic therapeutic interventions to become available in the last hundred years—Viagra.

Viagra (Sildenafil): Will It Help?

Until the Food and Drug Administration approved the oral medication Viagra, erectile dysfunction was a huge elephant in bedrooms across the world, with an estimated thirty million men in America suffering in silence. The drug has an interesting history. Scientists working for the drug company Pfizer were searching for a treatment for hypertension. One of the drugs they were testing was a pill that contained sildenafil, the main ingredient in what eventually became Viagra. The pill didn't lower blood pressure as well as they had hoped, so the scientists asked the men to return their samples. The men refused. They'd discovered that the pill was helping them achieve erections! Some research subjects even broke into labs to get more, and one scientist claims he had to change his phone number because he was so besieged with calls from men begging for more.

How does Viagra work? It increases blood flow to the penis by enhancing smooth muscle relaxation. More technically, it blocks the enzymes that destroy the body's natural substance for opening blood vessels—nitric oxide. It doesn't raise libido or cause an "instant" erection. Viagra is an enhancer; it has no effect without sexual stimulation.

The blue, diamond-shaped pills come in two doses, 50 mg and 100 mg. Pills are about ten dollars each, and of course, along with a million other Viagra jokes, there's the one about the husband who says to his wife, "Ten dollars a pill! That's terrible!" She replies, "Oh, honey, thirty dollars a year isn't so bad."

Men are directed to take it about an hour before they anticipate having intercourse. The effect is supposed to last for several hours. However, in some men it lasts a lot longer. Many patients have told me they still feel it working the following morning. Remember that most men awaken with an erection. But after Viagra the evening before, many men have commented to me that the morning erection is firmer and longer lasting, and that encourages them to want to have sex again. How often can you take it? Not more than once a day at most.

Viagra's popularity comes from the fact that it is effective in 80 percent of men who don't realize they have an organic or blood flow problem that is causing erectile dysfunction. Their concern is performance anxiety—it didn't work once, and now they're scared that it will never work again, and they're sure it's stress or something psychological. In fact, the majority do have some diminishment in blood flow. When Viagra improves matters, it's usually an indication that something organic has been going on.

Unlike other treatments, Viagra is a pill that can be taken quickly and discreetly. Although men have had some side effects, including headaches, flushing, nausea, nasal congestion, and visual changes, such as seeing a blue tinge, most users report these as minor. As one man said it, "Who cares if I see blue? Without it, I can't get hard. Small price to pay." Higher doses of the drug (e.g., 100 mg, the maximum dose) will intensify the side effects, and the long-term effect of Viagra on vision is unknown.

Performance anxiety is essentially cured provided the Viagra works for this person, because with Viagra he doesn't have to think, Will my erection go away? After a couple of successful experiences with Viagra, that's no longer an issue. He's reassured: "This stuff works for me, and I'm OK," and eventually he forgets about the problem. He now has the self-confidence of knowing that once the blood flows into the penis it's going to be there and stay there, and he doesn't have to worry. If he takes Viagra often enough at first and regains his confidence, he may be able to skip the Viagra and find that, because he's not a prisoner of this performance anxiety, he can perform even without the pill. With extended use of Viagra, which means essentially teaching the penis to respond again, there are men who may stop needing the medication.

There are plenty of men—and women, too—who have wondered, If this is so great for men who can't function at all, what might it do for *us*? Will our normal sex with Viagra be better, longer, more exciting? Viagra wasn't meant to make good better. But it can help a man last longer and have a shorter period of time between erections if he wants to make love again the same day. There are many men taking Viagra as recreation—or so they think in some cases. Many men have mild erection "differences" as they age—and that means thirty-five years old and up! It's not dysfunction. Everything "works." It's been such a gradual thing, like going to the eye doctor and having him or her say "You should think about bifocals" and wanting to jump out of your chair and scream "What do you mean, bifocals? I see fine! Let me try again—I'll do better." Similarly, he might not realize that the blood flow isn't as strong in getting there and staying there as it used to be. If he does notice it, he probably thinks that the reason he isn't as hard as he used to be is that he's distracted by too many other things or not as turned on. Tell him he has mild "erectile dysfunction" and watch him walk out the door, angry. Tell him there's a drug that will "enhance" his erections, and you recover a child of the sixties who isn't a stranger to the idea of experimentation with pharmaceuticals that promise a new kick.

Urologists across the country can document the fact that there are a lot more cases of "mild" erectile dysfunction due to aging that are passed off as stress, disinterest, or twenty years of marriage than most of us imagine. Many males who try Viagra as an "enhancer" aren't as "normal" and healthy as they think they are.

A discussion of the pros and cons of using Viagra as an enhancer follows in the next chapter. But the point here is that Viagra's incredible popularity wouldn't exist if it were used only by men who never function. The 1994 Massachusetts Male Aging Study estimated that 52 percent of American men between ages forty and seventy have minimal, moderate, or complete erectile dysfunction, and those numbers will rise steadily as the population ages.

Who *shouldn't* take Viagra? Anyone suffering from heart disease, especially those men taking medications such as nitroglycerin or any form of medical nitrates. Viagra intensifies the blood-pressure-lowering effect of these drugs, and this can make it a dangerous, even fatal combination. Be sure to consult with your cardiologist if you have such a history. Men with bleeding disorders, peptic ulcers, retinitis pigmentosa (a genetic eye disorder), or kidney or liver disease should use Viagra only with careful medical supervision, exactly as directed, and then with caution.

People who haven't tried Viagra often wonder what it's like. This was one man's experience: "The first time I took it, I was really scared shitless. I wasn't going to tell her that I took it, because I wanted to experiment alone and see what it did, but I ended up telling her, just in case she'd find me dead or something. I mean, everyone was talking about people who had died from this stuff, so I was really nervous; my heart was palpitating.

"After a little while I started to feel some congestion. My face was flushed, and I could feel my sinuses. I knew right then it was taking effect, so my pulse shot up, and I remember thinking, I wonder what else this is going to do. I could also see a little bluish-green tinge, especially in fluorescent light. I'd heard about that one, but it was a very strange sensation. Still, I wanted to see if it worked.

"By this time my wife was pretty curious, too. Was it going to work? It did. My wife and I were having intercourse, and even though I was still worried, the kind of worries that would have made me 'lose it' before didn't do a thing. In fact, I kind of started playing around, trying to think of things that would turn me off, but I stayed hard. I woke up the next morning harder than I'd been in years. Viagra was a pleasant surprise for both of us. Six months later, the side effects don't even bother me, and I don't worry about sex at all."

What was his partner's reaction? "He's much more loving now. He spends a lot more time trying to satisfy me." Many women report this reaction to Viagra. A man who is going through a bout of erectile dysfunction is often not a very loving man. For one thing, his mind is on *his* physical sensation and how he can "keep it going," leaving little attention for his partner. He doesn't want to stop and do things for her because he's too concerned about losing his erection. He may feel angry at her if he thinks something she did caused him to lose it. And, of course, the more concerned he becomes about the issue, the worse it gets. After Viagra, many men become much more loving again, because they feel much more confidence in *reacting to their partner* and can spend more time in pleasing her.

What About Viagra for Women?

There is ongoing research about Viagra's affect on female sexuality as this book goes to press. What's it showing? Mixed results. Most recent studies have shown that, among women who complain about sexual dysfunction, the most frequent complaint wasn't disinterest in sex but disinterest in their sexual partner. Loss of libido in general was less of a problem. Viagra's benefit is mainly on arousal and orgasm.

It has been demonstrated that Viagra increases the blood flow to the clitoris and the labia—88 percent of the women studied showed this improvement. Since increasing age means decreasing blood flow to the vagina, Viagra might be helpful in terms of heightening some sensitivity to stimulation. However, it has yet to be demonstrated that increased blood flow to the vagina does anything for arousal or orgasm.

Researchers are still in the midst of finding out how important this blood flow is for women. Viagra seems to enhance the erectile activity of the clitoris. Blood is trapped there, just as it is in an erect penis. Lubrication in the vagina also has to do with blood flow. So the potential for Viagra is to increase the blood flow, increase the vascular response, and therefore increase arousal and the ability to achieve orgasm. Newer studies are also demonstrating the critical need for a normal testosterone level in order for women to gain the full benefit of Viagra.

Getting Viagra: Exactly What Happens at the Doctor's Office?

Viagra is a prescription drug. Although there are doctors who provide it over the Internet, as already mentioned, erectile dysfunction can be a signal of a circulatory problem or other illness, and any man who experiences it frequently should have other medical causes explored and ruled out. A checkup with an internist or a urologist can make the difference between successful treatment and a haphazard, hit-and-miss bandage for trouble in bed.

Ideally, a couple will go together to talk to the doctor. Many doctors have said that when both partners come in, this type of "Let's work together" attitude is a springboard for success in overcoming the problem. In the real world, however, many men will see their doctors alone, some without even telling their partners. Their partners might not even be concerned yet. If the problem is minimal, performance anxiety may be his *real* concern.

Many men will seek out an internist first rather than a urologist for a prescription for Viagra, and there's nothing really wrong in going about it that way. The internist will make sure there is nothing in the man's medical history that would make Viagra dangerous, do a basic checkup, and then simply write the prescription. The idea here is that the doctor makes sure there is no reason a man shouldn't take it and then prescribes the drug. If the drug works, there's no need for a full urological workup. If the drug doesn't work, then the man should have a full workup, preferably with a urologist. It's similar to what I do with some women who are infertile, with irregular periods due to infrequent or absent ovulation, if nothing else in their medical history implies a cause for the infertility. Before doing a full workup, I recommend a drug to help her ovulate. It's the first step, and it may be enough on its own to solve the problem. In these instances, the drug is being used both therapeutically and diagnostically, meaning that if it works, you're all done. If it doesn't, you proceed with a more sophisticated workup. The expense and time of doing every test under the sun isn't necessary until it's clear that the problem isn't a simple one.

Some men prefer to see a urologist who specializes in erectile dysfunction. What will happen in the examination room? While the basics may differ a little from doctor to doctor, the exam generally includes a physical exam, a blood test for testosterone, a prostate exam, and an ultrasound exam to test the blood flow to the penis. Sometimes they will inject the patient with medication, usually Alprostadil, that causes an erection and then do the ultrasound exam to check the blood flow. The injection is usually not painful and has been described as feeling like a pinprick (interesting analogy!).

William, thirty-nine, had a typical experience: "I was placed in a small, individual waiting room and given some forms to fill out. I admit I was relieved to know that I wasn't going to run into someone I knew. Finally I was brought into a treatment room. The doctor asked me to describe the problem. He said, 'I've heard that one before,' and his whole attitude was that this isn't so unusual, so I started to calm down. He asked me a lot of questions, like do I wake up with an erection, how often do I masturbate. Pretty sharp. I've heard that urologists never ask you *if* you masturbate, so you don't have a chance to feel embarrassed or lie about it—they just ask how often!

"He told me to take off my pants. Then he put on plastic gloves, put a cold gel on my penis, and used an ultrasound device that measures the blood flow. Nothing was terribly uncomfortable. Next he used an instrument that emitted a slight vibration to test the sensitivity of my nerves, applying it to different spots on my penis. He asked me if I could feel the vibration. He said that everything looked intact. He wrote a prescription for Viagra and suggested that increasing the blood flow might be enough. 'Sort of a way to retrain the penis,' he told me. If it didn't work, I could go back for a more extensive series of tests. The whole thing was over in fifteen minutes."

Viagra worked for this man. It also removed a big secret and a great deal of stress in the bedroom.

What to Do If Viagra Doesn't Work

There are men who take Viagra, wait around for an hour, and wonder, Where's my erection? Without sexual stimulation, it isn't going to happen. Again, Viagra is an enhancer, not the "cause" of an erection. Viagra also isn't always the complete answer. Some men will not respond to

Viagra even with stimulation, and some will find that it doesn't improve their erections enough. Part of the workup at this point includes checking the blood level of testosterone to see if it's low. If that's the case, injections of testosterone ethanate or a new testosterone gel for the skin can be used to prompt a return to either normal function or function that will be enhanced with Viagra. Testosterone is also available in oral form, although injections or gel give a better and more consistent blood level.

There *are* other options beyond Viagra. In fact these options have been around quite a bit longer than Viagra. A little more complicated, a little less user-friendly, these methods may provide an erection when all else fails.

The "Erection Injection"

Caverject is a medication that is injected into the penis and is effective in 65 percent of cases in causing an erection that will often last for an hour or two. Once a man injects himself, the erection is there whether he wants it or not and requires no other stimulation. One might think, Ouch! but the surprising fact is that the injections don't hurt because the needle is so tiny. Obviously a man has to learn how and where to inject himself for the best results, and this means being taught by a urologist or other health-care provider. New trimix and bimix medications, even stronger than Caverject and also injected into the penis, are available and widely used, though not approved by the FDA.

The potential for an hour-long erection has a certain appeal to some men who don't really need Caverject, and the reasons are obvious. "It's like you have wood in there," admitted one man. Because this one-hour erection can turn into a five-hour erection and a medical condition called *priapism* where "what goes up doesn't come down," this is not something to borrow from a friend. The Internet is replete with personal stories of men who have used the "erection injection" out of curiosity.

The Pump

The pump is a device that applies suction to bring blood to the arteries. A vacuum chamber is placed over the penis, and the pump produces an erection that perhaps won't be full but is better than nothing. Then the man places a ring around the base of his penis to prevent blood from exiting, thereby maintaining the erection. There's even a new pump available for women to use on the clitoris to increase blood flow and cause enlargement.

Medicated Inserts

Medicated inserts are actually the same therapy the injections are. But the inserts are placed into the urethra with an applicator. When given the choice between an injection and simply inserting something into the opening in the penis, a man might assume "Hey, I'm not going to stick myself with a needle if this stuff will work." It works in about 30 to 40 percent of cases and thus is not as successful as injections. The most popular one men use today is called Muse.

Surgically Placed Implants

Two pliable plastic cylinders filled with saline are inserted through a one-inch incision on the scrotum. A small pump is inserted into the scrotum. The man squeezes the pump to inflate the implants. Although this will produce an erection in 95 percent of men, the procedure is irreversible.

Herbal Remedies

Erectile dysfunction or problems with libido may also respond to herbal medications. Refer to the cautionary advice in preceding chapters. These are the most widely used.

Yohimbe (Pausinystalia yohimbe)

WHAT IS IT? This medication, which comes from a West African evergreen tree, reportedly has been used by West Africans as an aphrodisiac for centuries. A few small clinical trials showed that yohimbe produced erections in about half of men with emotionally induced erectile dysfunction, such as performance anxiety, and in about 40 percent whose erection problems were physical. How they determined which men met the criteria for which group, since the two causes so often overlap, is sketchy at best. It's also been shown to have a positive effect on libido.

Yohimbe is available in capsules at health-food stores. Yohim*bine*, a pharmaceutical drug sold as Yocon or Yohimex, is a pure extract of the active compound and available through prescription. Pharmaceutical company trials found yohimbine caused improvement in one-third of the men studied. It is purported to work by opening up the blood vessels of the skin and mucous membranes, increasing blood flow to the penis.

What to watch out for. Although you can buy yohimbe at most health-food stores, even many staunch herbalists agree it is probably safer to use the prescription drug. Side effects include anxiety, increased heart rate, tremors, headaches, and high blood pressure — not exactly a blueprint for a great night in bed. The prescription version is said to cause fewer side effects than the raw herb. You should also be aware that Germany's Commission E does not approve either yohimbine or yohimbe as a medication for erectile dysfunction or a male aphrodisiac because of the lack of proven effectiveness and the high risk of side effects. The FDA simply rules it unsafe and ineffective. Some researchers feel that the biggest problem with the herb is that its effective dose is very close to a toxic dose. There are reports of men experiencing hallucinations from high doses of it. My advice is to use it only with medical supervision and not at all if you have low blood pressure, prostate problems, or heart, kidney or liver disease or if you are taking an antidepressant.

Ginkgo (Ginkgo biloba)

What is it? When you see bottles of ginkgo lined up at the cash registers of drugstores across America, you may wonder, What is it, and why does it seem like everyone is suddenly taking it? Not all of those men buying it at the checkout counter have erectile dysfunction. Many are purely interested in the claim that ginkgo can improve memory and cognitive functioning. This herb has grown for centuries in China, but only in the last decade has its use exploded across the Western world. It has been said to be helpful in treating heart disease, asthma, eye disorders, dizziness, ringing in the ears, and more. But what can it do for erections?

There is quite a bit of research showing that ginkgo opens up the blood vessels and improves the rate of blood flow. If your erectile dysfunction is caused by poor vasodilation and insufficient blood supply to the penis, it may help, although long-term treatment is often needed to get the desired effect.

Wʜᴀᴛ ᴛᴏ ᴡᴀᴛᴄʜ ᴏᴜᴛ ꜰᴏʀ. Side effects are not common if taken in recommended amounts. It's a promising herb not only for treatment of erectile dysfunction but also for many of the maladies of aging. The only warning is to those men who suffer from blood clotting disorders, since ginkgo will prolong the time for blood to clot.

DHEA (Dehydroepiandosterone)

Wʜᴀᴛ ɪs ɪᴛ? DHEA has achieved a lot of popularity since its release to the market in the mid nineties. It is a hormone normally produced by the adrenal glands. Human beings naturally produce less DHEA as they age. This caught the interest of researchers, who hypothesized that perhaps this lower level of DHEA is one of the causes of age-related ailments.

Proponents say that taking supplements of DHEA may slow the aging process, help prevent heart disease, burn fat, enhance athletic performance, help prevent osteoporosis, improve mood and cognitive function, improve strength, improve the immune system, and treat depression. Disbelievers listening to this dizzying list of claims say, "Wow, and I bet it even slices and dices!"

Sex researchers are interested in it because the body converts DHEA into testosterone and estrogen. Proponents say it can therefore improve libido as well as arousal and orgasm in women and men and diminish erectile dysfunction. The dosage varies but, most commonly, 25 mg twice a day is suggested. A recent small double-blind, placebo-controlled study showed DHEA in the above dosage significantly improved libido after three to four months of use. Still, the study had only twenty-two participants, so more research is needed.

The Department of Urology at the University of Vienna, Austria, provided forty men who suffered from erectile dysfunction but who were physically capable of having an erection with either 50 mg of

DHEA or a placebo. The patients taking DHEA saw improvement in their sexual functioning. These are the positive studies. There are some who say DHEA is ineffective. In my opinion, this is a supplement that appears to have real potential, but studies on the effectiveness and safety of taking supplements are conflicting. With so many people taking it, there are sure to be more studies in the future.

WHAT TO WATCH OUT FOR. We simply don't know what long-term effects taking DHEA supplements will have on the body. We do know that DHEA is converted into potent sex hormones in the body. It may interact with other drugs, so be sure to tell your physician that you are taking it.

How to Dispel the Erectile Dysfunction Secret

When Viagra was first released, it amazed people how many thousands of men had been suffering in silence about their problems. Even with so much talk about it, a man may have a great deal of difficulty admitting he has a problem or being open to seeking treatment. What can be done to break the pattern of secretiveness?

What She Can Do: Four Things Never to Say to a Lover with Erectile Dysfunction

1. **"It's OK, honey, it really doesn't matter."** First, if this is a lie, don't tell it. He might feel better for a moment, but you will never be able to keep that lie going forever, and if you try, you might erupt with the truth at some point during an argument, causing irrevocable damage to the trust in your relationship. Second, telling him it's OK with you may take away the motivation to get the help he needs. Remember, men have not been socialized to ask for help but to figure it out for themselves. Don't encourage him to relax by telling him not having sex is OK with you. Third, he may begin to avoid sex altogether if you don't push the issue. He may also stop touching you, cuddling with you,

or even kissing you good night, thinking, Why start something I can't finish?

It's especially tempting to say "It doesn't matter" when the relationship is new. One might think, Well, he obviously never got over his divorce, or His wife's illness must have sapped him of all his sexual energy. I don't want to put pressure on him. That's what Jacqueline, fifty-four, thought when she met Dave, fifty-seven. "I thought that we had so much else going for us that it would be enough without sex. We really were great together. We had so many of the same interests, we could talk for hours. I never pressured him about sex. Six months after we started dating, he told me he'd met someone else. I found out later that *she* wasn't willing to go without sex. She forced him to see a doctor, and eventually he loved her for it."

The take-home lesson is, be understanding, but if you want to be his lover and not just his friend, be up front about it. Instead of saying it doesn't matter if he isn't functioning in bed, tell him, "Of course it matters to both of us; I want to be lovers. How can I help?"

2. "I know you're having an affair! Admit it!" Don't put the idea in his head. As one man put it, "If you're having this kind of problem in a relationship, and you're worried that something is wrong with you, you have two choices—see a urologist or see another woman."

There is no question that many men think of an affair when they have erectile dysfunction just to see if it will "work" with a different woman. But don't promote such a solution by harping and accusing. As another man said, "She already thought I was guilty, so I figured, why not just do it?"

3. "You're under stress. I'm sure it will be better next time." There are a lot of alibis you can give him to make him feel better about what is happening. But the real key to feeling better is getting treatment. The longer he goes without it, the worse it is. There are many stories of couples who went on denying the problem for years, never having sex. Then the man discovered Viagra. Suddenly *she* had a massive problem. For one, her vagina might no longer have been equipped to receive him or respond to him. For another, she may have concentrated so long on burying her sexual feelings lest she upset him that she can't conjure them up anymore.

4. "?!??!?!" Never say nothing. If you don't talk about the problem, will it disappear? That's superstition. True, you don't want to shine a spotlight on the problem and cause even more performance anxiety the next time, but to leave him there, stewing in silence, wondering what you're thinking or if you really noticed benefits neither of you. Better to say "I guess it wasn't our night; good night, I love you" than to act like nothing is happening. If you aren't saying anything because you want to avoid conflict or protect him, realize that to ignore the problem may mean that you cheat yourself out of the sexual pleasure you need and deserve. Your growing resentment may eventually destroy the relationship you are trying to protect.

So, what *can* you say at that moment when things don't work and he's scared and embarrassed, other than promise him that everything will be OK? One woman found this attitude really helped keep communication open: "I told him, 'I know I hate it when I can't respond. These things happen. If it happens again, why don't you call your internist? It could mean nothing, but I think you'll feel better.'"

How Not to Fall into the Trap of Using Him as a Mirror of Your Own Sexual Adequacy

It's easy to begin wondering if the few pounds you've gained are causing the problem or if your partner isn't turned on because he doesn't love you anymore. To stay out of that trap, remind yourself as often as possible that 90 percent of sexual dysfunction has a physical cause. Just as your losing weight won't do anything about his diabetes, chances are there's nothing you can change about yourself to rid him of erectile problems. In this culture, people tend to think, I made her come twice, or I got him so hard, as if the partner had no responsibility whatsoever. In truth, each of us is responsible for our own pleasure. One of the challenges of midlife is to give up the myths that his orgasm is a sign of your sexual adequacy or that yours is a sign of his. Even more, one has to give up thinking orgasm and sexual adequacy mean the exact same thing. Try substituting the word *pleasure* for *orgasm* as you think about sex and think about the many different types of sexual pleasure you and your partner can give each other.

Remember, too, that while his bout of erectile dysfunction has been frightening and painful for him, you have also been through a lot. The next chapter discusses some of the emotional fallout that occurs over Viagra, but the information on how to cope is just as relevant to whatever treatment a couple embarks on.

Answers to Questions Women Most Frequently Ask

"My husband won't talk about this. He says talking about it makes it worse. What can I do?"

How are you talking about it? Sure, nagging about it or fighting about it isn't going to help. Emphasize that this is most probably a physical problem that affects men his age. When he says "Don't talk about it," calmly reply, "We need to talk about it so we can figure out what to do. This is usually a medical problem. It isn't going to respond one way or another to the sound of my voice!"

Try to get him to agree that if the problem doesn't solve itself within a specific period of time he'll go for help.

"My husband knows he has a problem, and he even knows it's because of his diabetes. But he won't go for help. Now what?"

There are men who feel enormous guilt over this type of problem. They secretly believe it's happened because they're bad lovers or even bad people. Unconsciously they won't seek treatment because they feel this is a just punishment. You may have to help him release some of his grief and anger. You have to help clarify his choice: He can go on just cuddling and hugging, or he can seek treatment and resume a sex life. Help him see that he really has only these two alternatives—everything else is a fantasy. Suggest going for counseling with a trained sex therapist. If he won't go, go by yourself.

"How can I get him to admit that he has a problem and that it's his problem and not my problem? He makes me feel like it's happening because I'm not attractive or sexy enough."

This is double trouble. You may have those sinking feelings yourself. He'd very much prefer to think that it's because of you, not because of him. Don't fall for it. Emphasize "I think this is a medical problem, and neither one of us is responsible. Why don't we go and find out?" If he persists in blaming you, seek counseling so that you don't lose your own self-esteem or sexual response. Continue to emphasize "I don't want to blame you, and I don't want to be blamed, I'd rather find a solution."

What He Can Do

What most men think about when erection problems happen is "Is it me? Is it my problem? Or is it her not turning me on?" Some men will blame their partners because they want to deny their own problems. Some will go and have an affair to prove the problem isn't theirs but hers. "I'm going to see if I can get an erection with somebody else."

Here's a better approach than blaming either you or your partner:

- **Realize how frequent and preventable this problem really is.** When it happens to you, you may feel like you're very much alone. The truth is, erectile dysfunction is such a frequent problem that doctors told reporters they were getting blisters on their fingers from writing prescriptions for Viagra the moment it became available in the United States! Remember the fifty-fifty rule: 50 percent of men over the age of fifty have this problem to some degree. You're not alone, it's not unusual, and it doesn't mean you're less of a man. It means you are aging the way men normally age. There's something you can do about it very simply, without all the guilt, anger, and frustration. It's better to go for a therapeutic trial of Viagra and see if it helps than to search for someone else to try to prove something. You'll also get a big bonus from seeing your doctor and getting a workup. You'll find out if there's blood flow obstruction elsewhere in your system. You'll make sure your heart is fine, your cholesterol is in the normal range, your blood pressure is normal. If it's not, you'll be given instructions for improving your health.

- **It's important to talk about it with your partner, even though this might be the last thing you want to discuss.** She needs to know that it isn't her fault and you gain little by letting her wonder if it is. It's a myth that talking about it makes it worse. Talking about it or not talking about it isn't going to increase the blood flow to your penis, which is almost always the problem. In fact, men have taken Viagra and tried to psych themselves out of erections by thinking of things that might ordinarily make them "lose it" and found the erection remains, as one man related earlier in this chapter.

- **Realize that you may not have to take Viagra forever.** There are men who simply feel bad that they have to take a pill to have sex. They feel it makes them less of a man. But they are in the minority. The vast majority of men who need this thank their lucky stars that something is available in a simple pill that allows them to function sexually once again.

I believe that as we understand the aging process better, men will begin to see erectile dysfunction much as they do the other unpleasant signs of aging, like losing hair. It's no fun, but what's the alternative? You can learn to make the most of what you have at any age.

You may not have to be on Viagra forever. There are studies that early usage "retrains" the penis and makes Viagra eventually unnecessary. More studies need to be done, but my advice would be to take one day at a time. Let Viagra decrease your performance anxiety. Let it help you get back to the real point of nonreproductive sex—to experience pleasure.

- **Realize that this secret isn't really a secret.** If she hasn't talked to you about the problem, trust me on one thing: *she knows*. She doesn't buy that you're tired, stressed, or having a bad day, even though she'd like to. I hear about this every day in my practice. What I don't usually hear is "I think he's less of a man" or "I can't believe he needs Viagra—what a loser." I hear "Is it me?" or "How can I help?"

She isn't looking for another man. She wants *you*. At least she does today. Ignore the problem or push it under the rug, and by next year at this time, it can be an enormous elephant in the bedroom, blotting out even the best times you've had together. She has her own problems with sexuality due to aging. She has her own different needs. She wants your understanding about how her body has changed and how her sexual needs have evolved. Chances are, she will give you *her* understanding about the changes you are experiencing if you are willing to take action. You don't have to be alone in this. You can revive midlife sexuality together.

10

THE SECRET

"The Little Blue Pill Is Causing More Problems in Our Relationship than It Solves."

 Facing the Emotional Side of Viagra

WHEN YOU ASK PAULA, fifty-six, what she'd like to do with her husband's bottle of Viagra, she'll tell you: "Flush it down the toilet!"

The other night was typical. She says, "I was in the den with my laptop, in the middle of an outline for a presentation, and he sat down and started kissing my neck. He said, 'Come on, let's do it. I took the pill.'

"There was no way. I had a presentation first thing tomorrow. I *needed* this outline.

"'Who told you to take it now, without asking me?' I asked him.

"'That pill cost ten bucks! Are we going to throw good money down the drain?'

"I just glared at him. There was no way I was in the mood to make love, and I couldn't believe he took that pill without asking me how I felt. I went to sleep in the den. He was a dark cloud for the next two days. You know what I'm beginning to think? Screwing with Viagra is screwing *us*."

Psychotherapists across the nation are documenting cases of relationships breaking down and sometimes breaking up completely over Viagra. The most common reason? Viagra addresses the erection problem but does nothing to address the anxieties and doubts both partners may have.

Let's look at some of the secrets couples become anxious about when he takes Viagra.

Hers

> "When we make love now, I wonder if it's me turning him on or the Viagra."

> "I simply don't want all the sex he wants now, but I worry that he'll go looking for it elsewhere."

> "I got used to repressing my sexual feelings because of his problem. How am I supposed to just forget all that and jump back into a sex life I haven't had for six years?"

> "I found some blue pills that I think are Viagra. My husband hasn't touched me in weeks. Is he having an affair?"

> "My lover wants to use Viagra even though he doesn't have any problems, because he thinks it will make him harder and last longer. I worry it's going to make him sick. Is this dangerous?"

His

> "Should I tell her I'm taking Viagra?"

> "Why doesn't she ever want to make love? You'd think that she'd be happy about this, but instead she acts angry."

> "Why does it take so much stimulation for me to get an erection even with the Viagra?"

> "Now that I've got my erection back, I have this urge to wander."

Let's look at these issues more closely.

Is It Her or the Viagra Turning Him On?

The ability to excite a man—to see pleasure or even admiration in his eyes and to feel the proof of it when you touch him—is a sexual self-esteem builder for most women. As Karen, forty-eight, put it, "There was always something about seeing him grow bigger and harder as I touched him that made sex fun even when nothing special was happening for me. It was like a game, to see how hard I could get him."

Then Karen's husband had a bout of difficulty sustaining his erection, and the couple turned to Viagra. "Without Viagra, he would lose his erection right in the middle of sex. Viagra solved the problem, but it doesn't make me as happy as I thought it would. I feel like it's not really me turning him on."

Experts note that when Viagra first works for couples like Karen and her husband, these are usually very happy moments full of relief. It's later, often months later, when both partners may have their moments of doubt.

Karen's uneasy thought every time her husband took Viagra was that his erection had nothing to do with her. Women who have the hardest time with their partner's use of Viagra often don't have the most solid understanding of how it works.

Viagra is not an aphrodisiac or passion pill. It doesn't work without sexual stimulation. As noted in the last chapter, Viagra is a vasodilator, which means it dilates the blood vessels. It allows the release of nitric oxide from the blood vessel walls, and that causes the blood vessels to open wider. An erection is caused when the penis fills with blood and the engorged muscles of the penis compress the veins, which prevents the blood from leaving. This trapped blood causes the male hardness. What Viagra does is allow the blood vessels to open better. It does not rush blood into the penis, and it doesn't keep it there. It simply allows blood to get in if stimulation occurs.

In sum, Viagra doesn't *give* men erections—it *allows* them to have an erection in response to stimulation. When a woman is making love to a man who has taken Viagra, she is a very important part of his stimulation. If nothing turns him on, Viagra isn't going to do much—except maybe cause sinus congestion.

Sex therapists Max and Della Fitz-Gerald believe that some of the fallout from Viagra comes from a larger misunderstanding about what really causes men and women to feel turned on. Max Fitz-Gerald explains, "A person aids and abets another person's orgasm, but no one gives anyone an orgasm. We really get tremendously hung up on this in our culture: *She gave me an erection. He gave me an orgasm.* We seem to believe that each of us is responsible for the other person's turn-on or orgasm. But eroticism is an inside job. No one can turn us on if we choose not to be erotic. When you're angry at your partner, for example, he or she may do things that are erotic until the cows come home, but it can still fall on deaf ears."

Della Fitz-Gerald agrees. "In our practice we emphasize that even with Viagra the man's mind has to be involved in creating erotic thoughts. He's got to be thinking sexy thoughts, fantasizing, doing the things he would normally have done to get erect. Viagra is simply an enhancer."

Women like Karen who worry that it's the Viagra, not *them*, turning their partner on may still be dealing with the emotional fallout of their partner's erectile difficulties, even though the problem is no longer there. Often, by the time Viagra was prescribed, there has been a great degree of hurt, misunderstanding, and anxiety. She may have felt responsible for her partner's problems. Now the problem is gone, but the fear lingers: "Do I really turn him on? Am I still attractive to him?"

When the problem first occurred, it may have coincided with doubts that she was already having about her sexual desirability now that she is no longer in her thirties. In addition, some women have a hard time letting go of the feeling that they should have been able to solve the problem on their own, even when told directly by a urologist that it had zero to do with them. As one woman put it, "I feel competitive with that blue pill at times. It's like it can do things I can't. When he takes it, it also reminds me of a partner I had in the past who had to get high every time we made love. It was like I wasn't enough."

What can women do?

Check Your Self-Esteem Issues

If your self-esteem has been knocked for a loop by the sexual difficulties you've experienced as a couple, look at that squarely. You may have focused so much on him and his trouble that your own needs have gone on the back burner. You may need extra reassurance from your partner.

Telling your partner "You care more about that pill than you do about me" isn't the way to get reassurance and will almost always elicit a defensive response. The direct approach—"Do you still find me attractive?"—works for some women but fails dismally for others, who don't believe him when he says yes and end up asking the question so frequently it only makes him mad, as in this scenario:

> **Him:** "I already said you look good."
>
> **Her:** "But what do you mean *good*? If Pamela Anderson is a ten, what would you give me?"
>
> **Him:** "Honey, Pamela Anderson is in her twenties."
>
> **Her:** "So you think I look old? I don't see Pamela Anderson working to put your two kids through college."
>
> **Him:** "Who brought this up anyway? You want to know how you look? You look fine. You really do."
>
> **Her:** "What do you mean by *fine*?"

It's not wrong to need a little admiration or to ask for it. There is no shortage of middle-aged men who are stingy with compliments and feel their partners should "just know" how they feel. But what has a better chance of getting you what you want? Usually a better reaction comes from statements like "The other night when you told me how great you thought I looked when we went out to dinner really made me feel good. You really make me feel wonderful when you say things like that."

One woman admitted she had to really go digging in the ashes for reassurance. "All talk between us about being attractive, about being sexy, about turning someone on—any flirtation at all—was off-limits for a year while we had all these sexual problems. After Viagra, I needed to know I was still attractive. He'd just roll his eyes.

"Instead I started to do things that would make me feel good about myself. I exercised. I had my hair highlighted. I joined a book club, where it felt great to have people listen to my opinions with interest.

"One day I was looking at an old photo album, and I said to him, 'Remember that time we were out at that beach and you wanted me to take the top of my swimsuit off? I told you that you were crazy, but I never told you what I honestly thought: I felt so sexy. I really felt special.' I wasn't really looking for a compliment. I was actually feeling pretty good about myself. There was no pressure, just the fun of remembering that vacation. He took me in his arms, and we had the first intimate talk we'd had in what seemed like years."

If you have great memories of times he was very reassuring to you, try mentioning those times and what it meant to you. He may very well recall all of the bonuses that come from that type of giving.

Recognize That You May Have Other Issues to Deal With

Beyond feeling you're no longer "needed" to give him an erection, many other feelings may be lurking. How important are you to him these days, period? How appreciated do you feel in general? Before the crisis that brought Viagra onto your personal scene, how fulfilling was your intimate life? As one woman put it, "I want a pill that will change him an hour *after* we've had sex. A pill that will make him want to hold me, talk to me, bring me flowers."

Couples often have their own unique ways of describing themselves and their relationships to themselves or anyone who asks: He's the smarter one. She's the calm one who is great in a crisis. He's the quieter one. She's the social one who knows how to strike up a conversation with anyone. He's the powerful one. She's the sexier, more attractive one. He's conventional. She knows the latest thing happening and confidently wears the latest styles. He's the one the kids really listen to. She's the only one who can handle their parents without getting a migraine. She's clever. He's pragmatic. The list can go on and on.

Therapists will tell you that sometimes these statements are very accurate and reflect different strengths in the union. They will also tell you that some of these statements can be totally inaccurate. They are ways couples unconsciously agree to different roles in the relationship. Sometimes these statements were true in a couple's twenties, when they met, but are not true anymore. If he's the smarter one, how did she get her Ph.D. while he has only a master's degree? If he's the conventional one, how come he calmly invests in risky stocks while she agonizes because their money isn't in a low-risk mutual fund? If he's the breadwinner, how come it's her commission that paid for their new car?

Sometimes couples mutually "agree" to see each other in certain roles, even as they grow and change and those roles no longer fit the way they used to. But when sexual dysfunction occurs, the whole train is knocked off the track. Who's the powerful one now? Who's the calmer one now?

He's thrown into a type of intense self-doubt that can affect more than just the way he sees himself sexually. She has her own doubts. They both begin to reevaluate who they really are.

When he takes Viagra and it works, sometimes it's difficult for her to assume her old, comfortable role. She no longer sees him as invincible. It's difficult for him to see her as he once did. He may no longer see her as the sexy wife he's always enjoyed making love to. Now she's someone he has to prove something to.

She may also have assumed what I think of as the Florence Nightingale role. I don't mean this negatively. He was in trouble. She was understanding and nurturing to the maximum. She waited, helped, and hoped. Frankly, her support may have pulled him through in more ways than he'll ever fully realize.

But now he's *back*. He doesn't even want to think about that time. He doesn't especially want to be grateful. He wants to show his prowess and go back to the way things were.

She may be reluctant to go backward. She may have felt that he finally really needed her for the first time. She may have found strengths in herself as they faced this crisis that she still wants him to appreciate. She stayed and saw him through this. Doesn't this count for something?

This is all normal. It's evidence of how complex our relationships become as we go through so many years together. Sometimes we never see who we really are and what we're really capable of until we're *tested*.

Couples I've worked with where Viagra has been successful over-all in allowing erections begin to realize, "Well, we've still got some other issues." No pill is going to take those issues away. Couples who face and address those issues and resolve them often find that the whole erectile dysfunction nightmare ends up being a win-win situation. They grow. They release themselves from relationship roles that no longer fit. They move forward and start anew.

Accept Your Ambivalence About the Little Blue Pill

Chances are, he feels it, too. Men who are taking Viagra wish they didn't have to rely on a pharmaceutical for an erection or still have hopes that the problem will disappear on its own. As one man put it, "I kept think-ing that there was something wrong with me that the doctors just couldn't find and that Viagra was covering up a major symptom of it." It isn't unusual for a couple to need an additional appointment with the urologist or doctor who prescribed Viagra after it's been successful. You're calmer now, better able to listen and take in the information. Have the doctor explain Viagra to you again and why it's necessary.

When Viagra Helps—but Only a Little

While some women feel less "needed" once Viagra comes on the scene, others are frustrated because he has Viagra and sex is still pretty infre-quent. After the initial relief of finding out that everything is working, some men still don't crave sex very often.

Other women will tell you that their partners are interested, but it still seems like sex is a real workout. One woman whose husband began taking Viagra admitted: "He needs what seems like a ton of stimulation to get an erection, even after he takes the pill. Sometimes I get so tired I want to say, 'Let's just forget the whole thing.' Is it supposed to be this difficult?"

There is a lot of misunderstanding about what Viagra is supposed to do. Sometimes a man will tell me, "The Viagra isn't working." Viagra is sometimes confused with the instant, four-hour "injection erection" men get from something like Caverject. After the injection, you have an erection whether you want it or not. What happens with the Viagra is much more subtle. Stimulation has to take place.

Some men's problems with blood flow are more severe than others. Viagra comes in two doses: 50 mg and 100 mg. If it still seems like it takes an inordinate amount of stimulation, consider increasing the dosage. If the dosage has been 50 mg, take one pill and cut another pill in half and take 75 mg.

Keep in mind that, for most men, Viagra really works in two ways. One is physically, helping blood flow to the penis. But it also has a psychological effect. It relieves the mental pressure of wondering every time he has sex, "Is it going to work?"

After that first failure, many men have that question in their minds every time they make love. Once he sees that he can get an erection and maintain it long enough for intercourse, that clears his mind a bit. In the beginning he may need a lot of stimulation, just to combat this mental hurdle. Each time it works, his mind becomes a little clearer. If he can get to a point where he's used the Viagra and it's worked frequently enough, and he's more confident about his ability to have erection and penetration, less direct stimulation may be necessary. He may even find that he gets turned on and everything works by itself, without taking the pill. It's almost like reteaching the penis to get the blood flow and reteaching the brain to accept the fact that everything is OK.

This is not to say, however, that one should take more and more Viagra if it clearly isn't working. As discussed in the last chapter, many factors can contribute to causing erectile dysfunction. Viagra is popular because it works very well in men whose problems are caused by reduced blood flow. If Viagra is clearly having no effect, or a very minimal one, reevaluate its continued use with a physician.

What if He *Isn't* Willing to Try Viagra?

There are entire books on the subject of how women can get the men they love to go to the doctor. Those books are merely talking about regular checkups. Getting him to go to a doctor and admit he isn't functioning in bed can be a major hurdle.

Charlene, thirty-seven, has been married for six years to Bill, fifty-eight. "I'm an adult, I need a sex life," Charlene complained bluntly. "I don't want to go looking for someone else, although it's crossed my mind. I think the least he could do is get a prescription for Viagra and try it once. He tells me there are side effects, that people see blue bubbles or feel like they can't breathe, or they have heart attacks, and he's not going to take something that could kill him. Finally he told me he isn't going to talk about it anymore. I feel cheated. My friends tell me this is what I get for marrying a much older man. But Bill looks thirty-five, works out every day, is in great shape, and we could be having great years ahead together instead of this constant fighting."

If you can identify with Charlene's story, keep in mind that your partner probably *will* experience side effects when he takes Viagra. He can be afraid for that reason. As with any medication, the first time he takes it he's in uncharted territory. Hundreds of thousands of men have persevered in spite of those fears. After all, this drug has rapidly become a best-seller. What do they know that you and he need to know?

Eddie, forty-eight, tells a story that can be enlightening to women who are having this battle with their partners. While some men will try any drug, any kick, anything that will enhance their sex drive, Eddie wasn't one of them. He says, "A couple of years ago I went through a bad time with my career. My parents were sick, one of my close friends had died, and I was really depressed. Over a pitcher of margaritas one night, I spilled the story to a friend from work, and he said, 'Listen, you've got to try Paxil. It's amazing. I feel like a new person.' And, of course, the next thing he did was give me a couple.

"That night I took one. Dumb thing to do. To make a long story short, I had a complete anxiety attack that went on for hours. My wife and I were up all night. We were on the hot line with the poison control people, and I was sure I was dying. My buddy forgot to tell me that you work up to a full dose—he'd been on it a year.

"For months after that, I didn't even want to take an aspirin. Two years later, I'm having this problem in bed. I can't get it up, or I can't keep it up. It's a real shot in the head to my ego. Everything in the newspapers I read is about this new drug, Viagra. On TV I hear an internist say he got a blister on his hand from writing so many prescriptions for

Viagra the first week it was approved. Then came those stories that men had died from it. I could only think, That'll be my luck.

"Then my wife came to bed one night in sexy lingerie. This was something she'd never done. She was standing there, dressed in something from Victoria's Secret, and I was feeling absolutely nothing.

"A week later she prepared this romantic dinner with candles and wine. That night we were cuddling in bed. She went to the bathroom, and I knew she was putting her diaphragm in. When she came out, I pretended I was asleep. She shook my shoulder. I turned over and buried myself under the covers. She left the bed. I heard her crying in the bathroom. I couldn't even go in there and hold her and try to explain. It was a turning point. I had to do something.

"The urologist appointment wasn't that big a deal. The first thing you learn is that urologists have seen and heard it all. He told me *he'd* tried Viagra and exactly what to expect. He explained that the men who had died from it had been on cardiac drugs. Still, I was nervous. I got ten fifty-milligram pills, and that night I broke one in half, just to see what would happen. I felt a little bit of what was going on, and I realized I wasn't going to die from it. Yes, I felt a little congestion in my face. More than that, I was anxious; my heart was beating fast and my mouth went dry. But twenty minutes later, I knew I wasn't going to die from it. The next night I tried a fifty-milligram, and I made love to my wife for the first time in months. My advice to men? On your first try, don't appear in front of your wife with a tray of cocktails and the little blue pill on a napkin, because the first time may not be that great."

Here are some other suggestions that have worked for women whose husbands were reluctant to seek help:

- Don't tell him his fears are nonsense and that he isn't going to have these side effects. He very well might. Say "I'm concerned about side effects, too. Why don't we find out more about them?" Emphasize the positive. Point out that urologists now have a number of years of monitoring their patients' experience with it—and many have experimented on their own with Viagra. A good physician can tell him exactly what it's like and point him to research that will be reassuring.

- Saying "If you really loved me, you'd be willing to try Viagra" probably won't help. He's liable to tell you that if you really loved him you'd stop harping on the problem. This is probably one time it really makes sense to separate sex from love. He's vulnerable, and he needs to know you love him, even if the two of you aren't having sex. Emphasize that you miss the sex in the relationship because of the fun the two of you used to have, not because it's the only way you or he expresses love.
- If he's convinced that he doesn't need help from the little blue pill, and the problem will go away by itself once he's under less stress, don't argue. Tell him that you wish the problem would go away by itself, too. Try to reach an agreement that if that isn't the case after a month or two, or whatever deadline you can both agree to, he'll at least read more of the research about Viagra. And resist the impulse to remind him of that deadline every day.
- One woman admitted that the way she finally convinced her husband to try Viagra after sex therapy and couple's therapy had failed was to say "If you take one, I'll take one, too."

When Viagra Is a Secret in the Bedroom

"I found these blue pills in my husband's shirt pocket. Are they Viagra? If they are, there's going to be trouble, because he hasn't touched me for months."

Just as there are women who aren't entirely honest about how aroused they feel or who may say "Honey, that was great!" when their mind was really making a grocery list, there are bound to be men who won't share the fact that they are using Viagra.

There are lots of blue pills. Paxil, a best-selling prescription anti-depressant, comes to mind. Even the amoxicillin tabs the vet prescribes for your cat's urinary infection are little blue pills! But you can tell a pill is Viagra if it is small, diamond shaped, and has the name *Pfizer* printed on it.

What's he doing with Viagra? Don't jump to quick conclusions. One of the latest gag gifts men report receiving these days for their fiftieth birthdays is a bottle of Viagra—it used to be a bottle of Geritol! But if your partner does have a prescription for Viagra, there is every chance he's opting to try it, and there can be many reasons why he hasn't told you. Many men—I suspect more men than not, although this is impossible to measure—try Viagra alone for the first time. In other words, they take the pill and see if they can stimulate themselves mentally and physically. If a man has been suffering from any degree of performance anxiety, it makes sense that he might want to see if it "works" and exactly how it works before he uses it with a partner.

Is he having an affair and using the Viagra with someone else? The woman who found Viagra in her husband's shirt pocket suspected that but opted to handle it this way. She said, "I found these. They're Viagra, right? I'd be interested in seeing what it does, too. It could be fun." Her partner, who had gotten the pills from a friend, was happy to oblige.

Every relationship is different, and for some women such a discovery would be intolerable. The best one can do is see the problem in terms of its possibilities. When was the last time you had a discussion with your partner about sex, what it means in your relationship, and what you can do together to make it better? If you can't discuss it, why not? What would it require for you to be able to have a meaningful conversation about your sex life? What are your wants and needs? If your partner hasn't shown any signs of needing Viagra, what does it mean that he's pursuing it? Is Viagra something one should use recreationally?

Should Men Who Don't Really Need Viagra Take It as an Enhancer?

"The man I've been involved with for two years is definitely a risk taker," sighs Sharon, forty-one. "He races around on his motorcycle, he hang glides, and he always says there's nothing he won't try once. On his forty-sixth birthday he comes home with a bottle of champagne and takes this blue pill out of his pocket. 'What do you need that for?' I said, absolutely amazed that he'd even think of such a thing. 'Come on, let's try it,' he said. 'Let's see if it does anything different.'

"He scared the hell out of me. I wouldn't let him take it. He still wants to. I keep telling him it'll make him sick. Will it?"

There are a number of issues to consider if you, like Sharon, have a partner who wants to experiment with Viagra recreationally. Obviously, if this is a man who borrowed a pill from a friend and has a serious heart condition and is taking nitroglycerin, it's a very dangerous way to get an extra "kick" in bed. But Sharon's partner didn't have a history of cardiac problems or medications.

There's no data on the number of men who have simply tried Viagra once to see if it would enhance their experience in bed. When Viagra was first released, droves of journalists—male and female—simply took one to enhance their own stories about it. It doesn't take much of a leap of faith to imagine that many of their readers simply followed suit.

Let's look at another issue, however. As men age, their erections are often less hard, their orgasms less intense. You might not notice it, but he knows the difference. The hope that he can get back that youthful feeling may be his real reason for experimenting with Viagra, even though he may not admit this and insist he is just doing it "to see what happens." It may or may not give him the added boost he desires.

A benefit of Viagra is that the recovery time—the time it takes a man to become erect again—may be shorter. The man who wants to have sex twice in one night and isn't able to may achieve some help from the little blue pill. Although many men awaken with an erection in the morning, some men find that the erection they wake up with the next morning is stronger, and it allows them to have sex again, because the drug is still in their system.

Does it endanger a man to take Viagra when he doesn't really need it? There's no evidence that it does. Most physicians' bias about medication is that it is for the people who really need it—and that they should take the lowest dose that will do the job. Viagra isn't meant to make good *better* but to make OK better or bad into good.

Some women have no problem with a partner who wants to experiment with drugs or other "enhancers" while making love. Some women crave it. Others have a big issue with it. "I don't want a man who needs to be high or needs to be drunk to have sex with me," says one woman. "Viagra falls into the same category, in my mind." Communication is key here. Ask him to explain what he thinks he's going to get out of using Viagra with as open a mind as you can muster.

"I Don't Want All the Sex He Wants Now That He's Taking Viagra"

This is one of the most common complaints psychotherapists hear about Viagra: *He never wanted sex, I got used to it, and now, with Viagra, he wants it every other day.* Leslie, fifty-six, is a case in point. "We had so much else going for us, to be honest, I just thought, So what? It's not the end of the world if we don't have sex anymore. We have our kids, my gift shop, his law practice, a beautiful grandchild. Like everyone else I know, sex was pretty hot in our twenties, but by the time we hit our forties, it was once a month. In our fifties, it was even less. So it wasn't like I was missing all that much. And we didn't talk about it. He just stopped initiating it, and I just put it out of my mind.

"Then he hears about Viagra. Who didn't? A couple of his friends started using it. They didn't even get it from a doctor, but off the Internet. He has dinner with his good friend, an internist, who prescribes it for him. My whole feeling was, why? Sex didn't seem to matter to him for the last ten years. He never said a word. Now he wants all of this sex all of a sudden. I don't understand it, and I don't want it."

First and foremost, it's wonderful if a couple can decide together that they want and need Viagra to achieve a common goal of better sex as they get older. Viagra can be the answer to what many people pray for. But it's not always that easy or that clear.

Women like Leslie whose husbands embrace Viagra and the new sexual strength it gives them sometimes feel like this pill has invaded a very settled, accept-life-as-it-comes-and-make-the-most-of-it marriage, which often took a lot of compromise to achieve. If they've submerged their sexual feelings and have had no sexual stimulation for a number

of years, starting all over again can be difficult both physically and emotionally. Chapter 1 includes a discussion of how to deal with physical challenges. But emotional challenges are often the greater hurdle.

If your partner is having success with Viagra, realize that there will
be a honeymoon period, perhaps lasting several months, where new sexual prowess is at the top of his mind. He may want you more than he's
wanted you in years. If you can muster a sense of humor about this, you
will probably find that, several months down the line, things will return
to a less frenzied need to have sex because suddenly it's working so well
again. You'll probably assume the pattern you had before there were sexual problems.

The bigger issue for the woman who finds her husband to be
thrilled with Viagra, while she could take sex or leave it, is this: You may
have learned to accept what you thought was the end of sex with your
partner. You aren't alone if underneath that acceptance and compromise
was a lot of unspoken anger. Now that he wants to resume your sex life,
you may feel even angrier, and that's perfectly normal given what has
happened in your relationship. It's not unusual for a man to get so bold,
once Viagra helps him function again, that he gets a big attitude about
it: *If you don't want sex, I'll find someone who does.*

What do you do then? Dr. Della Fitz-Gerald has this advice:
"Underneath that indifference or turnoff there's often a very angry
woman. She's learned to deny her need for sexual pleasure as a way to
protect herself. When you get past that protective layer in therapy, you
often find a woman who is coping with a lot of hurt and a sense of rejection. There's a lot of injury here, and she needs help to get her back to
the feeling that she is an erotic person. She did whatever was very natural to protect herself, and now she has to ask, 'What do I really value
in the long run? Am I willing to work through the anger? Am I willing
to work through the turnoff? Am I willing to work through the hurt and
then literally learn to turn myself back on again? Do I choose to take
the risk to do whatever is necessary to tap back into what is erotic and
seductive to me and share that with my partner, and, in turn, together?'
It's really a risky business."

Max Fitz-Gerald adds, "The key is the desire to be erotic again.
We can't give that to anybody. We frequently see this in some older cou-

ples in their sixties and seventies where sex has never been pleasurable for her and she participated simply for him. When he could no longer maintain an erection, she was invested in this. She doesn't want him to use a product like Viagra and become erect again."

Regardless of what has gone on in the past, however, each day many women succeed in learning to tap back into their eroticism. If you have the desire, you can do it, too. You can find out what's blocking your natural function, look carefully at your different feelings and what you've done to protect yourself, and open yourself to eroticism again. At that point, Viagra becomes nothing more than what it is—something to help you enhance your sex lives when more than just desire is needed.

Getting the Viagra Secret Out of the Bedroom

I've discussed the impact Viagra has on the female partner, but there is no doubt that men have their own emotional issues that come up once the thrill of knowing that everything is working again wears off.

A man is usually so excited that this drug is working for him that his first impulse is to grab his partner and say essentially, "Hey, I want to show you what I can do!" That's probably the last thing on her mind. My advice to men is to treat your partner almost as if you were courting her on a first date. You can't just pounce. You've gradually got to get back to the tenderness, the touching, the kissing—to all of the things you avoided before because you felt that it would signal her sexually and you wouldn't be able to perform. You've recaptured what you lost. Now you need to recapture what the two of you have lost as a couple. It's going to take patience. She may have spent years repressing her own sexual feelings to protect you, and it may take time to bring them to the surface again. You may have pushed her away. Now you're inviting her back, but it shouldn't just be an invitation to go to bed. It should be an invitation to begin getting back the tenderness again, to begin sharing the relationship again that you both have put out of your minds for different reasons.

11

Ten Smart Ways to Age-Proof Your Sex Life

A Private Consultation with Dr. Altman

MIDLIFE, WHETHER IT includes perimenopause, menopause, or "manopause," can truly be *a signal for the future* from the point of view of health, sex, and quality of life. Midlife is a time to reevaluate and make important decisions—psychological, emotional, and medical—that will affect the second half of your life. There is a very good chance that if you're between the ages of forty and sixty, you've got a solid thirty-plus years left ahead of you.

Sexual fitness is, of course, tied directly to both physical and emotional fitness. In this last chapter, I'm going to reemphasize some of the points that have been made throughout the book and add some important suggestions that I think have helped my patients maintain their sexual fitness over the years.

Here are ten tips for lifelong sexual fitness.

1. Learn to Use All of Your Senses When You Make Love

John Denver got right to the point in his song "You Fill Up My Senses." In sex, romance, and life, follow his lead and fill up your senses. The more you use them, the more responsive you will become.

Touch

While all of the five senses are equally important, touch is one of the most sensual. Every square inch of your fingers has thirteen hundred nerve endings, and there are approximately seventy-five thousand nerve endings in your hands. Remember when we were little kids and our parents dragged us to dance class where we were supposed to dance with a member of the opposite sex? Well, the guys kind of stayed on one side of the room and the girls on the other until somebody got up enough nerve to walk across the room and ask for a dance. At most of the dances I went to, the girls were more socially adept and wound up coming across to ask the guys. Usually the first thing you did was stick out your hand and invite that person to dance. They, in turn, placed their hand in yours. It was very awkward, but it was the touching that everyone was afraid of. As you got older and began to date, one of the first things you did was hold hands. So why do we stop doing it now? Why do we stop holding hands in midlife? Touch—normal, everyday touching—is important. Not only holding hands when you get a chance to but what I call *walk-by touching*: simply walking by your partner or your lover and just touching him or her. It doesn't have to be skin to skin. You can touch your partner's arm or bottom as you walk by. Just touching says volumes even though not a word is spoken: *I acknowledge you. I acknowledge your presence in my life. I acknowledge how much I care about you.* All from a simple touch.

Dancing is another way of touching. It's said that men and women who dance well are great in bed. There's a well-known dance in North Carolina called the shag that is especially sensual and provocative. But any dance can encourage touch, regardless of speed, type, or location. If you don't know how to dance, it's never too late to learn.

Give your partner a massage. Do it with oils or in candlelight. Even if you don't know what you're doing, just the touch, just the squeezing of muscles, whether it's a light touch or a heavy touch, is delectably sensual. Some of the most sensual feelings can be gained even with massage of the hands or especially the feet.

Kissing is absolutely one of the most sensual practices that human beings can engage in, and there really is an art to it. It's time to learn or relearn how to kiss. Spend time kissing. Spend time licking and touching and enjoying the kiss and the caress, and remember that kissing doesn't necessarily have to be passionate. It can be soft, gentle kissing and wandering with the tongue inside your lover's mouth. Do it slowly, then reach a crescendo and do it with more passion and fervor and then come back to slow again. Remember that there are other places to kiss than the mouth. Kissing the erotic areas, such as the neck or the ears, can be incredibly sensual. Navigate his or her "love map." Even before the sexual areas that are incredibly sensitive to kissing, such as the nipples or clitoral area, start with the fingers. Kissing and sucking on someone's fingers or toes can be delightfully enticing and a wonderful turn-on. Spending time with your fingers in your lover's mouth and getting turned on by the feeling of his or her tongue is a sensual way to begin making love. Spend time doing this and you may find you'll have a wonderful lovemaking session that is only kissing. It's a fact that touching your partner causes the release of a hormone from the pituitary gland called *oxytocin*. It is believed that oxytocin is responsible for bonding and feelings of closeness and love. So "reach out and touch someone."

Finally, oral sex is the ultimate kissing, but it's so important to communicate with each other about what turns the other on. Many men are very resistant to hearing this because they feel it isn't macho to take directions. "I know what will turn you on," they think. Sometimes that's not the case, because sometimes oral sex enjoyment changes as you age. So follow directions and give directions.

During actual lovemaking, touching plays a very important role, whether it's gentle touching of the face or stroking or scratching of the back. Sensitive areas such as the anal area are also very important. If your partner likes it, putting pressure on the anal area during intercourse can drive him or her wild, especially during orgasm. Use all of these sensitive touching areas in your lovemaking and you'll make it far better.

Taste

Taste has to do with your ability both to taste and to smell. Without smell you couldn't taste, which is why you lose your sense of taste when you have a cold. Concentrate on the taste of your lover's mouth during a kiss or the skin when you're kissing your lover's body. Feeding your lover, even if it's just at the table and has nothing to do with the sex act, can be very sensual. We all remember Jennifer Beals in *Flashdance* teaching us how to eat lobster sensually. Bring food into your lovemaking. Feed each other. Share your food of lovemaking.

Drink wine. Take wine into your mouth and, as you kiss, deposit it into your lover's mouth. Spill wine on the skin and lick it off, especially around the breasts.

Smell

As I said, smell is very close to taste. It is a sense of its own, especially when it comes to love and lovemaking. There are some smells that stimulate us to make love, and there are other smells that stimulate us to stay as far away from each other as we can possibly get. Winifred Cutler, in her book *Love Cycles*, describes pheromones, which are smells or odors that can cause menstruation and cycles to become more regular or to become irregular. They are also smells that can cause sexual response in humans. Perfumes are generally based on this concept. Wear a perfume, cologne, or aftershave that your lover enjoys; and if it's one that you don't enjoy, say so. Find one you both love, and remember, while perfume or cologne can be a turn-on, it can also be a turnoff if you choke the room with it. Subtlety is far more sexual than hitting someone over the head with it. Use of fragrances during lovemaking can be very sensual as well. This includes the scent of a burning candle or incense.

Then, of course, we have the smell of lovemaking, the smell of the perspiration of lovemaking, and of course, the smell of your lover's body, especially the musky odor of the vagina. This smell should be a turn-on. If it's not, if there's something foul about it, look into why that odor is there. See your gynecologist about it.

Sight

Use your eyes. Watch each other. Watch each other dress. Watch each other undress. Watch each other when you're eating a meal together or just walking through a room. When you're shopping and he's with you, and he's watching you turn, look at him and wink or just lick your tongue around your lips while he is looking. Enjoy what you see. Get turned on by what you see, whether it's your lover or it's a beautiful day and you're with each other.

When it comes to lovemaking, use your sight for visual stimulation by experimenting with different types of lighting such as candles or colored lightbulbs. Experiment with sexy clothing. Just lower the lights when you make love rather than turning them off, because part of the wonderful sense of sight is watching each other directly or indirectly in a mirror. Watch your lover as he or she achieves an orgasm. Watch his or her facial expressions. Watch how your partner's body moves. It's one of the very few times you will see him or her out of control with nothing holding your lover back. Enjoy watching that. You're part of it. Watch and revel in what you see.

Sound

The most important sound is the sound of communicating with each other. The couple that loses communication will soon lose a relationship. Communicate what you like or dislike. Be as positive as you can in this communication. It's one of the hardest things for midlife couples to do, because they know each other so well, which can lead to a lot of negative communication. Stay positive. Compliment each other whenever you can: *That outfit looks beautiful on you. Your hair looks wonderful today. God, you look sexy. I love the smell of your aftershave.* Communicate about sex, what you want, what you like, what you're willing to try.

Laugh. The sound of laughter is a wonderful, wonderful sound. Make each other laugh. Make each other smile. There is passion even in laughter.

Stimulate your sense of sound with music, any kind of music, whatever music you or your lover likes. Make love to music. Have subtle music in the background. Or even without lovemaking, just listening to music with each other can be sensual. Whether it's symphony, rock music, country music, or any music you both enjoy, listen to music together and share it together.

During lovemaking itself, listen to the sounds of making love. Listen to each other's breathing. Listen to your own breathing. Listen to the noise of lovemaking. Talk to each other, whether you say sweet words or use dirty words. Use them. Listen. Say them. Enjoy them.

Finally, there is nothing more sensual than the sound of your lover's orgasm. Listen. Take it in. It's meant for you; no one else hears it (we hope). And when you achieve an orgasm, don't hold back with sound. Don't have a quiet orgasm. Explode. Let it out. It's a wonderful turn-on to your partner and an incredibly primal sound.

2. Make Sex Fun Again and Be Romantic

There are couples who report to me that the best sex of their lives has occurred in midlife and beyond. What do these couples know that the rest of us should know? Many couples feel that at midlife they're finally free to enjoy themselves. They are free to enjoy each other. Many pressures are gone. The concerns about pregnancy, the annoyances of menstruation or irregular bleeding and PMS are gone. This can be a wonderful sexual time in your life.

Get rid of the secret of boredom in the bedroom. Remember the term *sparkles*. While we can't get the fire back because that fire is a newness, a nervousness, an anxiety that enhances those early sexual experiences, we can get sparkles back. Use those sparkles to enhance the fun of sex.

First, the bubble bath. Bubble baths are sensual, wonderful, relaxing, and a time when you can escape all the pressures of the outside world. Men, I'm talking to you as well. Take a bubble bath with your lover, with your spouse. Sit in that bubble bath with those great big bubbles. Got a problem with your body image? In a bubble bath you can't see each other because of all those big, lovely bubbles. Stimulate your minds as you're sitting in the bubble bath as well as stimulating yourself sexually. Get that relaxation. A bubble bath is wonderful relaxation. It's sensual. It's stimulating, and it can be a wonderful break in the day to renew yourself and renew the time with your partner. Catch up where nobody can interrupt you and make sure of that by leaving the phone outside the bathroom. When you get out of the bath and you're warm and relaxed, what better time to dry off and make soft, gentle love.

Try leaving love notes or little pictures for your partner. Place them in your partner's clothing so when he or she reaches into a pocket during the day, your partner can take something out that says "Love you!" or "We made love here!" or whatever and bring a smile to his or her face.

An example of this was the old Polaroid commercial where a man is at his desk at work when his wife calls. She asks him to come home, and he responds, "Honey, I can't, I'm in the middle of a lot of work. When she asks again, his response is the same. She then tells him to look in his attaché case. When he does, he finds two Polaroid pictures that cause him to smile. He gets back on the phone and says, "I'll be right home." That's the kind of thing that would be a wonderful sparkle to a relationship.

Do the unexpected, whether it be surprising your lover with flowers or even a surprise weekend away. Preparing dinner at home when it's not expected, a lovely little candlelight dinner that either of you can prepare for the other, can be highly romantic.

Make out in a car. Make out or even go as far as to have sex in the changing room at your favorite department store — as long as you're sure no one's around and nobody's looking. Watch out for the cameras in those changing rooms!

Have a picnic on a hillside somewhere and make love on a tablecloth. Read poetry to each other under a tree somewhere. Poetry mixes music with words.

Another wonderfully romantic thing to do is have an affair in the afternoon with your spouse. Plan to meet one afternoon at a hotel, check in, and tell the people behind the desk that you want the room just for the afternoon and that you're going to be there with your wife. They'll all laugh at you and wink at you. If one of you happens to be away traveling on business or traveling for whatever reason, call and make love over the phone. Have phone sex. It's both sensual and an intellectual challenge to be able to talk through lovemaking, to describe your lovemaking to your lover accurately enough to turn him or her on. Choose your own sparkles, and whatever they are, allow them to make your sex life fun again.

3. Renew Your Life

It's difficult to renew the passion in our relationships if we're weary of everything else in our lives. Sometimes, boredom with a partner is really a symptom of an inner boredom and a secret wish that someone can magically take that feeling away and make us feel alive again. Unfortunately, no one can do it for you.

Begin a renewal process to your life. Try something you haven't tried before. Change your job, finish up your profession, and choose another one. Become more independent. If you haven't worked before, especially if you've been a mother bringing up children, go to work—paid or volunteer. Be exposed to other people and viewpoints. Enter midlife with that important triad of questions: Where have I been? Where am I going? Who am I going with? Sit down and reevaluate what's important to you. Reevaluate what's important to you and your partner together. Reevaluate the friends you have, where you live, how you spend your time. One patient excitedly told me, "I had such a wonderful feeling during my New Year's celebration. I'm going to go back to school or get a job. This is going to be the year of my renewal." Follow that example.

4. Exercise Daily

Exercise is very closely related to sexuality. Exercise can affect your body image, your capacity to make love and to last for a long lovemaking encounter. It can improve your sleep. It can improve your mood throughout the day. It can improve your general health. All of these are important to your sexuality.

Remember, there are two major kinds of exercises—aerobic exercise and strength training—and both are incredibly important for men and women at midlife.

There are two major benefits to aerobic exercise: cardiovascular benefits and fat burning. This kind of exercise is especially good for helping you get rid of that tire around your middle. The best way to do aerobic exercise is twenty to thirty minutes of strenuous aerobic exercise in the morning, before you eat or drink anything other than water. It can be done on a treadmill or a StairMaster. You can read or watch TV while you're doing it or listen to music. You can also walk or run outside. If you do it first thing in the morning after you've awakened, and before eating, you will lose three times as much fat tissue as if you do it at any other time during the day. This is because you have fasted for approximately six to nine hours since dinner the night before and you have no carbohydrate load available to burn for energy. Your body has to fuel itself from its storage of fat. You gain even more benefit if you minimize your carbohydrate intake at dinner the night before, especially if you're eating late. If you have to eat late in the evening for whatever reason, avoid the breads, pastas, potatoes, rice, and, of course, desserts, and eat mostly protein.

The other important kind of exercise, as I mentioned, is strength training, either using free weights or machines that give your muscles resistance. In my opinion, this is even more important than aerobic exercise. Strength training or resistance training means using your muscles against resistance, which builds muscle mass. The increase in muscle mass then increases your metabolic rate. I hear so many of my patients complain that they're not eating any more than they used to and they just can't lose any weight. "I used to be able to lose three or four pounds in a week if I just eased up on my diet so that I could fit into what I wanted to wear that weekend. Now I can't do that at all. What's wrong?" In truth, there's nothing wrong; it's just the normal natural slowing of metabolism as we age. If that metabolism is low enough, when you eat, what you take in will be less frequently burned for energy and more frequently stored as fat. So, use strength training to increase your metabolism. Strength training is also wonderful for your body image, for diminishing PMS and depression, and for increasing arousal and orgasm. It has also been shown to increase libido. Growth of muscle mass also increases your oxygen capacity, which means you'll be able to last longer in whatever you're doing. If you can't get to a gym or if you can't afford to join one, just buy a couple of sets of dumbbells, starting low, maybe at three, five, and eight pounds, even up to ten pounds, and you can exercise every muscle group using dumbbells in your own home. Strength training can be a very important choice in midlife.

5. Use It or Lose It

To most gynecologists, the phrase *use it or lose it* refers to the vagina. After menopause, the vagina can lose its elasticity due to the lack of estrogen. The blood flow to the vaginal tissues is diminished, also hampering the ability of estrogen to get to the vagina even in some women on hormone replacement therapy. *Use it or lose it* applies here to helping the vagina maintain its elasticity. One can "use it" by having intercourse or any kind of sexual activity, including masturbation if a partner is not available.

The same holds true for the bladder, because after menopause, without estrogen being present, the bladder can also become less elastic. This can cause more frequent urination, especially at night. Because of the loss of elasticity, the bladder is no longer able to fill to the extent that it used to be able to before, signaling that you have to empty the bladder. That signaling process occurs with a much smaller volume of urine in the bladder. So *use it or lose it* with respect to the bladder means drinking lots of water, making sure the bladder can stretch with increasing amounts of water to remain able to hold as much urine as it could prior to menopause.

But most important, *use it or lose it* goes far beyond just the vagina and bladder. It has to do with the use of your mind and your body during and after midlife. *Use it or lose it* applies to the eyes, the ears, the mind, the brain. You need to keep your mind stimulated. Don't sit passively in front of a TV set for long periods of time. Read. Do puzzles. Look at artwork. Go to museums. Be stimulated. Read poetry. Write poetry or prose. All of these things can help stimulate the mind and keep it working.

Remember that the body is a unique physiologic entity. It tends to put blood flow where that blood is needed, where the activity is happening. When you eat, blood flows to the gastrointestinal system. When you exercise, blood flows to the muscles. When you think, blood flows to your brain. Keep that blood flow going. When you're having sex, blood flows both to the brain and to the sexual organs. If blood is used to flowing to an organ or system, it will flow there more easily. That's one of the reasons some men find that after they use Viagra for extended amounts of time, they can sometimes go without it and still have the blood flow to the penis as it did with the Viagra, because the system was used to doing that. It's like training for any athletic event. Use it or lose it.

6. Maintain Your Vaginal Fitness

Vaginal fitness goes beyond *use it or lose it*. How do you keep the vagina fit? First of all, whether or not you've had vaginal deliveries of children, it is important to keep the muscles of the pelvic floor that surround the vagina healthy and strong. If they weaken, you may have to deal with *pelvic relaxation syndrome*, which can allow the bladder, uterus, or neighboring structures to protrude or hang out of the vagina. Keeping these muscles strong also can prevent leakage of urine or stress incontinence. You'll know you have this problem if you leak urine every time you cough, sneeze, laugh, or lift a heavy object.

How does one keep the vaginal muscles fit? Kegel exercises are often suggested. In these exercises, you contract the pelvic floor muscles to try to keep them strong. Women can learn to do Kegel exercises by teaching themselves to stop urination in midstream, holding the urine back. Kegel exercises are done when you're not urinating but sitting or standing. However, Kegel exercises don't often work as well as we wish they would, and there's a simple reason why. When you do strength training exercises in the gym, you need to put a weight in your arm when you're exercising your biceps or use a machine that gives resistance to the contraction of that muscle. An effective way to make Kegel exercises work better and faster is by doing those exercises against resistance. You may not believe this, or you may find it humorous, but there are special weights that can be placed inside the vagina against which Kegel exercises can be done, giving the needed resistance to strengthen the muscles. One might call this a *modified Kegel exercise* or a *Kegel with resistance*. Vaginal weights are fashioned after the ancient Chinese Ben Wah balls, which used to be used by Chinese nobility and royalty to strengthen the vaginas of the young women they used as concubines. This concept was then transformed in the 1950s by a Hungarian physician who produced these vaginal weights. They are tear-shaped, and each of the five vaginal weights used is a little heavier than the one before.

Here's how they're used: Weight number one is put into the vagina. It has a little nylon string attached, much like a tampon, so it can be removed. With it in the vagina, you walk or stand upright fifteen minutes twice a day. Be sure to wear panties, which can protect you in case it falls out, so it doesn't land on your foot and hurt your toe. When the weight is in the vagina, you will notice a sensation of wanting to hold it in. This is the resistance. As you hold in the weight, you'll be flexing your pelvic floor muscles and strengthening them. Do this twice a day, fifteen minutes at a time, with weight number one until you no longer feel an urge to hold that weight in. That means you're beyond that weight. Then you go to number two. You can keep advancing them until you get to number five. By the time you're holding number five in and no longer feeling the urge to hold it in, you've completed the series. At this point, you should definitely notice a difference either in your problem with loss of urine or during intercourse, especially the ability to squeeze on the penis.

But, as with any other weightlifting, if you stop doing it, the muscles will ultimately relax again. To avoid this, once you've surpassed number five, once a month put in number five twice a day for a week and you'll be able to restrengthen the pelvic floor muscles and keep them toned. Patients with urinary stress incontinence have often been able to avoid surgery after using these vaginal weights. They have also found intercourse far more pleasurable because they notice that they're able to tighten around the penis during intercourse, which gives a special sensation to their partner.

Somewhat related to this is jogging's effect on vaginal fitness. Ever since human beings stood up on two legs to look around and decided to stay upright, two major problems have evolved. One is lower back pain, and the second is pelvic relaxation because of the pull of gravity as we stay on our feet. When you jog regularly, you increase the pull of gravity on these pelvic organs every time your feet hit the pavement. Thus, while jogging is an excellent exercise for your heart, your brain, and your mood, it does have its downside as far as pelvic relaxation is concerned.

Another exercise to participate in with care is bicycling. Regular long-distance biking, especially using a narrow racing seat, can put a considerable amount of pressure on the area of your bottom where the nerves and blood supply to the clitoris or penis cross under the legs from behind on their way up to the organ they supply. Compressing the blood supply and injuring the nerves with chronic pressure can actually diminish or take away the ability to achieve orgasm in both men and women. I have had one patient whose specific orgasmic dysfunction was traced to a spinning class that she did five or six days a week. After stopping the class and removing the chronic pressure from the nerves and arteries over six months, she began to get her orgasmic capability back. I would caution those of you who are long-distance bikers or who take regular spinning classes to make sure that you're either out of the seat most of the time or using a wider, cushioned seat to minimize the pressure.

Maintaining vaginal fitness also means avoiding such practices as constantly washing the vagina with soap. This can wash away the natural oils that protect the vaginal lining. From time to time, a patient has come into my office with a yeast infection and told me that, because it wasn't getting better, she really scrubbed the vagina with soap to get it clean. Instead, she noticed it got worse. That was because the natural oils were washed away. The best way to cleanse the vagina is with water. That's why Europeans have bidets to wash it with water rather than using toilet paper, which can be terribly irritating to the vagina when you've got an infection to begin with. If you have chronic infections, it's better to use either a soft wash-cloth just to pat it dry or a spray of water from a squeeze bottle.

What about douching? There is no need to douche. If you find that you like to, especially after a period has been completed, use a physio-logic solution such as vinegar and water. And don't douche frequently. Also, be careful shaving around the vagina. It seems to be the in thing to shave your pubic hair or at least to tailor it. Others use depilatory solu-tions or laser therapy. This is a very sensitive area. Be careful no matter what method you are using so you can avoid the outbreak of pimples and small infections in the hair follicles.

Finally, a comment about the new "tighten me up" surgery. Many women's magazines have been writing about this kind of surgery, which is used to tighten up the vagina to allow it to look more cosmetically per-fect and to allow for better feeling during sexual intercourse. It began with women from Europe and the Middle East coming to this country for this kind of surgery: "Make me a virgin again, please." The loosening of the vaginal opening may have been caused by natural childbirth through the vagina or even by a very large partner. The operation is called a *perine-orrhaphy*, and it's similar to what is done after an episiotomy is cut dur-ing childbirth to repair the vaginal opening and muscles. But the kind of plastic surgery that is beginning to make the rounds now, such as trim-ming the labia and making the vagina tighter when the tightness is really not necessary, is something to be avoided simply because of the poten-tial complications of this kind of surgery, including bleeding, infection, and most of all, scarring. This scarring might lead to pain with intercourse that the woman didn't have before the surgery. So be careful and use com-mon sense. At the very least, seek out more than one opinion.

7. Drink Plenty of Water

Water is extremely good for your body. It replenishes all the fluids in your body, whether it be in your eyes, your vagina, or your joints. Water is very important. It's good for your kidneys and your bladder. It's also good for your skin. It keeps your skin moisturized. It keeps water in the layer beneath the skin to help prevent wrinkles. Water is also good in helping to prevent constipation. It's the best diuretic known to humans. In other words, if you drink water, you will urinate and remove water from the body. That's not to be confused with some other liquids such as coffee, which cause you to urinate but do so at the cost of drying out the rest of the body.

How do you know if you're adequately hydrated and drinking enough water? Just take a look when you urinate. If it's bright yellow, you need water. If it's clear or only slightly yellow, then you've got adequate water on board.

Carry a water bottle with you or keep one at your desk at work. Also remember that when you have a passionate episode of lovemaking or any kind of sexual activity, all the huffing and puffing and heavy breathing can make you dehydrated. Wouldn't it be wonderful if during this episode of passionate sex, your throat didn't suddenly feel so dry from the huffing and puffing because you were dehydrated to begin with? It's a small point but an important one.

8. Stop Smoking

Smoking is not only harmful to your health and a cause of lung cancer but also has impacts on sexuality and hormonal function. Smokers tend to have their menopause two years earlier than nonsmokers. Also, smokers tend to have more peripheral vascular disease, which means not only decreased blood flow to certain areas such as the extremities but also diminished blood flow to the vagina and clitoral area or the penile area, causing sexual dysfunction in both men and women. Don't forget how you smell after smoking. It lives in your breath. It lives on your skin and in your clothing. These odors can be a big turnoff sexually to your partner or someone you're trying to make into a partner.

9. Consider Hormone Replacement Once You Are Past Menopause

Most women will benefit from some sort of postmenopausal hormone replacement. This is a very important topic to discuss in depth with your health-care provider, who will review your personal and family history to help you make this important decision. The risk-benefit ratio will be discussed for you individually, because no two women have their menopause the same way. Remember there are many levels of hormone replacement therapy that can be tailored to your own needs and/or concerns. Alternative therapies can also be looked at. Make this an important topic, if you haven't before, when you visit your health-care provider.

10. Find the Right Doctor

To get the proper guidance in making this decision about hormone replacement therapy or especially obtaining information about sexual issues, you need to have a good physician or health-care provider with whom you can communicate. Having finished this book, you may still have questions that need to be answered, and you may need a professional to help you find those answers. I have intermixed a lot of terms here, such as *doctor, gynecologist,* and *health-care provider.* There are also nurse practitioners who are very capable and may be able to help you. At whatever level, the person you're looking for is the one who can give you the advice you need and the time to ask your questions. I'd like to cover a number of issues with respect to this topic.

See a Gynecologist

Every woman over the age of forty should have and continue to see a gynecologist yearly. This is true whether or not the woman is on hormone replacement therapy. With the intrusion of managed health care and the resurgence of what is known as the primary-care physician, many providers are doing gynecological care and pelvic exams as well as Pap smears. I have often heard primary-care physicians say, "Anyone can do a Pap smear." This is true, but that's not all that goes into a gynecological exam. A health-care provider must know how to determine whether something is a problem. He or she must be able to do more than just an adequate pelvic exam and know precisely what is being felt. Certainly many primary-care physicians can do an adequate pelvic exam, but they simply don't have the wide variety of experience in this area that the gynecologist does. As I travel around the country lecturing physicians and other health-care providers on peri- and postmenopausal care and hormone replacement therapy, many ask how they can keep up with so much information available today. As a specialist in this area, I even find that it's difficult to keep up with all the information. So to ask someone who is a primary-care physician and involved with so many other areas of health care for both men and for women to become an expert in peri- and postmenopausal care is unrealistic.

Given that, however, even the busy obstetrician/gynecologist often does not have the time to spend with a patient who needs the forty-five– to sixty-minute consultation about hormone replacement therapy to help her with this important decision. Also, physicians who have the time to do follow-up visits to go over any problems with hormone replacement or to take phone calls may be hard to find. That's why many women in midlife begin to seek out a physician who is just a gynecologist and no longer does obstetrics. It's often hard to leave that obstetrician with whom you spent so many years and who may have delivered your children, but if you have any concerns, ask the obstetrician what he or she would recommend.

Female Versus Male Gynecologists

I have sometimes heard it said that a woman needs to go to a female gynecologist to get the best care because that female gynecologist will have experienced what the patient is experiencing. Unfortunately, this is like saying that if you have cancer you should go only to an oncologist who has had cancer. I disagree with this premise. It's not about finding a male or female—it's about finding the best doctor for you.

Let me relate a story to you from one of my patients. We had just finished a forty-five-minute consultation on perimenopause, and this new patient looked at me and smiled and said, "Dr. Altman, I want to tell you a story. My male gynecologist and I weren't on the same page. I would talk with him and tell him about my symptoms, and it went right over his head. He looked disinterested. I finally decided that I was going to see a female gynecologist. I talked to a number of friends, and I came up with your name, but even so, I still decided that I would find a female gynecologist because of the experience I had had. I went on to do some more research and looked on the Internet, did some networking, and again came up with your name. Still, I insisted that I try to find a good female gynecologist. When I spoke to one of my closest friends, whom I hadn't seen in a while, she again gave me your name. I explained that I really wanted a female gynecologist. She said to me, 'Dr. Altman *is* a female gynecologist.' And you know, Dr. Altman, she was right."

That's probably one of the most meaningful compliments anyone has ever made to me professionally. The way I think of it is this: there is maleness and there is femaleness. Femaleness is being empathetic, being willing to sit and talk and, most of all, listen. Femaleness is caring about patients, allowing a softness that makes a patient feel she can enter into the physician's realm and feel comfortable. She can ask the question she needs to without being embarrassed—that's what femaleness is. Maleness, if you would, is a less open, less empathetic, "on a pedestal" kind of physician. There are many female gynecologists who have maleness. There are many male gynecologists who have femaleness. So don't base your choice of a gynecologist on the sex of the physician, but rather on the physician's ability to listen, counsel, and teach, as well as to empathize.

In this day and age, unfortunately, with managed care in control, some women are limited in their choice of physicians. This also holds for women using nurse practitioners or other health-care providers. If you find that your doctor or the doctor you want to see is not on your health-care plan, fight for the ability to be able to *see* that physician. If your health-care plan says you can't see a physician, it doesn't mean you can't actually see that physician. It means that plan will not cover seeing that physician. You have to weigh paying for what you require out of pocket against the disadvantages. Believe me, it can be well worth having a consultation with a doctor of your choice to help set you straight on important matters like sexuality or postmenopausal care.

Can You Talk to Your Doctor About Sex?

As has become obvious from reading this book, it is extremely important to make sure your doctor or health-care provider is willing and *able* to discuss sexual issues with you. There are two major reasons some doctors avoid discussing sexual issues with patients. The first is discomfort on the part of the physician because he or she is not confident giving advice on these issues. But more recently, the most common reason for physicians not bringing up sexual issues is that many doctors know that the patient will probably be happy to talk about his or her sexual issues and spend the next hour doing so. Again, with managed care encouraging the physician to spend less and less time with the patient, this would be an impossibility. So the challenge is there to find a gynecologist, a primary-care physician, or other health-care provider who will discuss sexual issues and who is comfortable and educated enough to be able to carry on an important advisory session. If the time is spent, the results can be rewarding. As an example, a patient of mine came in for her yearly visit, and while we were talking about sexual issues, she explained that her sex life had become boring. She asked for my advice. We went over a number of suggestions, but the one that seemed to interest her the most was my suggestion that she take a vibrator to bed and use it during sexual foreplay and intercourse with her partner. She said she would try it, and the next time I saw her was the following year, once again at her yearly exam. The remark I recall was "Dr. Altman, that vibrator idea was fabulous. What suggestion do you have for me this year?"

What About Getting Your Advice—or Medication— on the Internet?

This is such a new area, and the advice can be variable. I've mentioned in the book that men have been able to get Viagra on-line without even seeing a physician, which I do not advise. There are also some problems with taking advice on crucial matters from what you read on the Internet. There is no peer review of information that appears on-line. Peer review refers to other physicians or health-care professionals commenting on the information. Anyone can post a Web page and give advice. Without any regulation, one must be wary of information obtained from these sources. I have seen some excellent sources as well as some very dubious ones. A few of those that can be trusted to give you the best and most unbiased information are listed in the Appendix of this book.

I believe the best way to use the Internet is to gather information and *then* talk to your health-care provider about the veracity of what you've found. The upside of this worldwide information storehouse can be that anyone with access to the Internet can obtain some education and information he or she needs prior to seeing a physician so that the discussion with the physician can indeed be a dialogue instead of the usual monologue. This turns the short time that you'll wind up being with the physician into useful time.

In the same vein, I'm often approached by a patient who says, "I read this story in the newspaper or on the Internet, and does this mean I can't eat broccoli or else I'll get a heart attack?" A word about studies: Each study that appears in the medical literature is one piece of a multi-piece puzzle. Sometimes a hundred or more pieces are required for that puzzle to be finished. Until then, the real answers to the questions will not be known. The problem is, while physicians are aware that each study is only one piece of the puzzle, the lay public is not, and the media presents each study as a *completed* puzzle. This winds up confusing the public when another paper appears six months later saying something different. So it's important to have a physician who will take the time to answer your questions and try to clarify the confusion presented by these multiple sources of unregulated information.

One final word: Once you have learned about your sexuality, once you have age-proofed your sex life, once you've made use of these ten tips, don't keep them to yourself. Communicate with your friends about them if you're comfortable doing so. But most important of all, communicate with the next generation who will go through this. Be a bridge builder so that the next generation does not have to struggle for this information as we have. I am often amazed by the number of my patients who complain that their mothers or fathers never spoke to them about menopause and especially about sexuality. Teach the next generation what you have learned. Remember that the job of the student is to become the teacher.

No book can include everything. There is so much to cover and so little time and space. While I've presented a great deal of information, it's by no means all there is, but it's a good beginning. With new discoveries and continuing progress, there will be enough information for the sequel!

Appendix

Suggested Readings

Blum, Deborah. *Sex on the Brain*. New York: Viking, 1997.

Cash, Thomas F., Ph.D. *The Body Image Workbook*. Oakland, CA: New Harbinger, 1997.

Cutler, Winnifred B. *Love Cycles*. Haverford, PA: Athena Institute Press, 1991.

Davis, Martha, Ph.D, Eshelman, Elizabeth Robbins, M.S.W., and McKay, Matthew, Ph.D. *The Relaxation and Stress Reduction Workbook*. Oakland, CA: New Harbinger, 1988.

DeSalvo, Louise. *Adultery*. Boston: Beacon Press, 1999.

Diamond, Jared. *Why Is Sex Fun?* New York: Basic Books, 1997.

Dixon, Monica. *Love the Body You Were Born With*. New York: Perigee, 1994.

Hutchinson, Marcia Germaine. *Love the Body You Have*. Freedom, CA: The Crossing Press, 1985.

Meyerson, Mitch, and Ashner, Laurie. *Six Keys to Creating the Life You Desire*. Oakland, CA: New Harbinger, 1999.

Potts, Malcolm, and Short, Roger. *Ever Since Adam and Eve*. Boston: Cambridge University Press, 1999.

Shmuley, Boteach Rabbi. *Kosher Sex*. New York: Doubleday, 1999.

Whitehead, E. Douglas, and Nagler, Harris M. *Management of Impotence and Infertility*. Philadelphia: Lippincott, 1994.

Websites

www.power-surge.com
Award-winning site that features articles, on-line chats, Q&A, and interviews with authors on the subject of perimenopause and menopause.

www.pinksunrise.com
Within this site is HotFlash!, an information resource for women who want to learn about perimenopause and menopause.

www.sixkeys.com
Laurie Ashner's website, where you can download articles on a variety of subjects, read excerpts from her books, get information about midlife women's health and lifestyle issues, and contact Laurie.

www.AlanAltmanMD.com
Alan Altman's website for up-to-the-moment information about HRT, groundbreaking medical research on perimenopause, menopause, and women's health, and questions and answers about midlife sexuality.

www.body-images.com
Dr. Tom Cash's (author of *The Body Image Workbook*) website with all the latest information about body image therapy.

www.healthywomen.org
The National Women's Health Resource Center's website, which provides lots of great information on women's health.

Catalog

Good Vibrations
938 Howard Street, Suite 101
San Francisco, CA 94103
800-289-8423

Index